Al-Mughtaribūn

SUNY Series in Middle Eastern Studies
Shahrough Akhavi, editor

Al-Mughtaribūn

American Law and the Transformation of

Muslim Life in the United States

Kathleen M. Moore

STATE UNIVERSITY OF NEW YORK PRESS

Published by
State University of New York Press, Albany

Production by Bernadine Dawes
Marketing by Fran Keneston

Printed in the United States of America

For information, address State University of New York Press,
State University Plaza, Albany, NY 12246

Library of Congress Cataloging-in-Publication Data

Moore, Kathleen M., 1959–
    al-Mughtaribūn : American law and the transformation of Muslim
life in the United States / Kathleen M. Moore.
        p.   cm.—(SUNY series in Middle Eastern studies)
    Includes bibliographical references and index.
    ISBN 0–7914–2579–7 (HC : alk. paper).—ISBN 0–7914–2580–0 (PB :
alk. paper)
    1. Muslims—Legal status, laws, etc.—United States. 2. Muslims—
United States—Ethnic identity. 3. Religious tolerance—United
States. I. Title. II. Series.
KF4755.M66 1995
346.7301'3—dc20   95-16487
[347.30613]   CIP

10 9 8 7 6 5 4 3 2 1

CONTENTS

PREFACE

This book does not try to provide a sociological account of the assimilation in the United States of Muslims of various ethnic backgrounds and national origins. Others (e.g., Haddad and Lummis 1987) have begun to do that, and I have drawn on the valuable insights of their more comprehensive and detailed work in what follows. Rather, the central thesis in this book is that there is a distinctively American Muslim experience which is a product of a particular social environment with its characteristic political and legal institutions and values of religious liberty and tolerance. The focus of this work is on the gradual transformation of American Muslims' perceptions and self-identification coaxed by the ways American civil law has penetrated and come to dominate their daily lives. The analysis owes a heavy debt to scholars of the multidisciplinary Law and Society field—John Brigham (University of Massachusetts) and Sally Engle Merry (Wellesley College) in particular.

American Muslims' decisions whether and how to maintain a corporate life in a non-Muslim society have changed over time and through different types of contacts with American institutions. From encounters with changing standards for immigration and citizenship during the years between the Civil War and World War I, to the civil rights movement and the subsequent emergence of group rights—emphasizing promises of religious liberty and racial equality—the issues that have galvanized the Muslim community in the United States have been defined in large measure by broad sociolegal trends and transformations in the legal order of the nation. Nevertheless, as members of a minority faith living in a non-Islamic context, Muslims also have been subject to pressures presented by what Islam teaches about "marginality"—for example, the three classical models of hajj, hijrah, and jihad, and the thread of missionary activity, or da'wah. This raises an important question: What happens to the Muslim community as it develops the institutional organization it needs to preserve its identity in "diaspora"? The treatment here suggests that Muslims bring a distinctive and valuable contribution to the dialectical negotiation of what constitutes religious and cultural pluralism and tolerance in America.

This book will be of interest to a wide list of readers: anthropologists, cultural and social historians, legal scholars and civil libertarians, political scientists, students of world religions, and others who are interested in understanding the impact of the domestic experience of American Muslims both on the formation of their self-identification and on the global development of a "political" Islam.

This work has been nurtured by friendship. I thank all who made this book possible, beginning with my mentors, John Brigham and Yvonne Haddad, who each in their own way have gone beyond the call in providing me with guidance and motivation, as well as in setting excellent examples. Friends such as Gary Lehring, Tom Lalor, and Phyllis Farley Rippey have offered encouragement when I most needed it. My parents, Don and Kathleen, have given support in innumerable ways. My heart brims with love and gratitude for who they are.

Stephen Pelletier, my most intimate friend and partner, deserves more than my words can convey on these pages. Without his high intelligence, understanding and sensitivity, I have no doubt that this work—and much more—would not be possible.

INTRODUCTION

This book examines pluralism and religious tolerance in America, viewed from the vantage point offered by the history of Muslim life in the United States. A small but constant presence on the American landscape since the late nineteenth century, the Muslim community has grown steadily over the last twenty-five years due to the liberalization of American immigration laws and the rising number of native-born American converts. Once identified primarily by their "race" or national origins, Muslims in the United States are now becoming more public about their existence as a diverse faith community. An emerging *American* Muslim identity bears out that Muslims are a major new group in American life and a significant part of an increasingly pluralistic society. Now estimated to exceed four million, with roughly 1,100 mosques nationwide, American Muslims claim a past, present, and future in America.

This book attempts to show the influence of American law on Muslim life in the United States. Each word in the title has a specific meaning. The Arabic word, *al-Mughtaribūn*, refers to emigrants. It is derived from the Arabic root *gharaba*, from which proceed the following terms: strange, foreign, the West, and the verbs "to be far from one's homeland," "to become an occidental, become Westernized," and "to assimilate oneself to the Western way of life."[1] *Gharaba* and its derivatives have multiple implications, including a very strong spatial connotation. They mean, alternately, the distant place where the sun sets, the border with Christendom, and where people go when they venture beyond the boundaries of the familiar. Muslims experience their diaspora in Western countries, especially the United States, as a special challenge. By tracing the historical shift in the consciousness of American Muslims, precipitated by their interactions with the legal institutions of the dominant culture, this book demonstrates the transformative impact of law on a minority community seeking religious tolerance in a pluralistic society.

Concepts about national identity in post-bellum America and minority rights in American legal history have contributed to the construction of a complex host environment in which Muslims now attempt to assimilate without abandoning their religious and cultural traditions. As members of a minority faith living in a non-Islamic context, Muslims are subject to conflicting pressures presented by what Islam teaches about "marginality" and what the American civil tradition promises about religious liberty and racial equality. In this study I have focused on the interface between Muslims and the Western tradition of religious liberty, with its corollary promises of free exercise and toleration, which has had a profound impact on the development of Islam in the United States—its identity, institutions, doctrines and practices.

The analysis here offers an historical perspective drawn from court records, interviews, articles, and newspaper accounts. My concern in this book is with pluralism and, most directly, with the principle of religious tolerance in the context of changing social conditions. To examine this closely I have chosen to study a particular microcosm of the American religious scene, represented by the Muslim community in the United States.

American judicial opinions about Muslims date from at least as early as the 1811 New York State blasphemy case of *People v Ruggles*[2]—where Islam is called an "imposter" religion—to the present day criminal trial of the defendants in the World Trade Center bombing. Scholarly as well as popular representations of Islam and Muslims as antithetical to our civil democratic society are abundant.[3] These representations must be handled with care, as they tend to overgeneralize at the expense of the diverse and growing population of Muslims living in the United States. While many in the public arena would emphasize the American continent as a place of unprecedented religious tolerance,[4] some find it difficult to include Islam—"an ancient rival against our Judeo-Christian heritage"[5]—under the same umbrella. The point here is that these representations color our perceptions of what is acceptable, that is, legally protected, within the parameters of American society and suggest particular standards of treatment. These standards, articulated through such institutions as the courts, legislatures, and city planning boards, then influence the ways Muslims attempt to maintain an Islamic identity and lifestyle in the United States.

Recent events stemming from the World Trade Center bombing in February 1993 have piqued popular interest in the presence of Muslims in the United States. *The New York Times* published a series on Islam in America, reporting on the growing Islamic presence and the Muslims' current efforts to balance "the sacred and the secular while trying to find their place in the American mosiac."[6] Anxiety over terrorism, however, has often mitigated the willingness of the general public to accommodate Islam, and to reconcile a concern for security with the longstanding American tradition of pluralism. A poll conducted by the American Muslim Council in the wake of the bombing found that 43 percent of Americans think that Muslims are religious fanatics, while only 24 percent disagree.[7] An editorial by William F. Buckley Jr. argued that admission of Muslims into the United States ought to be reduced to a minimum or eliminated altogether. He wrote that, in light of recent events, we have to "take explicit notice of the incompatibility of our own culture and that of the fundamentalist Muhammadan, and that we need to organize our immigration laws with some reference to this problem."[8] Because of a prevailing, if inaccurate view that Islam is a violent and anti-American creed, it is a faith that is not easily accommodated.

This book looks at issues that have brought Muslims in the United States to the attention of various legal institutions. The erection of immigration and naturalization barriers at the end of the nineteenth and into the twentieth century, and responses of immigrants from the Muslim world to the emerging standards for citizenship; the religious liberty claims of Black Muslims in prisons during the 1960s and 1970s; federal hate crimes legislation at the close of the 1980s and the inclusion of mosques as protected religious property; and municipal zoning practices negotiated by Muslims where they sought to build mosques, are treated in the chapters that follow.

Scant literature is available on this growing community. The Muslims in the United States are treated in book-length studies of a sociological bent: Yvonne Y. Haddad and Adair T. Lummis' book, *Islamic Values in the United States: A Comparative Study* (1987), Haddad's edited volume, *The Muslims of America* (1991), and Earle H. Waugh's edited book, *The Muslim Community in North America* (1983) stand as groundbreaking works. This book differs from the three mentioned here in that it focuses on American law to shed some light on the character of the American Muslim experience, and to analyze the influence of American law on the expression of Muslim life in the United States. It looks at the emergence of the American Muslim minority against the background of American law and history. It examines both the responsiveness of legal institutions as Muslims claim rights, and the transformative impact of the American legal setting as many Muslims adopt the language and standards of these institutions. The first chapter presents a framework for studying the influence of American law on Muslim life in the United States. A central theme of this book focuses on the role of law in constructing an authoritative image of American society and in shaping popular consciousness in accordance with that image. This is illustrated by looking at the aspirations of Muslims to be included within the parameters of a pluralistic society. What happens to the Muslim religious community as it develops the organization it needs to preserve its identity in a non-Islamic setting? Changing circumstances require adaptation, and yet that adaptation involves the risk of loss of connection to the "orthodoxy" and original spiritual insight that were once central sources for identity and authenticity.

The claims that Muslims are making are conditioned by their historical experience as a religious minority in the United States. To understand this, it is necessary to look at the Muslims' experience over a relatively long period of time and to contextualize their claims. In the second and third chapters, this book reviews the immigration and naturalization debates at the end of the nineteenth century which continued well into the twentieth century. This era marks the end of open immigration to the United States and the erection of restrictions in the face of "new" immigration, principally from Central and Southern Europe but also, significantly, from the "Orient." The turn-of-the-century debates about immigration and naturalization are an essential part of the historical development of national identity in the United States. The purpose of chapter 2 is twofold: (1) to review how legal constructions have constituted an important element in shaping American ideologies; and (2) to show the ways race and culture, or race and moral character, are understood and linked in the discourse on citizenship.

Where it provides insight into the turn-of-the-century Muslim experience with emerging immigration restrictions in the United States, I have provided comparisons with the Canadian situation during the same period. As a member of the Commonwealth, Canada was the source of many Muslim—especially South Asian Muslim—immigrants to the United States. That Canada struggled with the same questions of national identity being debated in the United States meant that the development of a North American Islam was circumscribed for several years by nativist exclusionary impulses both north and south of the forty-ninth parallel.

Chapter 3 looks at the connections between what was being said about citizenship and how the Muslim community was affected.

The perennial question about who constitutes an acceptable if not ideal citizen is one which conditioned the voluntary arrival of Muslims to the United States. The first wave of Muslim immigrants to the United States (1875 to 1912) arrived when popular sentiments running toward exclusion of Asians from the United States were reaching their peak.[9] That Muslims began to arrive at the height of the anti-Asian furor in American politics is extremely significant. An important part of the affected community followed the courts' lead in adopting racialist and eugenicist criteria to construct a national identity which in effect denied equal access to citizenship to "Asiatics."

Chapter 4 reviews judicial considerations as to whether Islam and Muslim practices constitute protected "religion" under constitutional provisions in the United States. It investigates how Islam and Muslims have been treated by the courts when Muslims have made constitutional claims to maximize their religious freedom. Specifically the focus in this chapter is on religious liberty claims raised by Muslims in prisons. The circumstances of Muslim inmates came to the attention of the courts during the 1960s and early 1970s, when Black Muslims began to use law to challenge prison policies that denied them racial and religious equality. Black Muslims worked successfully, through litigation, to expand the individual rights of prisoners, including religious liberty. Their efforts have created precedents that have helped to establish broader prisoners' rights.[10]

Moreover, Black Muslim organizations have made significant inroads in the prison population, extending their outreach to serve the needs of African American male convicts as part of their overall religious mission. By the close of the 1970s, Muslims were estimated to comprise roughly six percent of the inmate population in federal prisons.[11] The notion that Black Muslims are subversive and members of a cult bent on the destruction of Anglo society has contributed to the outcome in many court cases involving Muslims in prisons and is considered in chapter 4 as a contributing factor.

The history of mosques as institutions of a faith community closely associated with immigrants in the United States is in many ways unique and in others quite typical. Chapter 5 focuses on the phenomenon of "hate crimes"—crimes motivated by hatred of race, religion, sexual orientation, or ethnicity—and discusses how mosques came to be included among the types of religious property protected by hate crimes laws.

Victims of vandalism, arson, and bombing motivated by hatred of religion now, by virtue of the hate crimes laws, would appear to have legal recourse. People who are victimized by more subtle forms of discrimination, such as exclusionary practices in zoning, however, have a more difficult obstacle to overcome. Thus, chapter 6 deals with the politics of municipal zoning during the 1980s, which in effect limited the operation of mosques. It looks at claims raised before zoning boards in suburban settings where efforts by Muslims to build and operate mosques in the communities in which they live provoked local resistance. This resistance was wielded through legal and political means, by using zoning systems and building codes to control what can be built. Municipal zoning affords suburbanites the power to define themselves and guide their growth as a community, which, in effect, allowed Muslims' efforts to be blocked in certain locales. These are historical moments which merit close attention, if only by virtue of the fact that they reinforce the instrumentality of local government in deciding who can live and worship within its jurisdiction and how their public life manifests itself.

The intention of this book is to bring the human factor into sharper focus by looking at the activity and views of a significant religious minority which has utilized legal structures in the United States to assert and protect its claims for religious tolerance. When we take into account the activity and views of Muslims as they interpret and act on law, we may apprehend the ways in which they, as a religious minority, signal and strengthen their relations with the dominant society. As Harvard law professor Martha Minow explains, "[t]hose claiming rights implicitly invest themselves in a larger community, even in the act of seeking to change it."[12] The last chapter, then, integrates the experiences of Muslims over time and shows how law has served as a mediating and transformative link between those who control institutions and those who are controlled.

1

Symbolism and Legal Institutions

In *The Myth of the Judeo-Christian Tradition,* Jewish theologian and philosopher Arthur A. Cohen questions the notion that a "Judeo-Christian" tradition even exists, and suggests it is an invention of twentieth-century American politics spawned by efforts to form a cultural consensus and, in the process, syncretize religious identification and promote interfaith harmony. The conception of such a tradition is, in Cohen's words, "mythological or, rather, not precisely mythological but *ideological* and hence, as in all ideologies, shot through with falsification, distortion, and untruth (emphasis mine)."[1]

An ideological use of the term "Judeo-Christian" has gained particular currency at the close of the twentieth century as reliance on certain religious values, symbols, and rhetoric in public discourse both generates and reflects popular approval. Recent attention focused on multiculturalism has accounted for, in some measure, an antithetical response represented in the use of the symbol of a Judeo-Christian nation and a reaffirmation of a shared Judeo-Christian cultural heritage.[2] Faced with the realities of religious and cultural pluralism, the American public is currently reevaluating common assumptions about the place of religion and morality in public life, and the nature of the relationship between church and state. For better or worse, religious symbols have become an important component in the dialectical statement of what constitutes "America."

Our two most recent U.S. Presidents provide illustrations of this phenomenon. George Bush, during his final days in office, declared January 16, 1993 to be Religious Freedom Day. He proclaimed:

> We Americans have long cherished our identity as one Nation under God. To this day American law and institutions have been

shaped by a view of man that recognizes the inherent rights and dignity of individuals. The Framers of our Government shared this view, and they never forgot the political and religious persecution that had forced their ancestors to flee Europe. Thus, it is not surprising that the first of all freedoms enumerated in our Bill of Rights is freedom of religion. . . . Over the years the exercise of our religious freedom has been instrumental in preserving the faith and the traditional values that are this Nation's greatest strengths. . . . In that spirit, the United States has continued to champion religious liberty around the world.[3]

Likewise, Bill Clinton, in acknowledging Religious Freedom Day on January 14, 1994, claimed:

It is no accident of authorship that the right to free exercise of religion is the first freedom granted by our Bill of Rights. . . . Religious freedom helps to give America's people a character independent of their government, fostering the formation of individual codes of ethics, without which a democracy cannot survive. . . . To be both the world's strongest democracy and its most truly multi-ethnic society is a victory of human spirit we must not take for granted. For as many issues as there are that divide us in this society, there remain values that all of us share.[4]

The reality that a reliance on the symbol of a strictly Judeo-Christian nation masks, however, is one of growth and complexity, both in the number and nature of religious faiths that have appeared on the American horizon of late. Several variables have changed the religious composition of the United States since World War II. Increased immigration from Asia[5] and the Middle East, declining religious membership in the conventional religious communities of Protestantism, Catholicism, and Judaism, and the concomitant growth of secularism have produced a vastly more pluralistic religious environment. A diverse assortment of faiths now represents a sizable number of American religious adherents.[6] Among these the Muslim community is growing the fastest, at a rate that will make it the second largest religious community in the United States by the twenty-first century,[7] when it will have nearly doubled the size it was estimated to have been in 1980.[8]

Islam, representing over four million adherents in the United States[9] is a significant minority religion in America. The rapid growth of the American Muslim community led a prominent Muslim scholar and activist, Isma'il Raji al-Faruqi (1921–1986), to call for its inclusion in the mainstream of American society, to be reflected in the reformulation of the concept "Judeo-Christian" to add "Islamic" to it. What al-Faruqi called for is an affirmation of the *Abrahamic* tradition, or a recognition of the common origin—God's covenant with Abraham—shared by Judaism, Christianity, and Islam.[10]

Symbols evolve and acquire new meaning as ideological understandings and demographic realities shift. This study grew out of the conviction that the Muslim experience in the United States has evolved out of a particular set of social forces with its characteristic values of religious liberty and tolerance, and yet has *not* been captured in the symbols of the dominant culture. A close look at the circumstances of Muslims in the United States can tell us something not only about the nature of that faith community but also about the social relations of the dominant culture.

Ronald Takaki, professor of ethnic studies at the University of California at Berkeley, analyzes racial domination in the United States in an effort to understand more fully its relationship to the development of American culture and to the political, social, and economic institutions the culture has helped to create and maintain.[11] He borrows from the thought of Italian theorist Antonio Gramsci when he identifies the phenomenon of cultural hegemony. The relationship between culture (the superstructure of ideology) and material conditions produces

> an order in which a certain way of life and thought is dominant, in which one concept of reality is diffused throughout society in all its institutional and private manifestations, informing with its spirit all taste, morality, customs, religious and political principles, and all social relations, particularly in their intellectual and moral connotation.[12]

Hegemony, then, is the organization of society along lines that benefit a particular class which has gained the loyalty of subordinate as well as dominant groups through a combination of coercion and consent. The exercise of hegemony, according to Takaki's analysis, consists of more than the simple dissemination of ruling-class ideas; it also includes the ability to define, through various media, the symbols and terms by which people understand themselves and the world they live in.

The network of symbols that filters our perceptions of the world and our places in it is fundamental to our culture. According to Takaki, those who control institutions and are chiefly concerned with the preservation of these institutions, are able to claim power because of the effective universalization of certain interests in the name of the collective good, reflected in cultural symbols. Those symbols whose imagery and vocabulary are universal remain predominant and substantially unaltered in the cultural realm, sustained and transmitted by active institutional custodians. This cultural hegemony exists at the expense of groups at the margins in the discursive production of state and society.[13]

The image of the United States as a Judeo-Christian nation implies a shared religious basis for the Western values at the core of the democratic ideal. As anthropologist Clifford Geertz puts it, "[r]eligious symbols formulate a basic congruence between a particular style of life and a specific (if, most often, implicit) metaphysic. . . ."[14] According to Geertz, religion relates a people's view of reality to a set of ideas about how they are expected or required to live. Religious and, more broadly, cultural symbols link ideologies and behavior and synthesize and disseminate a people's ethos. They are derived from common experiences and are fixed in identifiable forms; they are "embodiments of ideas, attitudes, judgments, longings or beliefs."[15] As such they must continue to make sense to the people who are meant to understand them.

However, reliance on the symbol of a Judeo-Christian nation has the effect of excluding other religious groups, such as Muslims, and non-religious groups from the mainstream of American society.[16] This symbol is of diminishing significance in an increasingly diverse society.

Political scientist Timothy Mitchell, informed by the philosophy of Michel Foucault,[17] warns against relying on the unexamined assumptions of the frameworks for analysis developed by such theorists of culture and ideology as Takaki and Geertz. While sharing their focus on relationships of domination and, like them, contributing to theories of power and resistance, Mitchell takes exception to the distinction they draw between material reality and culture, the concrete and the abstract, a practice which he sees as reinforcing the effect of a two-dimensional world constituted as something divided between two neatly opposed realms. This "binary" approach, as Mitchell calls it, is problematic and misleading because it replicates uncritically a larger dualism characteristic to modern means of domination. The distinction between material reality and culture conjures an image of an "unphysical realm of order that stands apart from the world of practice."[18] The apparent existence of such "frames of meaning" as described by Geertz is an artifact, "precisely the effect introduced by modern mechanisms of power"[19] which separate the material order on the one hand from the sphere of meaning or culture on the other. Through this structural effect, modern systems of domination are maintained. In Mitchell's estimation, Geertz's analysis, by reducing the world to a binary form, would ascribe to the "frames of meaning" a metaphysical authority, the power to persuade, which exists as something external to ordinary life, through which material reality and daily practices are perceived, understood, and justified.

Mitchell argues that this approach is overly simplistic: "the complexities of domination never quite fit the terms of the opposition between a physical and mental form of power... [and] many forms of exploitation and control cannot be reduced to this binary form."[20] The very image of a binary world itself inhibits political dissent by placing authority ultimately in the "unphysical realm" of order and meaning, communicated through symbols and terms congruent with publicly shared understandings of an imagined heritage. The parameters of society, or the boundaries around various arenas of action, are established not simply by "the agenda-setting of particular interests" who control access to institutions of power and the rhetoric of national debates, but also by social processes.[21] Meaning is context-bound and located in the social acts and attitudes of a given historical moment. Human activity vests symbols with meaning, which is continually reproduced. The analyses of many theorists of culture and ideology, according to Mitchell, are inherently flawed because they do not examine closely the ordinary social practices commonly taken for granted. In this sense, the theorists themselves are complicitous in reproducing a dualistic world view. When social scientists place the phenomena of physical coercion and ideological persuasion in two separate and opposing realms, we see how the binary world created by the methods of domination "works itself into the very vocabulary with which we speak of power."[22] The problem, then, becomes one of understanding the provenance and effect of this larger dualism.

Similarly, legal scholar Martha Minow suggests that the problem of dualism requires that we expose the:

> rigidity and limitations of patterns of thought that force perceptions into dualities: good/bad, same/different, white/black, male/female. Becoming adept at recognizing how each half of a given duality depends upon the other half in self-definition, and how crudely each duality divides varieties and ranges of perceptions

and experience, can help people challenge the seeming inevitability of dualisms in social practice.[23]

The discourse that reinforces the dichotomy between material reality and culture, or between the notions of a Judeo-Christian and a multicultural society, is both cause and effect.[24]

Values, including pluralism and tolerance, need to be seen and understood in the context of social relations. Political scientist John Brigham, in studying the U. S. Supreme Court, makes this point when he professes an interest in seeing the way values affect institutional arrangements. Brigham defines institutions broadly as sets of practices which accomplish certain tasks.[25] Institutions "amount to ways of acting."[26] In an important way, an institution is constituted through the interactive process of establishing, refining, and understanding the way things get done. Human activity vests institutions, as well as symbols, with meaning. Just as symbols are context-bound, so are institutions, located in the social acts and attitudes of a given historical moment. In turn institutions share "a capacity to order social life because people act as if they exist, as if they matter."[27] Thus, not only are institutions socially constructed but, in a dynamic process, are constitutive of social life. They rest firmly on social foundations, and their actions must be congruent with the values and expectations of the communities "who understand the practices [of the institution] and operate according to them."[28]

Brigham's approach is helpful in that it explores those practices which produce a social order. It traces how shared understandings about social reality become ingrained, are reinforced by, and, in turn, reinforce the authority of such institutions as the law courts in ordering social life. Secondly, the insights revealed in Brigham's analysis are useful for the present study because they help clarify the relationship between beliefs and practice, linking ideologies and legal institutions.

The ideologies[29] of a society find their most concrete expression in its legal institutions.[30] For that reason, the study of these institutions in the United States should provide some insights into the complicated ways in which culture and ideology interact with politics and law. In the United States, a struggle to move away from the amalgamation model of a melting pot in favor of a society which esteems pluralism continues, and a look at the institutions that reflect these notions—including religious tolerance—is in order. An examination of the record of legal institutions, which are often the location of contests over issues of rights and freedoms, can help to illuminate the production of ideologies.

A look at the reception of Islam and Muslims in America can help to elucidate the culturally productive role of law. The present study sheds some light on the character of the Muslim experience in America by examining the responsiveness of legal institutions as Muslims seek recognition and tolerance. It seeks to clarify "the role of law in constructing an authoritative image of social relations and shaping popular consciousness in accordance with that image" in the particular context of Muslim aspirations to be included within the parameters of a pluralistic society.[31] How the law has been used to fashion categories that may serve to exclude Muslims from full participation in society will be examined. This study focuses on the American experience of Muslims to: (1) provide a contemporary and concrete example that illustrates the functions of law in defining how society orders itself; (2) say something meaningful about the historical experience of a liminal group (a religious minority) in a liberal democratic state with a long tradition of text-based constitutional guarantees of free exercise of religion; and (3) contribute to the growing literature on Muslim life in the United States.

It has been noted that "Islamic scholars, students of religion, Middle East experts, and analysts of the American scene all tend to overlook the presence of Islam in America, or to dismiss it as of only marginal interest."[32] However, the growth of the Muslim community, not only in the United States but worldwide results in demographic changes and social, economic, and political tensions that can no longer be ignored by scholars, analysts, and government officials alike.

MUSLIMS IN THE UNITED STATES

The size of the American Muslim population is estimated at present to exceed four million.[33] The number of Muslim immigrants entering the United States has more than doubled since 1960. During the same period, the number of North American converts to Islam, both black and white, has also risen. This rate of growth, combined with the recent wave of religious resurgence in the Muslim world and the popular association of Islamic revival with terrorism, presents a challenge to the shape of American society and its commitment to the principle of tolerance. The February 1993 bombing of the World Trade Center in New York represents only the most recent rupture in the strained relations between the Muslim world and the West. Further, the evolution of the objectives of the indigenous African-American

Muslim community—from black separatism to accommodation and a stronger identification with the global community of orthodox Islam—is yet another factor which helps define the diverse Muslim community and Muslims' claims for greater tolerance within the American milieu.[34]

A careful look at the history of Muslim migration ought to disprove the prevailing misconception held by many in the West that Muslims and Arabs are synonymous. An accurate portrait shows that the Muslims of the United States come from diverse national origins and cultural backgrounds covering as many as sixty-five countries, not only in the Arab world but also South Asia—including Afghanistan, Pakistan, India, Bangladesh, the Maldive Islands, and Sri Lanka; Southeast Asia—including the Philippines, Indonesia, and Malaysia; as well as Europe, Africa, China, Iran, and Turkey. Additionally, indigenous African-American Muslims were estimated in 1980 to comprise roughly thirty percent of the total Muslim population living in the United States.[35] American Muslims are not restricted to any particular national origin, but represent a microcosm of the multi-national global community of Islam. In short, the migration of Muslims to the United States and the development of American-evolved Muslim groups have contributed to the contemporary diversity of American society.

In *Islamic Values in the United States: A Comparative Study*, Yvonne Haddad and Adair Lummis describe the pattern of Muslim migration as consisting of five "waves," the first arriving in the United States between 1875 and 1912. Most of these immigrants came from the Arabic-speaking provinces of the Ottoman Empire: Syria, Jordan, Lebanon, and Palestine. For the most part, those who stayed in the United States settled in urban communities. The second and third waves, between 1918 and 1922 and 1930 and 1938, respectively, consisted to a large degree of relatives, friends, and acquaintances of earlier immigrants but also included a very small number of immigrants from other parts of the Middle East and Eastern Europe.[36] Many who came as part of the second wave had experienced the disruptive effects of World War I. Some were enticed to immigrate to the United States by the reports of opportunities there from returning and visiting immigrants, letters from immigrants, or Americans visiting the region.[37] Isma'il al-Faruqi, himself an immigrant to the United States from Palestine, writes:

> For two hundred years the image of America in the minds of Muslims was one of a haven where the persecuted could lead

lives of religious freedom and piety and where they could earn from God's bounty to feed and clothe themselves and their families.[38]

The fourth wave of Muslim migration arrived to the United States between 1947 and 1960 and was more diverse in national origins. It contained immigrants from the Middle East plus South Asia, Eastern Europe, the Soviet Union and other parts of the Islamic world. Displaced by the upheavals of the post-World-War-II era, many of these arrivals differed from their predecessors in that they were less likely to be from unskilled, uneducated, or rural backgrounds. Many:

> were the children of the ruling elites in various countries, mostly urban in background, educated, and Westernized prior to their arrival in the United States. They came to America as refugees or in quest of a better life, higher education, or advanced technical training and specialized work opportunities, as well as for ideological fulfillment.[39]

The fifth wave began in 1967 and continues at present. The volume of this wave has been affected by the relaxation of immigration quotas. The U.S. Immigration Act of 1965 abolished national quotas and, at the same time, introduced standards of immigration selection which drew an occupational elite. Hence, according to Carol Stone's study of U.S. immigration and census statistics, the number of Muslim immigrants has more than doubled in an eighteen-year period, "increasing from 4% of all immigrants in 1968 to 10.5% in 1986."[40] A large proportion of these arrivals are professionals in medicine, engineering and other technical fields, and share the socio-economic background (i.e., middle-class, highly educated) of the immigrants of the fourth wave. Many come from the South Asian subcontinent and the Arab world, and, as a result of the 1979 Islamic Revolution in Iran, there are a substantial number of Iranian newcomers. The arrival of Afghanis also increased throughout the 1980s as a result of the war in Afghanistan.

The international scene has had its effects on the development of black nationalism and the indigenous African-American Muslim community, too. During the post-World-War-II period when several African nation-states achieved independence,[41] the popularity of black nationalism in the United States was enhanced. Africa became the symbol for liberation, a model for black Americans' efforts to deal with their own problems of daily existence in America. In the words of historian C. Eric Lincoln, "freedom for the Africans left the Blacks in America the only "colonized" peoples in the world."[42]

In these circumstances, under the leadership of Elijah Muhammed, the Nation of Islam grew. Called America's foremost black nationalist movement in Lincoln's classic study, *The Black Muslims in America*, the Nation of Islam appealed to the oppressed as "a protest directed at the whole value-construct of the white Christian society—a society in which the Black Muslims feel themselves (as Blacks) an isolated and unappreciated appendage."[43] Distinguished from orthodox Islam by their beliefs (e.g., that a black man named Fard was God-in-the-flesh and Elijah Muhammed was his Prophet; the White Man is Satan), members of the Nation of Islam, at least until the transformation of the movement in 1975,[44] adhered to doctrines about black supremacy and suspicions of white America and its institutions. Thus, the Nation of Islam cannot be understood as an isolated phenomenon, but as an important part of a larger liberation movement, or a mass protest against the state of race relations in North America.

The dynamics of the ideological and philosophical conversion of this American subculture, leading to its conformity with more orthodox Islamic beliefs and practices after the death of its charismatic leader, are a product of a particular set of forces. That the immigrant Muslim community is generally prosperous, educated, and middle-class isolated it from the experiences of the Black Muslim community of more humble socio-economic backgrounds. The mainstream Muslim groups in America, composed of immigrants and their descendants, by and large dissociated themselves from the Black Muslims prior to 1975, but the rift has since been mended. In 1976, the Nation of Islam was renamed the World Community of Islam in the West when Elijah Muhammed's son, Warith Deen Muhammed, assumed leadership of the movement, and the name was changed again in 1980 to the American Muslim Mission.[45] By 1985, the racialist tenets of the former Nation of Islam had been expunged from all but a few remnants, and the vast majority of African-American Muslims now consider themselves part of the mainstream Muslim community in the United States.[46] While relations between immigrant Muslim organizations and the African-American Muslim community remain somewhat tentative, both immigrant and African-American Muslim organizations have made greater efforts to extend their fellowship to embrace each other. The immigrant American Muslim community's recognition of African-American Muslims as part of the global Muslim community, rather than as strictly a black nationalist movement, was noted in the memorial banquet hosted by the Islamic Society of North America, held to honor Al Hajj Malik el-Shabazz, otherwise known as Malcolm X, at the Muslim American Political Awareness Conference in Washington, D.C. on August 5, 1989.

Islam in the United States is maturing. Religious consciousness in the Muslim community has been reawakened and intensified by Islamic resurgence in the Middle East, North Africa, and Asia. Generational differences appear to affect the degree to which immigrants from the Muslim world exhibit a strong religious identity. Arrivals prior to the mid–1960s tended to be absorbed into the local communities where they settled, sometimes intermarrying and Americanizing their names (for instance, Mohammed became Mike), while more recent immigrants have displayed a desire to maintain their separate identity. This recent propensity can be said to be due in part to increased numbers of immigrants, reaching critical mass in the United States under liberalized immigration policies. However, it is also related to significant changes in their countries of origin, where rising trends of a political Islam and movements of Islamic resurgence have forced many to grapple with the issue of identity, redefining what it means to be a Muslim. A key principle of this explicitly Islamic consciousness is that *religious* should prevail over *ethnic* identity. Thus, Muslim-Americans, bound by ties of a common religion regardless of their national origins, are being galvanized by events in the Muslim world at large as well as by their reception in the host society of the United States.

Drawn by the vision of a restored and resurgent Islam that began in the the early 1980s, many have affected changes in lifestyle, resulting in an increase in mosque attendance and daily prayer. At the same time, the American Muslim community, inexorably drawn by the promise of their new home, has become politically active, and is presently engaged in the process of articulating a collective agenda that reflects Islamic moral principles. Generally, Muslim political activity has been bipartisan, both Democratic and Republican, but is socially conservative—against abortion, pornography, gay rights, and permissive sexual standards.

The politicization of Muslims is evident in such events as the Muslim American Political Awareness Conference, organized by the Islamic Society of North America Political Action Committee and held August 4–6, 1989, in Washington, D.C.; the 26th Annual Convention of the Islamic Society of North America, held September 1–4, 1989, in Dayton, Ohio, to discuss ways of increasing public awareness of the Muslim presence in North America; and the American Muslim Conference held in the San Francisco-East Bay area on November 4, 1989.[47]

Further, the Islamic Society of North America,[48] whose stated purposes are "to foster unity and brotherhood among Muslims and to raise their Islamic consciousness as a people enjoining the right and forbidding wrong,"[49] has established three professional organizations: the Association of Muslim Social Scientists (AMSS), Association of Muslim Scientists and Engineers (AMSE), and the Islamic Medical Association (IMA). These associations seek to represent their respective constituencies in the political arena. The American Muslim Council operates to protect the civil rights of Muslims in the United States.

Although Islam has been practiced in America for more than one hundred years,[50] it has only recently received even nominal recognition as an American phenomenon. The presence of Muslims in the United States is gaining the attention of the larger society. *Time* magazine published an article entitled "Americans Facing Toward Mecca, The Fast-Growing Muslim Community is Invisible No Longer" in its May 23, 1988, issue. *USA Today* featured "A Growing Islam Community, Moslem Faithful in USA Tackle Misconceptions," in its September 3, 1989, edition. An article called "American Moslems" appeared in the October 5, 1990, edition of *The Wall Street Journal*. *U.S. News & World Report* followed suit by publishing an article on American-Muslims on October 8, 1990, which stated that "Islamic worship and lifestyles are becoming an increasingly familiar part of the American tableau."[51] Following the February 1993 World Trade Center bombing, *The New York Times* published a series on Islam in America.[52] However, Islam is still widely perceived to be a foreign creed and is maligned by its association in the media with terrorist activity, both domestic and abroad, and black separatism in the U.S. Because of a prevailing sense, however misguided, that Islam is a violent religion, intolerant of non-Muslims and a threat to society, it is a faith that is not easily accommodated.

The Muslim experience in America is considered in this study for several reasons. The impact of Muslims' experiences in the United States on their changing perceptions of the world and their ideas about social order merits attention. Muslim impressions of American society, and the unprecedented intellectual freedom many Muslims enjoy here, have been essential in shaping the contemporary resurgence of an Islamic identity. While the current trend of Islamic resurgence denounces the West, especially America, as imperialistic, corrupt, and corrupting, there is a burgeoning migration of Muslims to Western countries, especially the United States.[53] This holds immense implications into the next century, for American society as well as the development of a global Islam.

Yvonne Haddad, author of several articles and books on Muslims in the United States, notes that Muslim students, having enrolled in American universities in increasing numbers since the mid-sixties (estimated to be over one hundred thousand per year in some years), have the opportunity to explore ideas and structures "away from the watchful eyes of wary governments and the criticism of [Muslim] traditionalists," and can critically assess their heritage, religious beliefs, and the global role of Islam.[54] The benefits of relative religious and intellectual freedom available in North America have proven to be crucial to the ideological formation of contemporary Islam. In Haddad's estimation, the United States in particular has of late become a center of "Islamic intellectual ferment" in the shaping of an Islamic world view.[55] Key individuals, such as Egyptian opposition leader Sayyid Qutb,[56] who was angered by what he "experienced as strong racial prejudice in the United States," have returned to their home countries to become catalysts in the conception of contemporary Islamic ideology and Islamic responses to the challenges of the present.[57] They have adhered to an alternative vision, based on an Islamic ideology, which is deemed to be more appropriate for their societies than the Western secular paradigm with Westernized political and social institutions adopted by previous generations.

The global implications of Muslims' experiences in and observations of North America have been profound.[58] The rising popularity of Islamic revival and the intensification of Islamic identity abroad has, in turn, affected the goals and identity of the Muslim community remaining in the United States. Muslims who stay permanently and those who are North American converts are encouraged by the global resurgence of Islam to assert their religious identity more publicly and to be more religiously observant. The ideal that unity (*tawhid*) of the Muslim community (*ummah*) overrides all other forms of national and ethnic affiliation, constitutes a challenge to other focuses of identity. Global and local factors combine to constitute the American milieu in which Muslims now emerge as new claimants for religious tolerance and protection.

As Muslims become more involved in the American political process, the character of the community is subject to change. Political involvement may tempt a religious community to compromise or even ultimately to eschew their religious mission. Once the attention of the Muslim community has been diverted from the internal concerns of interpreting the past and present in accordance with scripture, and prescribing the normative Islamic lifestyle, and has been broadened to include a functional understanding of American society, the nature and identity of the community will have evolved. As the Muslim community interacts with the surrounding legal and political systems, and becomes attentive to the authoritative institutions in them, it is likely that the institutional setting will have a transformative impact on the community.[59] The concerns of Muslims as participants in American political life will alter to some extent their practices and adherence to literal interpretations of scripture. How Muslims retain an Islamic identity while being part of the mainstream of American society will merit greater attention as the American Muslim community continues to grow and develop.

An example of this happening can be seen in the fact that the Islamic Society of North America (ISNA) now issues Islamic marriage certificates to Muslims only if the following provisions are met: (1) *a "proper" marriage license has already been secured from a court in the United States or Canada*; and (2) an Islamic marriage has been performed by or in the presence of an ISNA representative in the United States or Canada.[60] The first requirement indicates compliance with an American civil practice. The two provisions together demonstrate the intertwining of different normative orders, one official (i.e., the courts, state law) and the other unofficial (i.e., a voluntary association), in identifying plural sources of authority for the sanctioning of a marriage. This may be seen as an instance in which aspects of the dominant legal order are replicated in the rules of ISNA, which, as a voluntary association, might appear to be remote from the processes of state law.

Another example, which is examined in detail in chapter 6, is the cautious approach recently taken by the Islamic Society of East Bay-San Francisco in building a mosque in Fremont, California.[61] The Islamic Society has worked closely with the Fremont architectural review board and made sure that the size and height of the dome on the proposed mosque was acceptable to the board, the Fremont city planning department and neighborhood groups. Further, the mosque is being built on a site adjacent to the United Methodist Church in Fremont and, to insure their success, the Islamic Society has cultivated an amicable relationship with their neighbors. The church and the mosque have a formal arrangement to share in the construction and maintenance of parking and landscape and in the cost of sewer service. With this arrangement, the Islamic Society has gained a strong ally before the planning board and other municipal boards, including the City Council, as well as neighborhood groups from whom approval is necessary for the construction and operation of the mosque.[62]

The Islamic Society found that gaining approval was not a simple matter. It was "a task in educating not only the City Staff, but also the public" about the functions of a mosque and the intention of its prospective worshipers. To accomplish this task the Society utilized the print media. Plans for the mosque were published in such newspapers as the Fremont *Argus*, the San Jose *Mercury*, the Oakland *Tribune* and the San Francisco *Chronicle*.[63]

MAPPING THE TERRAIN

The principle of religious tolerance becomes valid and meaningful only through its elaboration within the particular circumstances of time and place. Muslim aspirations to be recognized as full members of American society, to assimilate without jeopardizing their Islamic identity, and to gain political and civil rights, raise questions about the meaning of religious tolerance. To date, relatively little scholarly attention has been paid to the circumstances of Muslim communities in the United States.[64] Most of what has been written have been sociological case studies of specific immigrant communities, which do not differentiate clearly between the influence of religious and ethnic factors. These offer valuable insights into the patterns of assimilation and acculturation of certain immigrant communities that happen to be Muslim, and begin to discuss Muslim responses to challenges presented by the host society. However, they do not deal in any systematic or analytical way with the responsiveness of the host society—the United States—to the special circumstances presented by Muslims.

Moreover, these studies have a fragmentary nature. That is to say, they have broken apart the totality of the Muslim experience by treating various national groups as hyphenated Americans going through essentially the same acculturation process as every other immigrant. These virtually, if not completely, ignore the religious element of identity and the historical dimension of experience. There is a need to overcome excessive fragmentation, heal the fractured approach, and focus on the meaning of religious tolerance in relation to what we constitute as state and society. An analysis of legal institutions in the United States can contribute to this endeavor. The point has been made elsewhere that "the fact remains that the chances of acculturation and recognition essentially depend on the kind of welcome which the host society provides for immigrants and their descendants."[65]

The paucity of information and studies about the reception of Islam and Muslims in the United States conceals an important aspect of the evolution of American society, ideology and institutions. While scholarly literature tends to focus on the experiences of Protestants, Catholics and Jews as the mainstream faiths, and of Jehovah's Witnesses, Mormons, Native Americans, Hutterites and Amish as minority faiths, nothing has been written about the reception of Islam as a faith that seems to many people to be foreign to, if not at odds with, the dominant Judeo-Christian tradition. Most people are in favor of religious freedom and tolerance in principle, but are less supportive of these norms in specific situations. Popular conceptions of Muslims and Islam may mitigate the willingness of Americans to adhere to the espoused principles of religious freedom and tolerance when called for by Muslims in the United States.

Studies of memoirs, articles, and letters written by immigrants from the Arab[66] countries and from other areas of the Muslim world,[67] as well as African-American Muslims[68] reveal early Muslim experiences with discrimination in the United States. Several recent works have examined negative stereotyping of Muslims, especially Arabs, and of media distortions of the Muslim image.[69] Problems of misunderstanding, prejudice, and hatred have become acute during the last quarter of the twentieth century, as Islam and Muslims have been maligned by association with terrorist acts.[70]

Crude caricatures of Muslims appear abundantly in the production and organization of popular culture. Events and situations, whether fictional or real, are presented to us within a framework of symbols, concepts, and images through which we mediate our understanding of reality. Our common sense ideas about race, ethnicity, and religion help us order social life in a way that is easily understood and meaningful, and provide us with clues about appropriate behavior and shared expectations. The news and entertainment media both generate stereotypes and rely on our familiarity with them in order to formulate the world in their terms and communicate ideas and information in an efficient, i.e., timely, fashion. Discussion of the effects of such overt manifestations of prejudice on Muslims has only just begun, although the primary focus to date has been almost exclusively on the distorted image of the Arab.[71]

A study of the particular circumstances and claims of Muslim communities for tolerance and acceptance as part of the American landscape will help illustrate the extent to which these misconceptions have been operationalized through the legal institutions of the United States. Ultimately, such work will reveal the degree to which the secular state in the United States has the capacity to accommodate pluralistic forms of community and can sustain a truly heterogeneous society. It will also attempt to show the connections between concepts of race, religion, and culture, on the one hand, and national identity on the other. In essence, it seeks to show how Muslims' claims are a constituent element of the discussion about who Americans are, and how the cultural setting—its characteristics and arrangements—both suggest and inhibit behavior.

2

Immigration and Citizenship
in Turn-of-the-Century United States

The first influx of Muslim immigrants to the United States began when popular sentiments running toward exclusion of Asians were reaching their peak. The exclusionary impulses that shaped public policy from the late nineteenth through the mid-twentieth centuries, while directed primarily against Chinese and Japanese immigrants, affected the lives and prospects of other Asian immigrants as well. This included many who professed the Islamic faith. The first wave of Muslim migration, between about 1875 and 1912, consisted mainly of Arabic-speaking immigrants from Syria, Lebanon, Jordan, and Palestine, then under Ottoman rule.[1] Just as the flow of Muslim arrivals (from South and Southeast Asia and the Middle East) was gaining momentum, it was interrupted by the racially inspired immigration and naturalization policies of the United States.

Immigration and naturalization policies have both reflected basic principles of social organization (e.g., pluralistic vs. homogeneous) and contributed to particular self-definitions in the United States. In this chapter and the next, we will consider the debates about immigration and citizenship generated by the influx of new immigrants in the late nineteenth century and the early part of this century. In particular, we hope to gain some insight into the American responses to the problem of national identity and see how these responses delimit the outer boundaries of the polity. This chapter takes as its starting point the considerable literature about the nativist movement in the United States, and proceeds to look at legislative and court records at the turn of the century for expressions of a hierarchical social order and ideals of citizenship. It attempts to show the influence racialist and eugenics arguments had in constituting national identity by, for instance, linking "race" and national character. It also shows how laws were used to deny citizenship to certain categories of people. The purpose of chapter 3 then will be to consider the consequences of the debates about citizenship for a particular faith community (Muslims) that is not discussed in the standard works on immigration.[2]

While the focus of chapters 2 and 3 remains the United States, illustrations will be drawn, when appropriate, from Canadian immigration and naturalization debates. Because Canada has been an important source of immigrants to the United States, especially from former British colonies and protectorates, the treatment of early Muslim arrivals to Canada must be included in order to understand the Muslim-American experience as well as the larger issues of Muslim migration to the West. It shall be demonstrated in what follows that restrictive measures were adopted in Canada during the late nineteenth and early twentieth centuries that paralleled American efforts to restrict immigration.

The legislative and court records discussed below are illustrative of the debates that have colored political discourse. They are useful not only because they say something fundamental about the standards for citizenship but also because they reveal how an ethnocentric or nativist conception of civic identity influences political debate. As concepts of rights, obligations, and social order evolve, various tensions are reflected in law. We can observe in law the mutual interaction "between the values . . . [of] a nation and the institutions which both reflect and shape them."[3] Here the interaction is between the values of ethnic and cultural homogeneity and the restrictive measures enacted by legislatures and upheld by courts.

MEMBERSHIP IN THE POLITICAL COMMUNITY

Several scholars[4] contend that American civic identity has been based on universalistic notions of citizenship. Technically, citizenship is acquired in one of three ways: *jus soli* (birth within the boundaries of a nation); *jus sanguinis* (through the nationality of parents); or the process of naturalization. As legal scholar T. Alexander Aleinikoff notes, the last of these methods, citizenship by naturalization, reveals the preeminent place accorded the Constitution of the United States in the configuration of loyalties. He writes,

> to obtain naturalization, an alien does not pledge allegiance to
> the American people or to the land mass of the United States.

Rather, she must promise "to support and defend the Constitution" and "to bear true faith and allegiance to the same." Becoming a citizen means joining a national political association—one founded by, dedicated to, and united around the Constitution.[5]

According to this standard, those who aspire to become American citizens simply are required to pronounce "a voluntary pledge of allegiance and an agreement to follow the laws of the country's sovereign government. In return, the government confers legal, constitutional status and political privileges on its citizens."[6]

Yet the history of the rules governing citizenship reveals the influence as well of an ethnocultural conception of identity, both in the United States and Canada.[7] More particularistic criteria than simply an adherence to liberal democratic principles—place of birth, gender, race, disease, special skills, domicile, and political beliefs— all have figured prominently in immigration and naturalization laws. Such laws were systematically defended in the historic traditions of discourse, which is evident in the legislative and court records of the turn of the century.

In the United States, immigration policy has long been thought of as "membership rules. . . [which] lie at the core of national self-determination and self-definition."[8] As Aleinikoff points out in his description of the citizenship-as-membership model prevalent in the United States, immigration policy is concerned with "membership in a national community. . . . Immigration decisions are membership decisions, and the immigration system is a process of selecting and evaluating candidates for membership."[9] Admission of immigrants implies their eventual acceptance as full members (i.e., citizens) of the political community, barring exceptional circumstances.[10] Thus, immigration policy serves as a "quantitative and qualitative screen. . . . Citizenship is clearly the intended end of the immigration process."[11]

Further, Aleinikoff cites an 1874 U.S. Supreme Court decision: "The very idea of a political community, such as a nation is, implies an association of persons for the promotion of their general welfare."[12] The stress is placed on the word "their" for, Aleinikoff writes, a nation is not a community "established for the benefit of non-members."[13] The concept of national membership is exclusive, for it designates non-members by defining members.[14]

Restrictive immigration and naturalization laws would seem inconsistent with the premises of liberal democracy, and historians and ideologues of American political thought have had trouble reconciling them. The problem, as immigration historian John Higham sees it, is that immigration policy inevitably entails discrimination, "and a system of discrimination that does not offend the democratic conscience has proved as yet unattainable."[15] In spite of what he acknowledges as "America's traditional susceptibility to race feelings," Higham persists in the argument that free immigration is a cornerstone of American society that can not be dislodged easily.[16] Essentially, exclusion based on race is portrayed as an aberration from the general adherence to Enlightenment ideals.[17]

Historically, the political struggle to develop and continually reconstitute a national identity in the United States has been characterized by racialist thought. Scholars of the history of race and ethnic relations, such as Ronald Takaki, have pointed out that while blacks and Indians were the prototypical oppressed racial groups, the social reality in the United States has been more complex than that. It was, and is, multifarious. It is

> dynamically multiracial. What whites did to one racial group had direct consequences for others. And whites did not artificially view each group in a vacuum; rather, in their minds, they lumped the different groups together or counterpointed them against each other.[18]

Yet, while the basis for social organization along racial lines has been more complex than a simple black-white dichotomy, the traditional expression of American race consciousness has been predominantly bi-racial. The presence of blacks and Indians in the New World was the central factor in the development of racial theories in the nineteenth century.[19] Reginald Horsman points out that the "new racial ideas which influenced the whole of Western society in the first half of the nineteenth century fell on especially fertile ground" in North America.[20] Racialist thought was stimulated by overt contacts between the dominant group—whites—on the one hand and the oppressed groups—blacks and Indians—on the other. Grassroots antipathies toward blacks and Indians were expressed in intellectual-scientific circles which "found necessary empirical evidence to confirm views that had become increasingly common . . . since the last decades of the eighteenth century" and helped articulate the idea that blacks and Indians were inferior varieties of humankind.[21]

It was in this historical context that racialist thought arose in the United States. Social relations between whites on the one hand

and blacks and Indians on the other were the genesis for systemic racism. Before the Fourteenth Amendment was ratified in 1868, blacks, both enslaved and free, were denied the status of American citizen.[22] By the end of the nineteenth century, despite efforts to expand the rights of blacks through post-Civil War legislation and amendments,[23] the persistence of a dual system of justice based on race was reaffirmed by the Supreme Court in the *Plessy* decision (1896) enunciating the "separate but equal" doctrine.[24] Segregationist law continued to operate in the southern United States effectively unchallenged by federal interdiction.[25]

It was in this light that racially-based concepts of social order endured, and, as they were developed and refined, they came to stress racial differentiation among Caucasian groups as well. The publication of William Z. Ripley's *The Races of Europe* (1899) popularized a classification of Europeans into three physical types: Nordic (Northern European); Alpine (Eastern European); and Mediterranean (Southern European). Anglo-Saxonism as a superior race was exalted and other national and cultural groups were, in comparison, debased. Race, not environment, was the independent variable accounting for the inequality of peoples. Thus, in light of the general scholarly and popular interest in the study of race, the arrival of new immigrant groups from southern and eastern Europe and Asia in the late nineteenth century took on special significance. Restrictionist writers such as Madison Grant (*The Passing of the Great Race*, 1916) warned that Nordics had to close the gates against the flood of the latter two, inferior, types that were pouring in from southern and eastern Europe.[26] The new influx "forced open the boundary of American citizenship" and renewed debates about membership in the political community.[27]

Ethnic and racial heterogeneity has elicited various responses, which clarify, define, and substantiate visceral racial anxieties expressing underlying concern for national identity and homogeneity. Newcomers alter the questions, but the fundamental issues remain unchanged. In his work on migration patterns and ethnic conflict in India, Myron Weiner has looked at social movements and government policy to show "how indigenous ethnic groups attempt to use power to overcome their fears of economic defeat and cultural subordination by more enterprising, more skilled, better educated migrant communities."[28] He suggests that policy is an instrument used to maintain or transform the ethnic division of labor, rather than a disinterested attempt on the part of government to ameliorate inter-ethnic tensions.[29] Thus, Weiner understands the motivations behind policy-making regarding migration as efforts either to uphold or challenge the status quo, motivations that may be fueled by irrational fears. Elsewhere, Weiner notes that, globally, neither notions of what constitutes "excessive" immigration nor responses to "excessive" immigration are uniform:

> As the world-wide flow of refugees and migrants continues, each country decides whether to accept immigrants, how many, under what terms, how it will treat those who have already entered, and whether it will force its migrants to go home.[30]

Thus, he contends, explanations for anti-migrant movements and policies must be provided on a case-by-case basis: "Contextual explanations seem more appropriate than a general theory in determining what constitutes a politically acceptable level of immigration."[31]

A tension between nativists, who advocate a homogeneous society, and pluralists, who emphasize the value of cultural diversity, is "at the heart of the controversy" in several countries faced with difficult migration problems.[32] While the debate about the desirability of particular migrants is often cast in economic terms—opposition is especially strong during periods of high unemployment—it is important to recognize that fears about the social, cultural and political impact of migrants and additional migration lie not far beneath the surface. Consciousness of kind, that "state of mind in which a [person] is vividly aware of [being] a member of a group different from other groups," is aroused especially when a dominant group feels that its prized values (e.g., social status, racial purity, religious cohesion) are threatened by the aspirations of newcomers or a minority group.[33]

Economic security and physical survival may be under a real or imagined threat, but this is not necessary nor even central to elicit group consciousness. For instance, V. S. McClatchy, former editor of the Sacramento *Bee* and a vocal leader of the Asian exclusion movement on the Pacific Coast of the United States and Canada during the early twentieth century, argued that the fundamental objection to immigration was racial, not economic. He writes, "local [i.e., Californian] opposition to this class of immigration had its inception in economic considerations, but basically the opposition is racial."[34] As Weiner observes,

> Nativism in the USA was only marginally linked to the issue of job competition, for the target of the nativists was not the number of migrants who came, but their composition. Nativists regarded Catholic, Greek Orthodox, Oriental and Jewish

migrants as disrupting a pre-existing American culture which they regarded as "Nordic," white and Protestant.[35]

A practical rejection of the ideal of tolerance is evident in some instances where discrete groups, distinguishable from one another on some basis (e.g., skin color), live in close proximity. As W. Peter Ward suggests, "racism and nativism are among the common consequences of interracial and cultural contact."[36] In Canada "it was because of the plural condition that whiteness came to form the core of the host community's identity."[37]

RACIAL AND EUGENICS CRITERIA

Anxieties over immigration are often expressed in the use of such terms as "cultural pollution," "over-foreignization," and "minoritization."[38] Anti-migrant sentiments are linked to concerns about preserving the composition of the social and political community, and cultural attitudes about the nature of the sending countries. The (real or perceived) possibility that foreigners might gain political control, or change the cultural or social order, is central in determining who is an "acceptable" immigrant and what constitutes an "acceptable" level of immigration. In the United States, beginning in the late nineteenth century, changes in thinking about immigration, and the erection of barriers to further immigration of specific types, gave governmental validation to the idea that immigration from places other than northwestern Europe was unacceptable.

Exclusionary politics in the context of constitutive debates about the membership of the American social and political communities acquired a very powerful conceptual tool by the late nineteenth century, whose provenance was in the ascendancy of genetics and evolutionary theory.[39] Racialist classification schemes were developed, borrowed from the apparently neutral fields of science and medicine, and were applied in the realm of public policy. The subject of immigration control and the reform of the rules of naturalization was already a matter of great interest in American public discourse from the mid-nineteenth century on, as immigration from southern and eastern Europe and Asia began to rise. The application of scientific principles and methods in explicating the dangers presented by this influx was grasped with enthusiasm for the most part, for it provided the necessary justification to support the exclusion of unwanted immigrants. Science was used to reaffirm prejudices many already held.

"By the middle of the nineteenth century, science had become such a dominant cultural idea that it rivaled religion in its explanatory power."[40] As the principles of evolutionary biology were popularized and gained credibility, the conceptualization of taxonomies of peoples, like flora and fauna, became evident and reflected the biases of the day. Genetics inspired many to hope for the improvement of society by regulating the inheritance of bad traits.[41] The assumptions of such a classification scheme rested on the presupposition that acquired characteristics, such as moral character, could be inherited, and led to the use of genetically-based distinctions among people as a justification for systemic inequalities and racism.

The belief "that character, disease, and temperament were inherited was called diathesis, or more commonly a constitutional bent."[42] Tuberculosis, cancer, and mental illness were atavisms triggered not only by the sufferer's moral and physical conduct but by those of his ancestors. Miscegenation thus became a serious threat to the well-being of a healthy "stock" of people because it introduced the possibility of injecting moral as well as physical deficiencies into a sound genealogy. "Miscegenation between races was viewed as both biologically and morally corrupting, with both understood as having physical causes."[43] Any racial mixture weakened the superior "stock."

These beliefs rested on the scientific learning of the day, and the works of social theorists and natural scientists alike reinforced basic presumptions about race and culture. For instance, the works of the French scholar Gobineau were translated into English and published in Philadelphia in 1856, with an addendum by the American craniologist Josiah Nott that corroborated the scientific validity of Gobineau's theories. Gobineau's work gave

> an exposition of the laws of nature which revealed that races differed from one another in their physical beauty, in their cultural power, and in their spiritual capacity, as well as in language and body structure.[44]

It also delineated a relationship between racial characteristics and the rise and fall of civilizations. Throughout history, as inferior "blood" of the lesser "races" of a civilization came into preponderance, the civilization degenerated. Gobineau contended that, "In particular, the Semites had time and again injected Negro strains into the dominant race and thus enfeebled it beyond the power of recovery."[45] Handlin notes that, as empires disintegrated and populations shifted, "The moral for the nineteenth century was inescapable."[46] Gobineau's theories of race received increasing acclaim in the United States and Canada over the next four decades as both nations faced a transforming immigration situation.

This line was adopted and developed by other eugenics specialists and proponents of immigration restriction, who attempted to prove that no degenerate stock could "ever be converted into healthy and sound stock by the accumulated effects of education, good laws, and sanitary surroundings."[47] This argument had an intellectual as well as a popular vogue. By the middle of the nineteenth century, as Horsman points out,

> the very phrases of the new scientific defenders of innate racial differences appeared in the mouths of politicians. Americans were reminded constantly that the observable differences between races could be shown scientifically to be based on physical and mental factors which had remained the same throughout history and against which environment and education were helpless.[48]

Essentially, restrictionists found in scientific discourse what they wanted to find: confirmation of inherent racial differences and their connection to supposedly observed cultural traits.[49] The science of the day "made the language of race an impelling vehicle for thinking and talking about culture."[50]

The idea that character and physical flaws were inherited served as a basis not only for racial distinctions but to discriminate politically and socially against the poor, the insane, and certain ethnic minorities. In the growing xenophobic atmosphere of the mid to late nineteenth century, the meaning of "race" expanded to include a variety of national groups. Southern and eastern Europeans were viewed as distinct and inferior racial groups, and Asians, whether classified as Caucasian or Mongolian, constituted distinct and inferior racial groups. The "concept of race had become a basic category of social analysis," in Canada as well as the United States.[51]

Thus, scientific principles and the newly-popularized knowledge of investigatory methods based on empirical evidence were borrowed and applied to social and political problems. The appearance of what in the natural sciences were "objective" measures was "incredibly persuasive, and this apparently benign clinical tool was suddenly crucial for legitimating prejudice."[52] Problems of race, crime, poverty, insanity, or deviation of any kind fit into a very simple explanatory category: genetic disease. The simplicity of the explanatory model enhanced its acceptability, as did expanding public knowledge about disease and its transmission. These ideas became a vital part of the eugenics arguments of the turn of the century, and became an integral part of public policy, as shall be demonstrated below.

LEGISLATIVE RECORD

Race

During the middle years of the nineteenth century, arguments began to circulate about the dangers of "race suicide" and the risk that the Anglo-Saxon "stock" would not survive if current immigration from southern and eastern Europe and Asia continued.[53] Heterogeneity of race was considered to be damaging and the "unassimilability" of peoples of dark complexions, etc., was emphasized.[54] These arguments generally ignored the fact that the Anglo-Saxons were themselves the product of 2,500 years of racial mixture.

By the 1850s, racial and eugenics arguments had firmly fixed the idea that the vast majority of the world's populations were incapable of creating democratic governments or living in a republican society.[55] Restrictionists, who wished to prove that people who were not Anglo-Saxon were innately incapable of comprehending or benefiting from democratic freedoms, helped to advance the popular acceptance of theories about general racial distinctions. Pressures for stricter enforcement of immigration regulations already on the books and for the legislation of further restrictions increased as the campaign for exclusion won popular support.

Advocates for the exclusion of objectionable immigrants (i.e., from southern and eastern Europe and Asia) were plentiful. Restrictionists preyed on fears about job competition, the unassimilability of newcomers, and cultural degradation, which were broadly based. The primary vehicles for expressing public anxieties over immigration were trade unionism and exclusion leagues. The Farmers Educational and Cooperative Union of America passed a resolution in 1908 calling on the U.S. government to exclude

> the present alien influx from Southeast Europe and Western Asia, and urge upon our federal officials the vigorous enforcement of all immigration laws in order to properly protect the country's welfare and to preserve its institutions, safeguard its citizenship, and preserve its Anglo-Saxon civilization for posterity.[56]

The potential to actualize this exclusion rested in earlier legislation and court decisions. In the United States the Chinese Exclusion Act of 1882 prohibited Chinese laborers from entering the country, and those who were already here became ineligible for naturalized citizenship.[57] This statute introduced a new category into immigration laws: "aliens ineligible for citizenship."[58] The Supreme Court's affirmation of the Act's constitutionality in the *Chinese Exclusion* cases contained the potential for exclusion of non-Chinese Asian immigrants as well.[59] These decisions laid the groundwork for various statutes in later years which restricted the rights of such aliens. For instance, in 1913 the California legislature enacted the Alien Land Law, a statute that prohibited Asians from owning and cultivating agricultural land. While the law was directed primarily at the Japanese it also affected other Asians, including "the few hundred [Asian] Indians" who farmed in the Sacramento, San Joaquin, and Imperial Valleys.[60] In 1914, a letter from the U.S. Secretary of Labor was appended to a Congressional bill on "Hindu" immigration which explained in full detail the implications of the *Chinese Exclusion* cases for Caucasian immigrants such as South Asians who were, like the Chinese, undesirable.[61]

In 1917, the enactment of new immigration restrictions provided the legal means, including a literacy test, to exclude more of the new immigrants. The "Barred Zone" provision of the Immigration Act of 1917 (39 Stat. 874) explicitly prohibited virtually all Asian immigration to the United States. Excluded from admission into the United States were immigrants from India, Siam, Arabia, Indo-China, the Malay Peninsula, Afghanistan, New Guinea, Borneo, Java, Ceylon, Sumatra, Celebes, and parts of Russian Turkestan and Siberia.

Canadian legislation similarly excluded Asian immigrants. As early as 1884, the British Columbia legislature passed a Chinese Immigration Act that forbade further immigration and imposed draconian restrictions on all Chinese residents of the province. However the federal government of Canada disallowed the Act, largely because the transcontinental railroad was not yet completed and Chinese labor was in demand. Further, the courts struck down one of the discriminatory restrictions, a poll tax on Chinese, although a prohibition on Chinese land acquisition remained in effect.[62] In 1885, the federal Franchise Act was amended to prohibit all Asians, including Chinese, from voting.[63]

At the same time that he nullified the Chinese Immigration Act, Canadian Prime Minister MacDonald promised an investigation of Chinese immigration and possible federal measures to regulate it. As Ward puts it, West Coast pressures forced MacDonald "to accept the principle of immigration restriction, although he would not enforce it until the railway's end was in sight."[64]

After years of acrimonious debates, the federal government of Canada promulgated the 1902 Immigration Act in the midst of growing concerns about diseases purportedly transmitted by immigrants. The statute divided all sick immigrants into three categories: the unfit; the fit; and the curable sick who were otherwise fit.[65] Further, the broad authority to make distinctions within and among these classifications was given to medical officers, appointed by the federal government to regulate immigration at all ports of entry. In short, the mounting immigration problem for Canada at the turn of the century was thought of as a medical one, and physicians were seen as having the appropriate expertise to protect the general welfare. The doctors' job was not simply to limit the number of entrants, but to select among them.

The 1903 report of the Bryce investigation into immigration articulated a scientific rationale for the exclusion and deportation of unwanted immigrants, "based on the latest ideas of eugenics and medical professionalism. . . . Racial notions concerning desirable sending countries were linked to scientific investigation" of social problems.[66] Doctors argued that race was a more important criterion than disease in determining immigration policies, since many diseases were curable and there was "no point in excluding from Canada someone of otherwise sound stock."[67] Those who were inherently incapable of becoming good Canadians, who would transfer their "foreign customs and morals," should be rejected. It was generally accepted that "medical reasons were an unimpeachable professional and scientific justification for racially based exclusion."[68]

The newly formed labor unions in Canada discriminated against Asians just as their American counterparts had in the early 1900s.[69] A call for restrictive measures appeared in such Canadian labor journals as the *Industrial World*, which queried,

> Is nothing to be done to stop the influx of mongols into this province [i.e., British Columbia]? What is in store for us as an Anglo-Saxon community? . . . The workers of British Columbia may be forced to give the government to understand, once and for all, that they intend this community shall remain Anglo-Saxon.[70]

About South Asians, the secretary of Victoria Trades and Labour Council in British Columbia argued in 1906 that

The people of India, in common with all Asiatic races, are reared and nurtured in and under the influence of civilization and environments that seem to be, in principle, totally opposed to the civilization and environments under which we of the Western civilization are born and reared. In practice they certainly are found to be both unwilling and incapable of assimilating with the people of the western races who have settled and developed this country, and who, for very justifiable reasons, aspire to control the future destiny of this broad and fair land, with the hope that civilization in the best and truest sense may advance and develop to a fuller degree than has yet been achieved. But the invitation or admission of these people, the Hindus [sic], would threaten and even make impossible the realization of such hopes.[71]

Similarly, the Liberal MP for Vancouver and vocal opponent of Asian immigration, R.G. MacPherson, reiterated this sentiment when addressing the question of South Asian immigration. He defines his sense of Canadian nationality in the following words, and places South Asians beyond the pale:

It is not enough to call it a question of cheap labour; it is not enough to raise the question of colour, race or creed. To be a Canadian citizen, at the beginning of this twentieth century, is no small thing. The men who built up this country, who hewed homes out of the forest, were men of first class, A 1 stock, and the responsibility they left us was great. The sentiment expressed in the proud phrase, *Civis Romanus sum*, becomes the citizen of Canada as well as it became the citizen of Rome. A race of men who cannot appreciate our mode of life, our mode of education, all that goes to make up Canadian citizenship, are not fit immigrants of this country. On the grounds of Canadian citizenship I attack this question.[72]

In the construction of the category of citizen, MacPherson makes it clear that, in his estimation, South Asians are excluded.

The 1908 report of MacKenzie King, the royal commissioner appointed to investigate the problem of "oriental" immigration, was only slightly less harsh in its assessment of South Asians in Canada. King framed his objections to the anticipated consequences of South Asian immigration in terms of the welfare of the South Asians themselves and the best interests of the nation. He writes,

That Canada should desire to restrict immigration from the Orient is regarded as natural; that Canada should remain a white

man's country is believed not only desirable for economic and
social reasons, but highly necessary on political and national
grounds. . . . It is clearly recognized in regard to emigration from
India to Canada that the native of India is not a person suited to
this country; that, accustomed, as many of them are, to conditions of a tropical climate and possessing manners and customs
so unlike those of our own people, their inability to readily adapt
themselves to surroundings entirely different could not do other
than entail an amount of privation and suffering which render a
discontinuance of such immigration most desirable in the interest of the Indians themselves. It was recognized, too, that the
competition of this class of labour, though not likely to prove
effective, if left to itself, might, none the less, were the numbers
to become considerable (as conceivably could happen were self-
interest on the part of individuals be allowed to override considerations of humanity and national well-being and the importa-
tion of labour under contract be permitted), occasion considerable unrest among the workingmen whose standard of comfort is
of a higher order, and who, as citizens with family and civic obligations, have expenditures to meet and a status quo to maintain
which the coolie immigrant is in a position wholly to ignore.[73]

Thus, the protection of the interest of Canadian citizens, "whose
standard of comfort is of a higher order" than South Asians, requires
that South Asians, who are *not* citizens, be excluded from Canada.

In addition to disease and race, the concept of the "continuous
journey" was used in Canadian immigration law to ban unwanted
newcomers. New restrictions were legislated in 1908 that prohibited
immigrants from entering Canada "unless they came from the country of their birth or citizenship by a "continuous journey and on
through tickets" purchased in their home country."[74] While these
restrictions appear to be nondiscriminatory, they were legislated
with Asians, particularly South Asians, in mind. Since there were no
direct routes from India to Canada at the time, the legislation eliminated virtually all South Asian immigration.

While Canada used what were *prima facie* neutral means of
discriminating among potential newcomers by requiring a "continuous journey," political pressures in the United States focused on
other means to restrict the flow, including the use of a literacy test.
The use of a literacy test and a poll tax were also proposed and, in
some cases, tested in Canada but received much less emphasis than
in the United States.

A Boston-based group known as the Immigration Restriction
League[75] began in the 1890s to pressure Congress for tighter control

of immigration, through such means as the imposition of higher head taxes and a literacy test. Advocates of the literacy-test idea argued that the test would be an objective device which would have the desired effect of ethnic discrimination. A literacy test "would cut in half the influx from southern and eastern Europe, without seriously interfering with the older immigration from the more literate areas of Europe."[76] The League's stated objective was to prevent the immigration "of large numbers of aliens of low intelligence, poor physique, deficient in energy, ability and thrift." Its spokespersons argued that the use of ethnically neutral policies—e.g., further tests for immigrants, such as a literacy test and a requirement that, upon arrival, each immigrant possess a minimum amount of money for self-support until employed—would accomplish the goal of excluding undesirable immigrants, for "experience shows that poverty, ignorance, and incapacity in general go together." They argued that, "from a eugenic standpoint" restrictions against the immigrant from southeastern Europe and Asia were justified. In 1911, the Immigration Restriction League claimed before the House Immigration Commission that "[r]ecent investigations in biology show that heredity is a far more important factor in the progress of any species than environment. Education can develop what is in an immigrant, but cannot supply what is not there."[77]

Congress passed a League-sponsored literacy bill as early as the 1896–97 legislative session, but President Grover Cleveland vetoed the bill.[78] The Immigration Restriction League continued its antiforeign agitation into the twentieth century, as the composition of the new immigration changed and "more and more remote cultures were drawn into the current. . . . [For the first time] a considerable number of Russian peasants, Greeks, Syrians and Armenians appeared" among the immigrant population.[79] As Higham notes, the elaboration of difference which began at least as early as the 1890s with the literacy-test campaign, came to fruition in the early twentieth century, for it was then that "the major theoretical effort of restrictionists" consisted in the transformation of relative cultural differences into an absolute line of cleavage, which was then used to explain the present danger of immigration "in terms of the change in its sources."[80]

A three-year study of the consequences of immigration from new "sources" was commissioned by the United States Congress as a result of continued pressures by restrictionists for the introduction of a literacy test. By calling for an investigation of the entire immigration problem, opponents of restriction hoped to block, or at least

postpone, the legislation of such a test.[81] But the outcome of the
study frustrated the aims of those who opposed the restrictionists
and underscored the eugenics arguments of the day. The United
States Immigration Commission, known as the Dillingham Commission, investigated immigration problems from 1907 to 1910, and
issued a forty-two-volume report, which attested to the "unfavorable
contrast between the northwestern and southeastern Europeans in
the United States" that restrictionists had struggled to articulate.[82]
The Commission's report served to reinforce rather than dispel
eugenics beliefs. Part of the report was a Dictionary of Races, which
distinguished among immigrants on the basis of physical features
and linguistic differences, creating fixed categories of immigrants.[83]
Moreover, the report had a direct impact on subsequent legislation;
it was widely cited in the congressional debates which produced the
Johnson Act of 1921, the immigration act which put in place a
national quotas system.[84]

Opponents of restrictionist measures argued that heterogeneity of race is actually better than homogeneity because racial mixture contributes to the genetic strengthening, rather than weaken-
ing, of a people. In its recommendation to Congress, the Immigration
Restriction League responds to this line of reasoning and turns it to
their own use:

> Assuming what is by no means proved, that a mixed race is a bet-
> ter race, we should do as we do in breeding any other species
> than the human, *viz.*, secure the best specimens to breed from.
> The same arguments which induce us to segregate criminals and
> feeble-minded and thus prevent their breeding apply to exclud-
> ing from our borders individuals whose multiplying here is likely
> to lower the average of our people. We should exercise at least as
> much care in admitting human beings as we exercise in relation
> to animals or insect pests or disease germs . . .
>
> We should see to it that the breeding of the human race in this
> country receives the attention which it so surely deserves. We
> should see to it that we are protected, not merely from the bur-
> den of supporting alien dependents, delinquents, and defectives,
> but from what George William Curtis called "that watering of
> the nation's lifeblood," which results from their breeding after
> admission.[85]

The League was successful in marshaling the support of influential citizens in its struggle to secure legislation of tighter restrictions.[86] Letters of support were solicited and submitted to Congress

along with the League's recommendation. In one such letter John Pomeroy, a prominent San Francisco attorney, favors the "extension of the Chinese-exclusion act to embrace all Asiatics, including subjects of the Turkish Empire." He asserts that the "fundamental objection to the immigration we wish to exclude is racial." He objects to "the racial character of three-fifths of the present immigration," which he illustrates by reference to a "Hindoo" (i.e., someone from South Asia) and an Arab.[87] Samuel G. W. Benjamin, the first U.S. Ambassador to Persia, also provided a letter of support. He avers, based on his long experience living abroad, that

> As for the Asiatic races, however brilliant they may be in certain directions, they have never had any clear notion of self-government, as understood by many of the Caucasian people of northern Europe, a matter of blood rather than education in its origin.[88]

Fear of racial deterioration was added to arguments in favor of greater restriction. Alabama Representative John L. Burnett, a member of the House Committee on Immigration and Naturalization during the nineteen-teens, advocated the restriction of immigration on the basis that southern and eastern European as well as Asian peoples were not assimilable with the "old stock" of America, descendants of northwestern Europeans. In stating his case he makes reference to Syrians among others:

> The people against whom my principal objection is aimed are of a different race and of a different color from those of America and northwestern Europe, and in my judgment they can never be perfectly assimilated. They may be amalgamated. History shows than whenever a superior race has been amalgamated with an inferior the superior has been pulled down and the inferior not lifted up.
>
> We have evidence of this in some of the very people about whom I have spoken. Who can detect the courage, the intelligence, or the honor of the ancient Greek in the people who now dwell amid the ruins of that splendid empire? *Who can detect the culture and the learning of the ancient Phoenician in the dirty Syrian to-day?* Who can see a trace of Caesar's triumphant legions among the beggars of Naples as they wallow to-day in filth and grime? [*Emphasis added.*][89]

Rep. Burnett argues that miscegenation is disastrous and results in the degeneration of civilizations. He illustrates this point in the following:

> It seems to me that when you can contrast the north Italian with
> the south Italian we find only one cause for the difference [in lit-
> eracy]. They have the same king, the same Parliament, the same
> laws; and yet the man north of the mountains is of the Cauca-
> sian, white race, and the other is of mixed race. . . . The Greeks
> are the same way; *the Syrians are the same way, mixed up with
> the Arabians and the people of African and western Asiatic coun-
> tries, until they are not our kind of people;* and they are not the
> kind of people from which those who settled this country sprang.
> [*Emphasis added.*][90]

This negative attitude toward immigrants from the Ottoman
Empire was also reflected in the press. For example, in the July 11,
1890, issue of the *Mail and Express,* Maronites (Roman Catholics
from the territories of modern-day Lebanon) who had emigrated
from Cyprus are described as:

> a fierce, war-like body of people but densely ignorant and
> imbruted by long battles against the Moslems. They are nominal
> Christians . . . [and] the movement for transporting them to the
> United States has the sanction and the support of the Roman
> Catholic Church. By nature, by training, by hereditary instinct,
> these predatory, half-savage mountaineers are totally unquali-
> fied for American citizenship . . . [and] their arrival among us
> would add still greater weight to the evil burden of foreign-born
> ignorance with which we are already afflicted. . . . A large num-
> ber of Armenians have made preparations for emigrating to the
> United States. . . . All of them are utterly unfitted to become
> American citizens.[91]

Clearly, by the turn of the century, if not before, the idea that
the mixing of blood results in the degeneracy of a people had captured "both the scholarly mind and the public imagination."[92] Moreover, the concept that "blood" and "culture" were intimately related
became powerful and influenced the legislation of immigration and
naturalization restrictions. The attitude that culture is an expression of race; that some races are more highly endowed than others,
and that superficial and striking physical characteristics, such as
differences in skin color, were visual signs denoting ability, intelligence, and morality (or the absence thereof), became operative in the
laws of the land.

Polygamy

The question of moral character was one which influenced ideas
about the acceptability of many of the "new" immigrants, and the

issue of polygamy had a particular effect for immigrants from the Muslim world. As a consequence of the anti-Mormon campaign of the late nineteenth century, immigration statutes added polygamists to the list of classes excluded from admission into the United States. Although directed primarily against Mormons, this stipulation created a legal means by which immigrants from the Muslim world were held suspect because what many Americans "knew" about Islam is that it allowed men to take many wives.

The Mormon experience in nineteenth-century United States reveals certain parallels with, and was influential in shaping, the experience of immigrants from the Muslim world. It has been noted that

> Outsiders saw the Mormons as the antithesis in almost every respect of what patriotic Americans should be and viewed the Mormon system as more akin to oriental despotism than to American democracy. This exotic image was enhanced by Mormon polygamy, practiced secretly since the 1840s and openly after 1852.[93]

While it is clear that many adherents of the Mormon faith are of Northwestern European origins, and that the religion originated in the United States, it is equally clear that from the perspective of the larger society at the turn of the century Mormons were distinctive. Further, "ethnicity is an immensely complex phenomenon," and to equate "ethnic" with "foreign" is a mistake.[94] Thus sociologist Thomas F. O'Dea asserts that the Mormons "represent the clearest example to be found in our national history of the evolution of a native and indigenously developed *ethnic* minority. [Emphasis added.]"[95] While the concern here is not with ethnicity *per se*, the point is that while Mormons did not differ from the dominant society in terms of national origins, they were viewed as a distinctive and inferior subculture. In the connotations of the lay meanings of such widely-used terms as "blood" and "moral character," nineteenth-century practices sanctioned by the Mormon church were perceived as threatening the cultural homogeneity and Anglo-conformity of America. With respect to the practice of polygamy the Mormon experience conditioned the American reception of arrivals from the Muslim world.

In 1882, the U.S. House of Representatives appointed a committee, known as the Ford Committee, to investigate the state of immigration. The committee submitted a report to Congress the following year in which it "praised the immigrant of the past, but said that it could not praise the immigrant then coming;" it recommended that Congress amend immigration laws in order to exclude from admission idiots, paupers, lunatics and convicts, polygamists, anarchists and persons having a "loathsome or dangerous contagious disease." Congress did not act upon the recommendations of the Ford Committee at that time, and pressure for immigration reforms continued.[96] Eight years later, in an immigration statute enacted on March 3 1891, polygamists were added alongside persons guilty of crimes of "moral turpitude" as aliens to be denied admission into the United States.[97]

The eugenics arguments of the day, especially the notion that "blood" and "moral character" were interrelated, were persuasive in matters other than immigration as well. This is evident in the following case involving anti-Mormon sentiment, presented before the House of Representatives Committee on the Judiciary. In a 1902 congressional hearing considering a proposal to adopt a constitutional amendment prohibiting polygamy, a witness, Mrs. Fanny Hallock Carpenter, testified that a state, like a living organism, can suffer from "degeneration." The description she provides is analogous to the descriptions of degeneracy of human "races" evident in the debates on immigration. She warns against the harboring of atavistic "moral evil," inherent in polygamy and the Mormon Church, that will deplete the moral forces of the country. "Evil has a wonderful capacity for growth," she avers. "Whatever appeals to the baser side of mankind seems to be all-powerful. Evil is catching in the way that goodness never is."[98] Mrs. Carpenter urges Congress to add the proposed anti-polygamy amendment, saying that

> the spirit of this amendment is already the unwritten law of the great mass of the nation, but to give it practical power in those States where the moral character seems weak it must be plainly written. . . . Our Constitution may be called our moral character. The world looks to it to learn what are the traditions of our blood, what are our principles, what constitutes our honor, and wherein lies our nobility of soul.[99]

In this brief statement various points are made: (1) Americans of strong moral character, i.e., those who constitute the "great mass of the nation," oppose polygamy; (2) in some states (those in which Mormons live) polygamy is practiced, the moral character is weakened, and the power of law is needed to enforce morality (i.e., monogamy); (3) to give them "practical power," we must reaffirm existing notions of morality in written form; and (4) the Constitution is analogous to the American "moral character," reflects the American "nobility of soul" and is the repository of American principles and the cultural heritage ("traditions") of "our blood." This last point connects the Constitution, representing "moral character," with "our blood," through which traditions and principles are transmitted.

This final point is directly related to our inquiry. If the Constitution is our "moral character," containing our principles and the "traditions of our blood," then presumably people not of "our blood" may not be included in the community giving its allegiance to the Constitution. The possibility of others acquiring an understanding of and loyalty to democratic institutions is foreclosed when "tradition" is tied to genetics. While Mrs. Carpenter does not define whom she means, it seems from the context and the meaning of "our blood" in the discourse of the day that by "our blood" she refers to Americans descending from northwestern Europeans. To take the point a bit further: Since it is plural marriage she objects to, it seems that Mrs. Carpenter connects the "immorality" polygamy embodies to people of another "blood" not represented by the moral character of the Constitution. Although she developed her argument with Mormons in mind, Mrs. Carpenter could as easily have directed it at Muslims. In the context of immigration and naturalization, the potential for exclusion of immigrants from the Muslim world, where polygamy is acceptable under certain circumstances, lies in the repudiation of Mormon practices.

Even without an anti-polygamy amendment, the loyalty of Mormons to the nation and, by association, the Constitution, was suspect in the late nineteenth century.[100] As Sanford Levinson has pointed out in *Constitutional Faith*, the Mormons were required to defer to the civil religion of the United States over the demands of their religious faith. For instance, voters in the Territory of Idaho had to take an oath declaring

> that I am not a bigamist or polygamist . . . [and] I do regard the Constitution of the United States and the laws thereof . . . , as interpreted by the courts, as the supreme laws of the land, the teachings of any order, organization or association to the contrary notwithstanding. . . .[101]

Thus "one's devotion to the civil religion [was viewed] as a predicate condition" for the ability to vote in national, territorial, and local elections.[102] Essentially, Mormons had to either disavow or amend their faith to conform with American principles, as reflected in the Constitution, and the failure to do so placed one outside the political community.[103]

Fanny Carpenter's words did not refer to, or even contemplate, the presence of Muslims, yet her words are pertinent to them. The implications of the anti-polygamy phenomenon for immigrants from the Muslim world were not lost on the general public or public officials. For instance, a Congressman made the point in the context of the following exchange. In a House hearing about Near East refugees held in 1922, an "expert" invited to speak to the Committee on Immigration and Naturalization, Mr. Lothrop Stoddard,[104] opposed the admission of refugees from Turkey—mostly Armenians fleeing massacres at the hands of the Ottomans—because of the "national character" of the refugees. They "are a result of an extraordinary racial mixture which has been going on for at least 2,500 years," and have characteristics that make them extremely undesirable:

> For one thing, they are very largely a parasitic population, living by their wits, by unproductive means of labor, by petty trading, by graft, and by similar equivocal methods. Wherever they have gone in great numbers they have exercised a very baneful influence on whatever country they have entered. . . . They have brought in the destruction of ideals, and various destructive religious and other ideas. . . .[105]

The people of whom Mr. Stoddard spoke were not necessarily Muslim but came from the Muslim world. When asked by the Chairman of the House Committee on Immigration and Naturalization whether there was "any pressure from Mohammedans [i.e., Muslims] to enter the United States," Mr. Stoddard replied, "Very few Mohammedans come in."[106] The Chairman then stated that the reason for this was

> that the laws of the United States prevent the admission of those who preach and practice polygamy, and most true Mohammedans are unable to deny that when they are asked . . . [and that] Mohammedans can not very well come in unless *they deny the faith to which they adhere*. [*Emphasis added.*][107]

Here it is very clear that a "predicate condition" for admission of Muslim immigrants into the United States is the disavowal of Islam because the faith allows for polygamy. Neither the possibility that one may embrace Islam without condoning the practice of plural marriage, nor the actual incidence of polygamy in the Muslim world, nor the limited circumstances in which polygamy is sanctioned, enters into consideration. Polygamists, and by extension Muslims, according to the Chairman's thinking, simply are not allowed by law to be members of the American political community.

Significantly, from this statement another point becomes clear. An element of *non*-recognition rings in what the Chairman of the House Committee has said. In other words, he has described a world and Muslims are not in it. Muslims simply do not exist within the boundaries of the American polity because their presence would violate the law. Of course, this description does not fit well with reality, as we know from the records that many Muslims actually were already here.

The opportunities for many potential immigrants from the Muslim world to enter the United States were severely restricted as a result of the Immigration Act of 1917. Others who were not affected by the "Barred Zone" provision, such as Syrians and Palestinians, were limited by the Johnson Act of 1921,[108] which allotted quotas for admission of immigrants on the basis of nationality. The 1921 act allowed for the annual admission of immigrants not to exceed three percent of the number of aliens of the same "national origins" already residing in the United States at the time of the 1910 census. This act was replaced by a new quota act in 1924 which designated 1890 as the census year of reference and reduced the quota from three to two percent.[109]

Muslims as a religious group were adversely affected by the quota scheme. Most immigrants from the Muslim world arrived in the United States between 1900 and 1914. Their numbers were exceedingly small in the 1890 census. Furthermore, the "national origins" of many had not been classified in the immigration and census records of 1890, because until 1899 Syrians, Greeks, Armenians, Palestinians, Turks, and others from Western Asia were all considered together to be from that part of the Ottoman Empire known as "Turkey in Asia." The quotas were not lifted until 1965, after which Muslim immigration reached unprecedented heights.

Together, exclusion on the basis of race and culture enabled Americans and Canadians to delineate their own identity—to affirm the virtues of self-control and a republican form of government, set apart from the presumed libidinous and despotic qualities of other cultures. The campaign for exclusion reflected notions of racial superiority which were ubiquitous by the mid-nineteenth century. Law, in its proscriptions and prescriptions, symbolizes dominant social relations. Beliefs about the ideological and moral character of persons from distant places, which are at variance with the prevailing conceptions of who we are and what constitutes our character, became embodied in law. Despotism, monarchism, and licentiousness all were anathema, and those whose origins lay in the lands where such vices presumably went unchecked were, by association, tainted.[110]

The court cases examined here demonstrate the authority courts have in defining the parameters of possible action and in "channel[ing] human action."[111] We have looked at appellate court decisions about the question of citizenship to see what impact the courts have in providing structure to political life (e.g., defining who is entitled to citizenship). By paying some attention to the influence they have had in constituting political reality and articulating "doctrines and perceptions of what is possible," we begin to see the role played by the courts in "interpreting the authoritative concepts governing politics"—in this case, racialist and eugenicist theories that validated exclusion of certain people from citizenship—and associating them with the authority of the state.[112]

As Takaki points out, many studies of race relations in America fail to recognize "how the oppression of different groups served common needs of white men," and have "tended to focus on the outgroups rather than those responsible for the plight of the oppressed."[113] However, while this is true in some measure, it can also be argued that a dominant group never completely determines the actions of a subordinate group; rather, it is the process of interaction that determines the result.[114] It is with this in mind that we turn our attention next to the actions taken by immigrants from the Muslim world in response to standards of citizenship.

3

Other Asian
Immigrants from the Muslim World

Interwoven into the general Asian experience in the United States is the particular experience of immigrants from the Muslim world. The collateral effects of racial exclusion, as it was operationalized via immigration and naturalization policies at the end of the nineteenth and well into the twentieth centuries, has had important implications for the development of the Muslim community in the United States. Muslim immigrants have come from more than sixty countries, most of which are in Asia.[1] Subject to restriction as "Turks," "Syrians," and "Other Asians" at the turn of the century, they were hindered in the process of setting down roots in the United States. As we shall see in what follows, restriction was critical in the formation of American Islam.

The purpose of this chapter is to place the responses of immigrants from the Muslim world at the center of the analysis of citizenship debates. Specifically, the chapter looks at the connections between what the courts said about citizenship, as well as the enforcement of immigration and naturalization laws, and what the affected community, reactively, has done. An attempt is made to show that at least part of this community followed the courts' lead in adopting racialist and eugenicist criteria to construct a national identity which in effect denied equal access to citizenship to "Asiatics." By such actions, the immigrants have taken part in the mediation of social consciousness along lines that made racialist distinctions central in the self-definition of the American people.

DESCRIPTION OF THE COMMUNITY

The first of the five waves of Muslim migration to the United States, identified by Haddad and Lummis, arrived from 1875 to 1912. Most of these immigrants came from the Arabic-speaking provinces of the Ottoman Empire: Syria, Jordan, Palestine, and Lebanon. During the same period a small number of Indian immigrants, mistakenly called "Hindus," were Muslims.[2] Before World War II, Muslim immigrants were attracted primarily for economic reasons.[3] Both the "pull" of employment and prosperity with the industrialization of America, and the "push" factor of socioeconomic deterioration at home affected outward migration.[4] According to Akbar Muhammad, "the first immigrants were more concerned with finding a comfortable economic niche in America than with propagating their faith."[5] Similarly, the first Muslim arrivals to Canada were "mostly young men from farming communities with little formal education" who came in search of work.[6] For the sake of economic survival, many of the more traditional Islamic observances of the old world were neglected in the new world. Haddad found that the first generations of immigrants "were less likely to be actively involved in organized religious activities. Congregational prayer, if practiced at all, was often held in homes or small mosques. . . ."[7]

The initial migratory pattern from the Arabic-speaking part of the Muslim world was overwhelmingly a Christian phenomenon. The ratio of Christians to Muslims in pre World War II Canada was believed to have been more than two to one.[8] By using Ottoman emigration records as well as U.S. immigration statistics, Kemal Karpat judges that fifteen to twenty percent of immigration of this type was Muslim. However, Philip Hitti gives a lower figure, estimating that, in 1924, more than 95 percent of all "Syrian" immigrants to the United States were Christian. "Their Muslim counterparts, as several historians have pointed out, faced psychological, religious, and cultural obstacles, and hence initially displayed considerable reluctance to immigrate to the West."[9] Paradoxically, the very *absence* of familiar Islamic symbols in the new world has been cited as one of the factors which discouraged further immigration from parts of the Muslim world. Anecdotal evidence is told and retold about Muslims who were informed, once aboard American-bound ships, that there were no mosques in the United States or that "America was *bilad kufr*, a land of unbelief," and changed their minds about immigrating.[10] According to the biography of one Muslim immigrant, in a shipboard conversation he "was told that Muslims were not allowed to enter America." In response he changed his name from Mohammed to two names easily recognized from a Judeo-Christian perspective: Abraham and Joseph.[11]

Albeit slowly at first, Muslims overcame these obstacles and joined their Christian counterparts in growing numbers. For this analysis, however, the focus is not on the actual numbers of Muslims but the beliefs many Americans held about life in the Muslim world that became operative in debates about immigration and naturalization. Regardless of religious affiliation, immigrants from the Muslim world were suspect in part because of the Western image of the Orient, including Islam, and were the object of efforts to restrict their entry and exclude them from access to citizenship. How Muslims reformed themselves and their lives around the (mis)conceptions other people held about them and were influenced by those beliefs will be examined below.

LEGAL STANDING OF IMMIGRANTS FROM THE MUSLIM WORLD

How did immigrants from the Muslim world fare in the midst of these racialist and eugenics arguments? In the United States the question whether many could become naturalized citizens remained to be settled at the turn of the century. Post-Civil War legislation and amendments, designed to extend protection of the law to all those of African descent, including freed slaves, influenced efforts to resolve this question as well. How the question was answered—through the application of law to a slightly different context, presented by "new" immigrants—was crucial, because, as John Brigham notes, "small changes in the inclusiveness of categories or their application can have a tremendous effect on political life."[12] In the record examined below we will see the impact of the judicial answer to the question whether particular aliens were acceptable citizens. In essence, it produced a political struggle to invoke the rights of citizenship for another category of people.

The governing statute, the 1790 Naturalization Act,[13] provided "that any alien being a free white person may be admitted to become a citizen" of the United States, provided that she was of good moral character, pledged an oath to support the Constitution, and had resided in the United States for two years before applying for citizenship by naturalization. In 1870, "aliens of African nativity and . . . persons of African descent" were added by amendment of the original statute.[14] When the statute was enacted in 1790, most immigration came from Europe and the courts, interpreting the act more than one hundred years later, decided on an *ad hoc* basis whether the new immigrants applying for naturalization fell within the meaning of the term "white persons," ostensibly as the framers of the statute would have intended.

When Congress amended the statute in 1870 to extend full citizenship to persons of African origin, an element of confusion was added to the debates affecting the legal status of immigrants from the Muslim world. Under the revised law "Arabs and Hindus from Africa, but not necessarily Asia," theoretically could qualify for naturalization. This measure "laid the basis for future problems by mixing geographic with ethnic or racial qualifications for citizenship," as shown in the court records discussed below.[15]

Further, in their efforts to include a new category of eligibility for citizenship, the lawmakers made a crucial omission. By identifying "whites" and persons of African provenance as suitable for naturalization, they did not provide for the possibility that persons who did not fit within the limits of the construction, who were neither white nor from Africa, might apply. Thus the courts, unable to deduce satisfactorily from the literal terminology of an earlier statute what the lawmakers meant precisely by "white," tended to rely on popular opinion and other, often contradictory, criteria such as anthropological evidence to decide which ethnic groups qualified for naturalization. Immigrants from the Middle East were quite literally an interstitial group, since geographically the region straddles the three continents of Europe, Asia, and Africa; as such, they were "subjected to close scrutiny and in several cases were denied citizenship."[16] After a directive was issued from the U.S. Bureau of Immigration and Naturalization in 1911 telling court clerks to reject declarations from applicants for naturalization who were neither white nor of African descent or nativity, some immigrants from the Middle East "encountered difficulty in securing citizenship."[17]

The two groups of immigrants from the Muslim world whose presence raised questions about the desirability of their admission were the Syrians and the South Asians. It should be noted that, although the terms are used here for the sake of convenience, these designations are not very accurate and are easily misconstrued. Syrians included those who came from the territories of modern-day Lebanon, Israel, and Jordan, as well as Syria,[18] and South Asians, also known as Asian Indians, were popularly but mistakenly called "Hindus" both in popular discourse and in official records. As one scholar recently observed, this (mis)construction of South Asians was adopted by the affected community itself: "Punjabis and other Indians in Canada were called Hindus by the host community; and they not only accepted the term but used it themselves until the 1960s, even though the majority were Sikhs."[19]

Syrians

Until 1899, many immigrants from the Arab Muslim world were recorded in American immigration and census statistics as "Turks from Asia."[20] But because the numbers of immigrants arriving from "Turkey in Asia" began to rise steadily in 1895, this category became too broad and imprecise for accurate recordkeeping. This factor, coupled with the growing domestic political pressures for classification of immigration by source discussed earlier, led the U.S. Bureau of Immigration to compile data by race as well as country of origin. Thus, immigrants hailing from the Ottoman Empire were classified as Syrians, Palestinians, Armenians, etc., under the general category of "Turkey in Asia."

According to Bureau statistics, Syrians arrived in unprecedented numbers during the fifteen years preceding World War I: "A total of 86,111 Syrians, recorded between 1899 and 1914, joined those who had come previously and uncountable hundreds of their unrecorded countrymen."[21] By 1910, Syrians accounted for nearly one-third of all the U.S. population born in Asia.[22] Syrian immigration was at its peak between 1900 and 1914.[23] But when travel was restricted during the years of World War I, the number on record of Syrian entries into the United States dropped to only approximately 3,700. After the war ended 12,288 arrivals were recorded in the four-year period between 1920 and 1924. With the imposition of the Quota Act in 1924,[24] the number of Syrians allowed to enter the United States annually was reduced to 100.

The appearance of the Syrian immigrant community in Canada, although of smaller size, roughly paralleled that of the United States. Syrian immigration in Canada reached an estimated 2,000 at the turn of the century, and was at its pre-world war peak between 1900 and 1911.[25]

Popular representations of Syrians as something other than white abounded in the United States. Philip Hitti cites the example of a 1920 election campaign in Birmingham, Alabama, in which the candidate for coroner billed himself as "the white man's candidate." "They have disqualified the negro, an American citizen, from voting in the white primary," the campaign flier read. "The Greek and Syrian should also be disqualified. I DON'T WANT THEIR VOTE. If I can't be elected by the white men, I don't want the office."[26]

In 1909, the U.S. District Court of St. Louis held that Syrians could not be naturalized because they are not white. This decision was reversed on appeal,[27] but the lower-court decision and others like it had a ripple effect within the Syrian community. The fact that the law did not easily recognize the rights of Syrians as aspirants to full citizenship generated a political struggle. The decision that Syrians were not white, even though repudiated, shaped the subsequent actions taken by the Syrian community. As Michael Suleiman notes, "the problem of racial identification and citizenship traumatized the Arabic-speaking community for several years early in the century."[28]

Many Syrians were naturalized, but some courts denied them citizenship. Collectively, Syrians took an interest in the fate of those who were rejected based on an interpretation of the 1790 Naturalization statute that held that the term "white persons" really meant people of European descent. The subject of Syrian eligibility for American citizenship was taken up in several articles appearing in the Arabic-language press in the early twentieth century. Many authors reiterated the racialist arguments of the day. An effort was made to place Syrians closer to Europeans than Africans on a phrenological chart depicting the shape of the head and facial angles of different "races."

The Arabic-language press in the United States, which first appeared during the closing years of the nineteenth century, yields evidence of changing, often conflicting, feelings about national identity. As George Tumeh points out in his 1965 study, *Al-Mughtaribūn al-Arab fi Amrika al-Shamaliyyah (The Arab Immigrants in North America)*,[29] this press, consisting of newspapers, magazines, books and poetry, "in its origins and development, reflected the development of the immigrants' life itself." Its first stage reveals the immigrant community's preoccupation with and longing for the homeland. In its second phase, at the beginning of this century, the output of the Arabic-language press reflected "what characterized [the community] in terms of parochial or confessionalist feelings, family loyalties, and particularistic, regional affiliations, all of which led to bitter [internecine] feuds and fanned the flames of discord within the immigrant community." In order to illustrate his point Tumeh, without providing details, refers to an altercation among some immigrants in New York in 1904 that "resulted in a number of injuries and the intervention of the American police and reports in the big New York City newspapers." He suggests that the discord this incident illustrated was expressed in the pages of the immigrant press.[30]

On a more sanguine note, however, Tumeh emphasizes the potential of the Arabic-language press to have a salubrious effect in dispelling factionalism. In the same period, he argues, the press strengthened ties among Syrian immigrants in the United States, Canada, and South America, and encouraged readers to rise above ancient divisions and narrow affiliations.[31]

A Syrian immigrant named Kalil A. Bishara was prompted by court decisions denying American citizenship to Syrian applicants on the grounds of "race" to research his background and, "discovering" that Syrians were Arabs, argued that as Arabs they were the "purest type of Semitic race," and had a "better claim upon the White Race than that of any modern nation of Europe."[32] Thus, he contends, Syrians were "white persons" within the meaning of the 1790 Naturalization statute. In support of the fitness of Syrians for American citizenship, Bishara wrote in the English-language edition of his study, *Origin of the Modern Syrian*:

> I most emphatically declare that our [American] national character needs the Semitic element in it. That "pliability combined with iron fixity of purpose," which has developed a Moses, an Elijah, a Hannibal, an Amos, a Paul, a Peter, a John, not to begin to enumerate that large host of Fathers, Prophets and Apostles.[33]

Noticeably missing from the list is the "name of one major prophet, namely Muhammad," the Prophet of Islam.[34] As Suleiman points out, this omission seems to have been intentional, for the Arabic-language edition of the same study includes Muhammad's name. While we lack hard evidence to prove this supposition, it is possible that Bishara omitted mention of Muhammad in the English edition because he was apprehensive about American sentiments against Muslims and felt it was necessary to distance Syrians from Islam.

Syrian activity in researching their background and asserting their fitness for citizenship was spurred principally by court cases involving Syrians applying for naturalization. The Syrian American Associations of the United States argued their position in court cases interpreting the 1790 Naturalization statute, both where Syrians were applicants for citizenship and where other, non-Syrian, applicants faced the same legal challenges. Syrians went to the courts, chiefly as interveners or *amici curiae*, in cases involving Armenians—for instance in *In re Halladjian*[35]—and another involving the eligibility of Parsees for citizenship, in *United States v Balsara*.[36]

The court records of Syrian applicants for naturalization include the cases of *Ex Parte Shahid*[37] and *In re Dow*,[38] heard on appeal as *Dow v United States*.[39] These cases are reviewed below.

Ex Parte Shahid. District Court Judge Henry A. M. Smith of Charleston, South Carolina, considered in *Ex Parte Shahid* whether the applicant, Mr. Faras Shahid, was "a fit subject to be naturalized." Mr. Shahid's circumstances presented Judge Smith with the opportunity to speak to two issues: polygamy, and the meaning of the term "white person."

At the outset, Smith describes Mr. Shahid. He comes from "Zahle, in Asia Minor, in Syria" and is a Christian. He writes in Arabic but cannot read or write English, and understands English "very imperfectly." He failed to understand questions put to him—in English—about "the manner and method of government in America, and of the responsibilities of a citizen." When asked in English if he were a "disbeliever in organized government," he answered in the affirmative. He also admitted (probably falsely) to being a polygamist.[40]

This portrayal of Mr. Shahid casts him as an alien without, presumably, the mettle to make a suitable citizen of the United States. He neither understands questions regarding the American government and the responsibilities of a citizen, nor believes in any form of organized government. The likelihood that Mr. Shahid simply misunderstood the questions put to him because of the language barrier, and, as a result, was mistaken in his replies, does not detract from the credibility of his answers. He is taken at his word because his very word leads to his inadmissability.

Despite the answers he gave in his naturalization hearings, it is highly unlikely that Mr. Shahid was a polygamist himself or even believed in the practice of polygamy. Mr. Shahid was a Christian who emigrated from Zahle, a town in the Beka'a Valley that historically has been a Christian enclave in what was then "Syria," a province under Ottoman (Muslim) rule. Yet his affiliation with the larger (Muslim), rather than the smaller (Christian) political and social community in his homeland determined the court official's perception of Mr. Shahid.

In holding this perception, Judge Smith was not alone. It appears that the U.S. Attorney's office, representing the federal government, objected to the naturalization of Syrians in many cases in the early years of this century because it attached "some importance to the fact that the applicant was born within the dominions of Turkey [*aka* Ottoman Empire], and was heretofore a subject of the Sultan of Turkey."[41]

On the point of Mr. Shahid's positive response to the question about polygamy, and the fact that Judge Smith found it to be noteworthy, we have what is probably a more accurate indicator of the American understanding of Islam and life in "the Orient" than of Mr. Shahid's personal situation. Polygamy was a (in this case, Muslim) practice that had been repudiated by American society. The Supreme Court had reinforced the belief that polygamy was outside the realm of acceptable practice less than a generation before in the so-called "anti-Mormon" cases.[42] Whether or not Mr. Shahid himself was a polygamist was not relevant; the fact that the immigration laws of the United States stipulated that polygamists were among the excluded classes gave the judge a legal device with which he could reject Mr. Shahid's petition for naturalization.[43]

The court's interpretation of the term "white person" reinforced the inclination to exclude Mr. Shahid from the American citizenry on the grounds of polygamy. Judge Smith ruled that, even though the language of the 1790 Naturalization statute is ambiguous and other courts treating similar cases reached different decisions, a "modern Syrian of Asiatic birth and descent" was not eligible for citizenship. Smith narrowly construed "white person" to mean exclusively someone of European descent and provided the following interpretation of the statutory language:

> It would mean such persons as were in 1790 known as white Europeans, with their descendants, including as their descendants their descendants in other countries to which they have emigrated, such as the descendants of the English in Africa or Australia, or of the French and Germans and Russians in other countries.[44]

Smith admits that this is not, "ethnologically or physiologically speaking," a very clearly defined group. He acknowledges that too much mixing among populations had already gone on and that his definition "includes many peoples containing many of them blood of very mixed races, but the governing or controlling element or strain in all is supposed to be that of *a fair-complexioned people of European descent.*" [*Emphasis added.*][45]

While he attempts to base his definition on a (pseudo)scientific genetic concept—"blood"—Smith does not give up the idea of skin color, although he protests "the uncertainties of shades of color" and the futility of drawing "the dividing line between white and colored."[46] Further, his standard for citizenship is connected not simply to color—fair-complexioned—but to cultural origin—European descent. Smith merges the notions of "blood" and "culture" by relying on complexion as an outward expression, and European descent as a cultivated expression, of "race." He assumes that culture is one manifestation of blood, and differences in blood parallel differences in culture. Therefore one is European by virtue of blood, not by virtue of place of birth. Thus a "pure-blooded Chinaman," even if born in England or France, is not European.[47] Moreover, the concept of "Jewish, Turkish, or Greek blood" remains central to his argument.[48] Excluded from citizenship are not only Syrians but "all inhabitants of Asia, Australia, the South Seas, the Malaysian Islands and territories, and of South America" who are not, by blood or culture, of European provenance.

In re Dow. In this case the court denied naturalization to Mr. George Dow, a Syrian, on the grounds that he was not a "white person" within the meaning of the 1790 Naturalization statute. South Carolina District Court Judge Smith, the same judge who denied citizenship to Mr. Shahid in *Ex Parte Shahid,* initially rejected Dow's application for citizenship but later granted a rehearing of the matter at the request of "other Syrians interested."[49] At the rehearing, the attorneys for the Syrian American Associations of the United States stated their argument alongside the argument of Mr. Dow's counsel.

In his opinion Judge Smith took note of the Syrians' position, writing that

> Deep feeling has been manifested on the part of the Syrian immigrants because of what has been termed by them the humiliation inflicted upon, and mortification suffered by, Syrians in America by the previous decree in this matter which they construe as deciding that they do not belong to the "white" race.[50]

Judge Smith rejects Dow's application again, not because Mr. Dow definitely falls outside of the "Caucasian" or "white" race, but because Smith interprets the term "white persons" in the 1790 Naturalization statute to mean only persons of European descent. Asiatics, by definition non-Europeans, do not qualify for citizenship. Rather than contest the statute, the Syrians offer an alternative interpretation and argue that the decision ought to be reversed because (1) the term "white persons" means Caucasians and not persons white in color; (2) Mr. Dow is a Semite; (3) all Semites are Caucasians; (4) the courts had already decided in their favor by admitting European Jews under the terms of the statute, and Jews are Semites (thereby creating a precedent for their acceptance as well); and (5) "the history and position of the Syrians, their connection through all time with the peoples to whom the Jewish and Christian people owe their religion, makes it inconceivable that the statute could have intended to exclude them."[51]

By this line of reasoning, the Syrians distance themselves from Mongolians, or the "yellow" race of Asia as it was commonly called, and emphasize their Caucasian origin. They also affirm the authority of the courts in making naturalization rulings on the basis of a racial scheme by proving that they are white, and by pointing to the precedents of the naturalization of Jews. They argue on that basis that Syrians, who, like Jews, are Semites, should be included as citizens. Finally, by inference, the Syrians' argument serves to distance them from Muslims by asserting their connection instead to Jewish and Christian history and omitting any mention of Islam.

Judge Smith does not find their argument persuasive, although he gives lengthy consideration to the validity of its tenets. In an attempt to shed some light on the claims about Syrian racial origins, Smith cites the works of several ethnologists and geneticists of the day, and discusses the bases of racial classifications. After a long and confused account, in which he avers that "a Syrian not only would not appear to be of a Caucasian race, but it does not appear that he is of a Semitic race,"[52] Smith rejects the Syrians claims and returns to his original position that "white persons" for the purposes of naturalization means only European descendants. Thus Mr. Dow, as "an Asiatic, whether Chinese, Japanese, Hindoo, Parsee, Persian, Mongol, Malay, or Syrian, . . . is not entitled to the privilege of naturalization, no matter what his fitness otherwise may be."[53]

Judge Smith's decision was overturned at the Appeals Court level on September 14, 1915, in *Dow v United States*. Circuit Judge Woods based his decision not on racial distinctions draped with "scientific" evidence although he does cite many of the specialists of ethnology and genetics referred to in the *In re Dow* decision; instead he relies on the popular understanding of the term "white persons." At the time of the most recent amendment of the Naturalization statute, in 1870, it was the "generally received opinion . . . that the inhabitants of a portion of Asia, including Syria, were to be classed as white persons."[54] The consensus of opinion was that Syrians "were so closely related to their neighbors on the European side of the Mediterranean that they should be classed as white,"[55] and thus, according to a more liberal interpretation of the statute based on the date of amendment rather than adoption, were held to fall within the meaning of the term "white persons" eligible for citizenship.

The crucial factor in Judge Woods' opinion was that Syrians resembled closely "their European neighbors." For this reason they are admissible as members of the American polity, as distinct from others—e.g., the Chinese—who perhaps differ more strikingly in terms of such visible signs as complexion and body type. Also Woods notes briefly that many Syrians had already been naturalized by the courts,[56] some without question, and sees no reason why this should not continue.

The problem of legal treatment of Syrians as something other than white, and thus potentially ineligible for citizenship, forced persons into an either/or construction: a given individual was either treated as a white person or not. Essentially, there were only two solutions to the problem of citizenship, "each defined in reference to the other."[57] As Syrian applicants for naturalization attempted to define themselves as eligible for citizenship, they effectively submerged that part of their heritage that presented a problem. There were at least two interrelated consequences of this legal treatment of difference. First, the possibility of individualized solutions existed, in which case courts reviewed the applicant's eligibility on an *ad hoc* basis, leaving the larger pattern of racially based discrimination in place. Second, Syrians, such as Khalil A. Bishara discussed earlier, in promoting their claims to the requisite status, illustrated the power of the dichotomy between white and nonwhite, drawn by the distinct legal treatment of racial difference.[58] With respect to negative associations, Minow puts it this way: "When individuals who have been labeled try to resist the demeaning consequences of those labels, they encounter complex layers of meanings that they cannot control. One strategy of resistance is to separate oneself from the group given the negative label and to demand treatment as an individual. Yet this response leaves in place the negative meaning of the label."[59] Justice Thurgood Marshall emphasized the same point when referring to the impact of racial discrimination in the latter half of this century. He wrote: "Members of minority groups frequently respond to discrimination and prejudice by attempting to dissociate themselves from the group, even to the point of adopting the majority's negative attitudes toward the minority."[60]

South Asians

South Asians—or "Hindus," as they were called regardless of religion—began to migrate to the United States in the first decade of the twentieth century.[61] A small number of Muslims were among the earliest South Asian arrivals to the United States. Karen Leonard, in her article on the effect of the 1913 California Alien Land Law on immigrants from India, notes that about ten percent of the South Asian population in California's agricultural valleys in the early twentieth century were Muslim.[62] According to Joan Jensen, South Asians earned a reputation as keen competitors in California agriculture during the early years of this century. White workers and landowners alike made their impressions of South Asians explicit. E. E. Chandler, a chemistry professor at Occidental College in the nineteen-teens who owned a ranch near Brawley, California, which he leased to tenant farmers, had this to say: "The Hindu resembles us except he is black—and we are shocked to see a black white man."[63] Prior to the Land Law, Muslim South Asians were especially successful in becoming land tenants and leasing land to grow rice in Butte, Sutter, and Colusa Counties in Northern California. One California (white) farm woman, who attested to the skills of these Muslims in growing rice, said they lived in what she called "Hindu Camp."[64] Another account, by a migrant worker of Indian (Hindu) origin, describes Muslims "from the northwestern border of India" at work in the hop fields of California. This account tells of the Muslims praying, fasting, feasting and reciting the Qur'an in the midst of the hops.[65]

The first trickle of South Asian immigrants in the United States came indirectly by way of Canada; many farmers and laborers from the Punjab, the northwestern province of India, were attracted by the economic opportunities advertised by Canadian companies seeking to import contract labor. In Canada, an estimated 95 percent of South Asian immigrants at the turn of the century were Sikhs, while the remainder were Muslim and Hindu.[66] In the four years from 1904, when official records of "Hindu" immigration were first kept, to 1908, more than 5,000 South Asians entered Canada, almost all through British Columbia.[67] Once in Canada, however, Indian nationals were subjected to racial prejudice and harassment, and the Canadian government ended Indian immigration in 1909.[68] Many Indians in Canada returned home, but some migrated south to the United States. Their numbers were quite small—averaging "about thirty per year from 1898 to 1903 and then two hundred fifty annually from 1904 to 1906"—but as Canadian persecution increased, so did the volume of Indian migration to the U.S., reaching nearly 2,000 per year by 1908.[69] The flow of South Asian immigrants to the United States was unsteady thereafter—dropping to less than 200 per year between 1911 and 1913—until the Immigration Act of 1917 barred further immigration altogether.[70]

While the situation of Syrians who wanted to become naturalized American citizens was generally favorable, if somewhat uncertain, the situation for South Asians was clearly less so. The arrival of South Asian immigrants met with opposition in the United States just as it had in Canada. The so-called "Hindus" suffered from the general anti-Asian bias prevalent in the Pacific coast states at the close of the nineteenth and the beginning of the twentieth centuries. Popular magazines and leading newspapers decried the arrival of South Asians and characterized it as a "Hindu invasion" and a "tide of turbans." One journal warned its readers that the United States was about to be inundated with "Hindus" because the Vedas, scriptures of Hinduism, enjoins them to "cover the earth."[71]

Evidence of organized and official efforts toward exclusion of South Asians is ample. Under the influence of nativist arguments of the day, immigration officials began to turn away many South Asian immigrants, ostensibly because of illness and the supposition that they would become public charges. The Japanese and Korean Exclusion League, an association whose goal was to press for greater restrictions on immigration, widened its scope to meet the challenge of increased South Asian immigration and, accordingly, changed its name to the Asiatic Exclusion League. In 1910, the League called for the resignation of Hart H. North, the Immigration Commissioner in San Francisco, because he allegedly encouraged "Hindu" immigration.[72] The League and its prominent supporters were quoted in San Francisco newspapers, charging that North allowed the admission of South Asians having communicable diseases. According to Gary R. Hess, "these pressures resulted in North's resignation and rigid enforcement of immigration regulations."[73]

In 1910, H. A. Millis, chief investigator for the Immigration Commission on the Pacific Coast, conducted a study of the growing South Asian community. In his findings, he claimed that the South Asian was "the most undesirable of all Asiatics and the peoples of the Pacific states were unanimous in their desires for exclusion."[74] Similarly, in Canada, despite the fact that South Asians were British subjects and argued that they were members of the Aryan "race," they "created as much, if not more, opposition as the Chinese and Japanese on the West Coast."[75] In 1907, they were the object of riots in parts of the state of Washington where they worked in the lumber industry. The Asiatic Exclusion League claimed that the South Asians themselves were responsible for causing the riots because they were willing to work for low wages and kept "filthy and immodest habits," presumably offensive enough to invite reprisals.[76] In the same year, California farmers began to agitate for legislation excluding Asians from agriculture. In 1913, their demands were met; the California legislature enacted the Alien Land Law which prevented the leasing and owning of agricultural land by "aliens ineligible for citizenship," a term first introduced into U.S. law by the Chinese Exclusion Act of 1882. While the law was directed primarily at the Japanese, it raised questions about the status of South Asian immigrant farmers. Until 1922 it was not clear whether South Asians were "ineligible for citizenship," and, in spite of popular resentment and discrimination, South Asians continued to farm. By 1919 they had some 100,000 acres of California land under cultivation and "were among the pioneers who developed [California's Imperial Valley] . . . growing cantaloupe, cotton, and lettuce."[77]

In 1907, U.S. Attorney General Charles Bonaparte advised the courts that South Asian applicants for citizenship were ineligible since naturalization was restricted to "free white persons" and persons of African nativity or descent.[78] Many courts, however, continued to allow South Asians to be naturalized on the basis that the applicants had proved that they were of the same "racial" origins as Europeans (i.e., Aryan) and were members of the Caucasian "race."[79] The U.S. District Court in New Orleans adopted this line of reasoning in 1908 and granted citizenship to two South Asian Muslims, Abdul Hamid and Bellal Houssain, over the objection of the Attorney General's office.[80]

The enactment of new immigration restrictions in 1917 adversely affected the situation of South Asians in the U.S. by serving as an effective barrier to further immigration from virtually all Asian countries.[81] The consequences for South Asians already in the U.S. were profound. Shortly after the passage of the Immigration Act, the federal government began to challenge all of the naturalizations of persons from India, arguing that former aliens of a class now barred from entry were not acceptable as citizens.

As a result of the government's renewed efforts to exclude South Asians, the citizenship of Mr. Baghat Singh Thind, granted by an Oregon court, was rescinded. The case reached the Supreme

Court which held in 1922 that Mr. Thind's naturalization was illegal. In *United States v Baghat Singh Thind* the Court ruled that "Hindus" were ineligible for citizenship because Congress had meant the words "white persons," used in the Naturalization statutes of 1790 and 1870 and the Immigration Law of 1917, to mean only Europeans and not "Hindus," whose descendants "would retain indefinitely the clear evidence of their ancestry."[82] While the Court accepted Mr. Thind's contention that South Asians were members of the Caucasian race, they were not, by virtue of their dark complexions, "white persons" in the popular understanding of the term. The Court held that, by comparison, immigrants from eastern, southern and central Europe who arrived in the United States after Thind, though "dark-eyed and swarthy," were perceived at the popular level as "white persons," and thus were eligible for citizenship. In this, the Court affirmed the idea that popular notions of acceptability and racial distinctions should decide who is eligible for citizenship; that the question of "assimilability" was crucial; and that through the "Barred Zone" provision of the Immigration Act of 1917, Congress opposed immigration from Asia and, by extension, the naturalization of Asians.[83]

In the *Thind* decision the Court quoted the "Barred Zone" provision of the 1917 Immigration Act as evidence that Congress was opposed to extending citizenship to Asians:

> It is not without significance in this connection that Congress by... (the Barred Zone Act)... has now excluded from admission into this country all natives of Asia... including the whole of India. This not only constitutes conclusive evidence of the congressional attitude of opposition to Asiatic immigration generally, but it is persuasive of a similar attitude towards Asiatic naturalization as well, since it is not likely that Congress would be willing to accept as citizens a class of persons whom it rejects as immigrants.[84]

The *Thind* case had certain ramifications in California, the state with the highest concentration of South Asian residents. Editorials in many newspapers in California "praised the ruling and most noted that the Alien Land Law could be enforced more readily against Indians."[85] The California Attorney General, a leader in the anti-Asian movement, promised to take swift action to stem "the menacing spread of Hindus holding our lands."[86]

Criticism also issued forth. A pamphlet entitled "An Examination of the Opinion of the Supreme Court of the United States Deciding

Against the Eligibility of Hindus for Citizenship," written by G. S. Pandit, a South Asian immigrant, and Raymond Chase, an American attorney, focused on the claim that Congress did not consider "Hindus" to be "white persons" at the time of enactment of the Naturalization Acts of 1790 and 1870. In response, the authors refuted the Court's claim and cited textbooks and popular literature from the periods in question which did characterize South Asians as "white."[87]

Many naturalization certificates granted to South Asians before the *Thind* decision were rescinded. Between 1923 and 1926, an estimated sixty to seventy South Asian-Americans lost their U.S. citizenship.[88] In effect, the *Thind* decision triggered a litigation campaign attacking the citizenship of a class of people previously admitted under the provisions of the 1790 Naturalization Act, amended in 1870. According to Hess, the restriction of Asian immigration provided for in the Immigration Act of 1917 was "accepted with less protest than the denial of American citizenship" to aliens from South Asia.[89] Many in the South Asian community residing in the United States were mobilized by the effects of the *Thind* decision, and a long struggle ensued to change the laws so as to allow South Asians to become naturalized citizens and to resume immigration. Eventually their efforts prevailed; Congress enacted legislation in 1946 that specifically allowed for Indian immigration and naturalization to resume.

The lower courts soon came to regard the *Thind* decision as the guiding precedent in deciding the naturalization cases of many other Asians as well, including Syrians, Afghanis, Arabs, and Persians. Thus, the consequences of the *Thind* decision were widespread. The immigration of many of the Islamic faith was adversely affected during the first five decades of this century, to a large extent because of the legislated restraints, judicially affirmed, placed on virtually all Asian immigration and naturalization.

For instance in *United States v Ali*,[90] the District Court of Michigan canceled the certificate of naturalization of John Mohammed Ali, an Arab Muslim who was born in the northwestern province of Punjab, India, and came to the United States on June 2, 1900. Ali had been naturalized on May 26, 1921. After the Supreme Court ruled against the naturalization of "Hindus" in the *Thind* decision, the court that issued Ali's citizenship certificate rescinded it at the government's request, on the grounds that it was "illegally procured."

At issue in Ali's case was whether he was a "Hindu" or an "Arabian." In Ali's 1921 naturalization hearing the district court held that the words "white persons" in the Naturalization statute included all persons of the Caucasian race and that "high-caste Hindus" belonged to the Caucasian race. Because he "was considered and referred to by all parties on the record as a high-caste Hindu"—a definition in which he "appeared to acquiesce"—Ali was admitted to citizenship.[91] When the U.S. Supreme Court decided in the *Thind* case that the words "white persons" were to be interpreted "in accordance with the understanding of the common man, from whose vocabulary they were taken, and were not to be converted into words of scientific terminology,"[92] and that "Hindus" were not included in the common man's understanding of the term "white persons," the U.S. attorney in Detroit asked the district court to reconsider Ali's fitness as an American citizen.

When Ali applied for and was admitted to citizenship, he did not make any objection to the court's description of him as a "high-caste Hindu." However, in the 1925 action to cancel his citizenship, Ali claimed that the *Thind* decision did not apply to him because he was not a "Hindu" but was "an Arabian of full Arabian blood."[93] Although Ali was native to India, and his family had lived in India for several generations, he asserted that his ancestors were Arab and that they had been careful not to intermingle with "the native stock of India" and had "kept their Arabian blood line clear and pure by intermarriage within the family."[94] District Judge Tuttle, in hearing this case, claims to be "unable to follow the argument" that Ali attempts to make. The question is not one of purity of blood, as Tuttle understands it, but whether or not Ali is a "white person." To determine this Tuttle relies on visual clues: "[Ali's] skin is certainly not white, but unmistakably dark, like that of other members of his race."[95] Further, Ali's argument merely proves that, "by reason of Arabian ancestry," he is a member of the Caucasian race, a fact which the *Thind* decision makes clear is not a sufficient basis for naturalization. For purposes of citizenship, it is possible to be Caucasian but not a "white person." Judge Tuttle ruled that Ali, although Caucasian, was not a "white person," and canceled his citizenship.

The District Court of San Francisco denied the petition for naturalization of Mr. Feroz Din, an Afghani, in a 1928 decision, *In re Feroz Din*.[96] District Judge Bourquin held that Feroz Din was "a typical Afghan . . . readily distinguishable from "white" persons of this country, and approximates to Hindus." Based on the *Thind* precedent, Bourquin held that Feroz Din was not eligible for citizenship. Bourquin ruled that "much of the comment in that case [*Thind*] is applicable to this." Further, he curtly dismisses the use of scientific evidence as a basis for considering the validity of racialist distinctions, as other courts had done, and claims to base his decision solely on the interpretation of statutes:

> What ethnologists, anthropologists, and other so-called scientists may speculate and conjecture in respect to races and origins may interest the curious and convince the credulous, but is of no moment in arriving at the intent of Congress in the statute aforesaid.[97]

In this, the judge emphasizes the exclusive authority of statutory language and the principle of *stare decisis*—adherence to past judicial decisions to guide present interpretations—in determining the outcome of legal issues.[98]

THE ANTI-POLYGAMY PROVISION OF IMMIGRATION LAW

The preceding court decisions turned on the question of "race," or skin color, and geographic origins. What of religion? In the case of Mufti Muhammad Sadiq, reviewed below, we have an instance where entry in the U.S. was denied—and the denial later overturned—strictly on the basis of the legal prohibition against polygamy, a social custom associated with Islam.

In January 1920, Mr. Sadiq, a Muslim of South Asian extraction, set sail from England, bound for the United States on the S.S. *Haverford*. Mr. Sadiq was a devoted member of the Ahmadiya movement, a largely middle-class, reformist Islamic sect that originated in the Punjab, India, in the late nineteenth century. The movement remained loyal to the British government in India and advocated accommodation of British rule. Initially its purpose was to rejuvenate Islam in the Punjab. However, by 1901 its agenda had expanded to include a worldwide missionary outreach program "to propagate Islam . . . [and to promote] the welfare of new converts to Islam in Europe and America."[99] Thus, the Ahmadiyas began to train missionaries for outreach work in England and North America, and to translate Islamic religious materials into English. By 1908, the official Ahmadiya publication, *The Review of Religions,* reported that approximately 2,000 people in England had been converted to Islam over the preceding twenty years.[100]

Mr. Sadiq, a philologist with a degree from the University of London, set out for the United States to propagate Islam and establish an Ahmadiya mission there. While crossing the Atlantic, he won six new converts to Islam among the ship's passengers.[101] When the S.S. *Haverford* docked in Philadelphia, U.S. Immigration authorities refused to allow Sadiq to enter the country and tried to send him back to England on the same ship. The officials rejected Sadiq's effort to enter the country because he was a "representative of a religious group that practiced polygamy."[102] As Sadiq relates the story, he told the immigration officer that

> I have not come here to teach plurality of wives. If a Moslem will ever preach or practice polygamy in America he will be committing a sin against his religion.[103]

He bases this argument on a distinction between what is mandatory in Islam and what is permitted. The commandments of Islam—e.g., the belief in one God—must be obeyed even when secular authority prohibits this, but the permissions of Islam—e.g., polygamy—can be avoided and, in fact, must be eschewed when they contradict the laws of the ruling government of the countries in which Muslims live. All Muslims must follow the commandments of their religion, but can abstain from what is permitted. Further, according to Sadiq, Islam commands that a Muslim obey the laws of the country in which he lives. Thus, in countries where polygamy is prohibited by law, Muslim men who marry more than one wife not only violate the laws of their countries but also a commandment of the faith which urges moderation. Islam

> PROHIBITS polygamy for the Mohammadans in Europe and America. No Moslem [man] can ever think of plurality of wives here. His religion does not allow it. [*Emphasis in original.*][104]

Unable to convince the immigration officers of his argument, after several hours of interrogation Sadiq nevertheless prevailed upon them not to return him to England. He was granted permission to appeal the decision to the Immigration Secretariat in Washington, D.C. However, pending the decision of the appeal, Sadiq was detained first in a Philadelphia and then a New Jersey jail for two months. During that time he wrote treatises in his own defense and hired lawyers to present his case in the capital, arguing that he could preach Islam in the United States without preaching polygamy. He won his appeal and was finally allowed to enter the United States in April 1920, on the condition that he would not preach polygamy.[105]

Being detained in jail did not entirely frustrate Sadiq's purpose. While confined, Sadiq won his first converts to Islam on American soil; he reports success in gaining twenty converts among his fellow detainees during his two-month confinement.[106] In addition, he attracted the attention of the press. Interviews with him from inside the jail appeared in American newspapers, with accounts of his message.[107]

Upon his release from jail, Sadiq settled in New York City, and began publishing a quarterly journal, *The Moslem Sunrise*, in 1921. The aims of this publication were to dispel misrepresentations of Islam that appeared in the American press and to propagate the faith. "The cover of each issue pictured a sunrise over North America which symbolized the rising sun of Islam in the United States."[108] Copies of the first issue were mailed to masonic lodges and major libraries.[109]

While Sadiq argues in the pages of *The Moslem Sunrise* against the practice of polygamy in North America because it violates the law, in the same essay he also maintains that the laws of Islam are superior to the North American civil laws that prohibit polygamy. The permission of polygamy, he contends, was allowed for practical reasons, for the protection of women. Historically, Muslim men were encouraged to marry more than one woman when women and children outnumbered men in a society, e.g., in times of war. Since "a Moslem does not do anything in vain," the practice of polygamy is limited even in Muslim countries where men are permitted to marry up to four women only under certain conditions:

> In cases of emergencies and for the protection of women, when necessary and allowed by the Government of the country as explained above, a man is permitted (and not commanded) to marry more than one, provided that he can keep them equally and justly in love, provision, and protection. But if he cannot be just, then only one, says the Holy Quran. This Restriction of "Justice" works in the majority of cases as an utter prohibition of more than one wife. Only those who are strong-minded, pious and with means enough to fulfill the orders of Justice and Equality can have the privilege.[110]

Sadiq offers this argument in part to refute the mistaken belief held by Americans that "every Muhammadan in the East marries more than one girl."[111]

A second purpose soon becomes apparent, however; Sadiq demonstrates his message—the practicability of polygamy even in the

United States—by pointing to evidence that it is already practiced. Immediately following his essay in *The Moslem Sunrise*, a reprint appears of an Akron, Ohio, newspaper account of a case of polygamy allowed in the United States under the heading, "Polygamy Sanctioned." With this account Sadiq expresses his views:

> With all the strict Laws and Statutes made by the United States Government against the plurality of wives, the authorities could not help allowing polygamy in at least one case. . . . [April 30, 1921]: "2 WIVES; WILL KEEP BOTH; COPS LET IT GO AT THAT." . . .[112]

The story is about an Italian immigrant. When reunited with his Italian wife after the First World War, the immigrant in question was allowed to remain married both to her and his second wife, whom he had married in Ohio when the war prevented his first wife from joining him in the United States. Sadiq avers that "there might have been other cases like that as well," and argues that this demonstrates the "desirability of the Law of Polygamy made by Islam in cases of emergency"[113] because it allows for just such exceptional circumstances and is designed to promote morality.

The juxtaposition of this news account and his essay on polygamy points to an unjust situation—the American government prohibiting Sadiq from preaching polygamy while sanctioning its practice in the case of an Italian—but Sadiq never explicitly states that an injustice has occurred. But such restraint is not shown by Sadiq's co-religionist and defender, Sher Ali, who writes of Sadiq's circumstances in *The Review of Religions*. In an essay entitled "America's Intolerance, Our Missionary in the Detention House," Sher Ali writes from England about "the treatment our brother has received at the hands of the United States authorities [which] is highly intolerant and inequitable." Sher Ali is quite indignant about the hypocrisy of the "children of the Pilgrim fathers [who] more than any other people should have held sacred the freedom of thought and speech." He exhorts, "you [i.e., Americans] have passed a law forbidding people who believe in the validity of polygamy admission into your country." Sadiq's missionary work in America, preaching Islam without "making any reference to polygamy," is, according to Sher Ali, "a concession to the intolerance of the American Government and will remain as a blot on the fair name of America."[114]

The Ahmadiya movement, established in the United States by Indian missionaries in the 1920s, had a special appeal for African-

Americans who at that time were looking for a new vision to lift them out of their demoralizing circumstances. It connected them to a worldwide, "non-white" religion, an attractive alternative to what were seen as the European religions of Judaism and Christianity.[115] The Ahmadiyas tapped into the growing groundswell of black nationalism, a social phenomenon discussed in the next chapter.

CONSEQUENCES

Small Muslim groups were founded to preserve the faith and to maintain social and cultural ties within the fledgling Muslim community: in Ross, North Dakota, as early as 1900; and in Cedar Rapids, Iowa, in the early 1920s. Islamic associations were established in Highland Park, Michigan, in 1919, and Detroit in 1922. A Young Men's Muslim Association was founded in Brooklyn, New York, in 1923.[116] Mosques were constructed for communal prayer in Highland Park, Michigan, in 1919 (but dismantled within five years); in Ross, North Dakota, in 1920; in Michigan City, Indiana, where "a dome was put atop a rented building in 1924"; and in Cedar Rapids, Iowa, in 1934.[117] The first Canadian mosque was built in Edmonton, Alberta, in 1938.[118] However, many of these organs of collective life vanished as the individuals involved became integrated into the dominant society or returned home, and the early Muslim communities dissipated.[119]

Whether because of their small numbers or because of the felt need to fit in with the surroundings, Muslims adapted their practices and institutions quickly and substituted "Americanized" symbols of collective life for the more familiar Islamic ones. In *The Moslem Sunrise,* the Ahmadiyas borrowed an image from the legends of the nineteenth century pioneer movement westward by comparing their missionary work in North America to that of the pioneers who settled the western frontier. They characterized themselves as "pioneers in the spiritual colonization of the western world."[120]

Two things happened as a result of the low profile of the early Muslim immigrant communities. First, the early generations of Muslims in the United States remained relatively invisible and showed little potential for influencing American society.[121] Evidence suggests that some of these Muslims concealed their religious affiliation to be less conspicuous and gain easier acceptance in the United States.[122] Second, potential immigrants from the Muslim world were unaware of the presence and level of organization, such as it was, of their co-religionists in the United States, and, as Abdo A. Elkholy observes, religion remained an important factor in delaying their immigration.[123] Centuries of accumulated misunderstanding and mistrust between Muslims and the West, dating from the Crusades,[124] had to be jettisoned somewhat before Muslim migration westward increased.

With respect to immigration and naturalization laws at the turn of the century, the increasing influx of newcomers generated a political struggle at the center of which was the question whether persons judged to be neither "white" nor "black" made acceptable members of the political community. A related question was whether the law, having extended recognition of citizenship rights to those of African origin, should extend the same recognition to others, notably of Asian origin. Legal exclusion on the basis primarily of skin color and geography, but also the issue of polygamy, enforced the prevailing beliefs of the day about moral character and public values. These standards governed the rules of citizenship well into the first half of the twentieth century.

It is necessary to keep in mind that while we may look upon the experiences discussed in this chapter as having involved a simple problem of public policy—namely, one of determining how to define standards for citizenship in the face of a changing immigrant population—it was clearly understood as a major *crisis* at the turn of the century. Fears of being inundated by outsiders, of racial deterioration, and the threats of disease and physical and moral degeneracy provoked not only by Syrian and South Asian, but also Japanese, Italian, and other suspect types of immigration, were rampant. The effort socially and politically to erect defensive barriers simply found in the state of the art of natural science what seemed like an effective, clinical tool to do so. Racial classifications legitimated exclusionary impulses by lending them a shroud of scientific expertise.

The role of the courts in refining the language of politics by linking empirical science with the authority of the state begins to become clear in the context of Asian applicants for citizenship. Although the courts are inconsistent in their application of scientific standards, relying on anthropological evidence in some places and resorting to the popular understanding of the common man at others, drawn into the discourse was the use of differing sources of authority. While popular opinion might be suspect and mutable, science appeared as an unimpugnable source. Many of the decisions discussed here provoked responses from the affected communities that were conditioned in particular ways by the courts. Syrians and South Asians both tailored their responses in terms of the language and issues enunciated by the courts, and called upon the legal system to extend recognition and rights to them.

In the political struggle that ensued, the Asian world was determined to be an unsuitable source of immigration. This was reflected in the laws governing admission of immigrants. The interaction between the early generations of Muslims in the United States and the constitutive debates that redefined the rules for citizenship at the turn of the century worked a profound impact on the shape of Islam in America—its identity, institutions, doctrines and practices. Where Muslims stood collectively *vis à vis* these debates, along with the fact that they came equipped with their own (Islamic) legal culture that had to be compromised if not abandoned in the process of assimilation, has had a lot to do with the way the issues of the Muslim-American community are framed today.[125]

The rules for citizenship in the United States, found in immigration and naturalization policies and judicial interpretation, express a peculiarly American consciousness, identity, and future. The rhetoric and outcome of the process of defining acceptable levels of immigration and the rules for citizenship provide the substance and texture of the self-definition of a people. As Weiner notes, "The question of who should be admitted has much to do with the self-definition that a people (and their government) have of themselves, a definition that is not immutable."[126]

4

Muslims in Prison
Constitutional Protection of Religious Liberty

The emergence of an African-American Muslim population in prisons has raised many questions concerning whether Islam is a religion worthy of constitutional protection in the federal courts. The responsiveness of the courts, as well as the Muslims' use of law, were shaped by a variety of factors which impinged not only on the changing role of the courts but also on the developing Muslim identity in North America. Specifically, the multiple historical contexts of the prisoners' and civil rights movements, evolving race relations, and the rise of black nationalism had a bearing on the legal status of Islam and Muslims. These factors also conditioned the way Muslims came to accept law as a legitimate social control mechanism, and accept its utility in creating "order" in everyday existence, both inside prison walls and beyond.

Three concurrent historical developments are central to, and inform, the analysis in this chapter: the prisoners' rights movement; black nationalism and the Nation of Islam; and the legal treatment of religion. While, as Malcolm Feeley and Roger Hanson point out, the federal courts have become one of the "principal agents of change in the nation's jails and prisons,"[1] the impetus behind efforts toward structural reform began with the inmates themselves. Thus, the purpose of this chapter is to provide an illustrative example of the transformation not only of legal concepts and the role of the judiciary, but, more importantly, of the very subjects themselves who have relied on the courts to maximize their religious freedom. We begin by reviewing the three historical developments mentioned above—the prisoners' rights movement, the Black Muslims, and the legal treatment of religion—before examining the court record.

PRISONERS' RIGHTS

While prisoners in the United States have gained recognition of their constitutional rights through court action, until the 1960s the judiciary, with few exceptions, followed a "hands-off" doctrine, refusing to intervene in matters of prison administration.[2] During the nineteenth century, prisoners rarely used the courts to challenge the conditions of their confinement. In many states, persons convicted of a crime suffered "civil death," and became temporarily "the slave of the state,"[3] effectively stripped of Constitutional protection. Prisoners' claims were denied by the courts well into the twentieth century on the grounds that the judiciary had no jurisdiction over the internal management of correctional institutions.[4]

Throughout much of its two-hundred year history, the prison reform movement understood the status of prisoners and their conditions of confinement as a religious or utilitarian problem.[5] Reformers held a benevolent regard for the criminal, as well as for the protection of society, and, like prison administrators, focused on the correctional institution's ability to rehabilitate the criminal. In the post-Civil War era until well into this century, the goal of the penal system was the "moral regeneration" of the criminal through incarceration.[6] Religion was believed to have a great rehabilitative potential, and religious services in prisons and jails were often mandated. However, in most instances, the opportunity to discuss religious ideas among themselves was forbidden to prisoners.[7]

The conditions of incarceration are seldom examined from the perspective of the kept, only of the keeper. A distinctive feature of the period from 1900 to the mid-1960s was its positivist approach to the treatment of the incarcerated; confidence was placed in the discretionary authority of public officials to understand and cure each "deviant," and to respond to the needs presented by each, on a case-by-case approach. Thus, prisoners were isolated from the rest of society by virtue of incarceration, and prison programs and practices were developed by prison officials who were given a great deal of latitude in corrections.

A reversal of this position was not clearly enunciated until 1961 when, in *Monroe v Pape*,[8] the Supreme Court resurrected nineteenth-century civil rights law to rule that plaintiffs could seek damages in federal court for state violations of their civil rights.[9] This legal development was applied soon thereafter to prisoners' cases. As Jim Thomas notes, the stimulus for this shift can be traced to the "changing social and political attitudes" of the New Deal era.[10] As early as "1941 the Supreme Court recognized that some Constitutional protections followed prisoners to prison (*ex parte Hull*, 312 U.S. 546, 1941). . . ."[11] Change came slowly and spasmodically, however, and the judicial stance toward prisoners was not fully metamorphosed until the 1960s. At the same time, many other courts continued to defend the discretion of prison authorities from the general erosion of the "hands-off" doctrine. Collectively, the courts were neither consistent nor enthusiastic about the overall drift toward an interventionist role by the courts. Through 1951, "most federal judges agreed with the decision in *Stroud v Swope* (187 F. 2d 820, 9th Cir., 1951), which explicitly rejected federal review of the discipline and treatment of prisoners."[12] In a 1953 case a federal district court in Illinois ruled against an African-American prisoner who "alleged racially motivated policies in restricting free speech," stating that prisoners cannot use the courts to challenge prison policies that they do not like.[13]

According to Thomas, the shift away from the official judicial "hands-off" policy toward a more activist stance was precipitated by the advent of the Warren Court and the incipient civil rights struggles in the 1950s. Generally, the courts became more receptive to the rights of minorities, and this openness extended to the rights of criminal defendants as well. In essence, the social activism beginning in the 1950s, which became widespread in the 1960s and 1970s, effectively expanded the concept of "civil rights" to include the protection of the incarcerated against substandard conditions. The growth of prisoners' rights, based on post-Civil War legislation, emerged slowly at first but expanded dramatically during the 1960s "impelled largely by social attitudes towards rights in general and the efforts of prisoners to translate these attitudes into legal action."[14] This shift resulted in the expansion of prisoners' access to legal resources, and effectively placed policies and actions of prison authorities under the purview of federal courts.

The 1960s are recognized as a watershed decade in the development of prisoners' rights, which, like the civil rights movement, were "part of a larger mosaic of social change."[15] The issues raised by prisoners and their advocates coincided with significant intervention by the federal judiciary in policy matters, the extension of rights to an increasing number of marginal groups, and the recognition of the legitimacy of group grievances, especially the demands by African-Americans for equal protection under the law in other contexts.

As James Jacobs has noted, "the preconditions for the emergence of a prisoners' rights movement in the United States was the recognition by the federal courts that prisoners were persons with cognizable constitutional rights."[16] Treatment of prisoners as legal subjects brought the movement into the courts, and led key actors, including prisoners, to concentrate their efforts at affecting change through legal remedies. Conversely, it brought the federal courts into the prisons, where court officials became deeply involved in defining and applying certain standards in disputes over prison practices, policies, and conditions. In effect, the *Monroe v Pape* decision opened access to the courts where prisoners could challenge their treatment by prison officials and demand that the courts intervene in setting standards for the conditions of their confinement. This action ushered in a new era of judicial intervention in prison administration which resulted in modest systemic change. Certain aspects of the closed world of prisons—especially the prison officials' absolute custodial power and the prisoners' isolation from the larger society—were brought under public scrutiny through the attention given to the legal status of individual prisoners. The litigation itself in turn "heightened prisoners' consciousness and politicized them."[17]

The consequences were "perhaps second in breadth and detail only to the courts' earlier role in dismantling segregation in the nation's public schools" following the 1954 ruling in *Brown v Board of Education*.[18] The Supreme Court's first modern prisoners' rights case, *Cooper v Pate* (1964),[19] which involved Muslim inmates, recognized that prisoners have constitutional rights that prison officials cannot violate, and that the federal courts are obligated to hear prisoners' allegations of religious discrimination. Jacobs asserts that "many legal victories followed after *Cooper v Pate* . . . [and] each contributed to the strength, self-confidence, and momentum of the prisoners' rights movement."[20] In 1974, the Supreme Court held in a landmark prisoners' rights case, *Wolff v McDonnell*,[21] that prisoners are entitled to certain minimal due process standards at disciplinary proceedings. Writing for the Court, Justice Byron White declared that

> though [the prisoner's] rights may be diminished by the needs and exigencies of the institutional environment, a prisoner is not wholly stripped of constitutional protections. . . . There is no iron curtain drawn between the Constitution and the prisons of this country.[22]

This case established a balancing test to weigh the merits of prisoners' claims against the institutional needs and objectives of the prisons.

While Supreme Court decisions have been influential in defining the contours of the law in the area of prisoners' rights, the number of cases reaching the Supreme Court are relatively small. Federal district courts not only serve as the forum for hearing prisoners' legal complaints, they also oversee the enforcement of judicial decrees stemming from court decisions in prisoners' litigation. During the 1970s the federal courts proved sympathetic to the need to bring prison conditions up to constitutional standards. Many courts appointed "special masters" or "compliance officers" to aid correctional officials in developing institutional remedies in response to court orders.[23] Lawsuits by prisoners increased at an unprecedented rate over the 1970s and 1980s; the total number of prisoner petitions in federal district courts increased from 15,997 in 1970 to 41,390 in 1989.[24]

In response to the volume of prisoners' litigation and the resulting increase in public attention given to prison conditions and policies, "an amalgam of statutes, regulations, and guidelines" has fostered dramatic changes in prison administration.[25] Many of these changes have placed prisons and prison officials under universal standards of accountability and have served as an impetus for the enhanced professionalization of corrections. For instance the American Correctional Association (ACA), the professional organization of correctional officials, with the support of the U.S. Department of Justice, has created an accreditation system of state prisons. Federal legislation of the Civil Rights of Institutionalized Persons Act (CRIPA) of 1980 authorizes the U.S. attorney general to sue state institutions that violate the constitutionally protected rights of inmates held in state correctional facilities, and to develop standards to evaluate state prison inmate grievance procedures.[26] Also, state legislatures have authored statutes which incorporate protections of prisoners' constitutional rights into state administrative law.[27]

The overall impact of this trend has been the transformation of the nation's correctional institutions and how they are run. A more general trend toward increased bureaucratization, legality, and attentiveness to "constitutional values as they affect public institutions," evident since 1960, has altered the operational life of prisons.[28] The emphasis has been on the professionalization of correctional officials "so that constitutional values are more fully appreciated" in the management of prisons and jails.[29]

However, the analysis in this chapter is not concerned primarily with the impact of prisoners' litigation, but with the influence of social trends and ideas about "rights" on the litigants themselves. Although I have not tried to analyze the litigation's impact in detail, it is clear that significant prison reform has resulted. Just as societal and institutional changes have altered the expectations and norms of prison staff, they have altered the expectations and norms of the prisoners as well.

Prisoners' litigation is but a recent development within the broader context of prison reform efforts, which, in effect, redefines the status of the incarcerated by focusing on its legal, rather than moral or economic, dimensions. It has cast the discussion of issues of prison management in constitutional terms, and has created expectations about rights and entitlements for prisoners, as well as the oversight role of the federal judiciary.

As Stuart Scheingold notes in his classic work, *The Politics of Rights* (1974), "a declaration of rights tends to politicize need by changing the way people think about their discontent."[30] The opportunity to pursue group grievances in the courts, and the encouragement of success, influenced the ideas of the prisoners who litigated. In what follows, we shall see how Muslim inmates adopted constitutional norms and language to change their environment and, ultimately, how this contributed to an overall transformation of their self-identification.

BLACK NATIONALISM AND THE NATION OF ISLAM

While few references explain how ideas about Islam became available in the black community, a variety of American scholars have proffered possible explanations as to the origins and appeal of Islam within the African American legacy.[31] Richard Brent Turner suggests that:

> As early as 1866, Edward Wilmot Blyden, Liberian scholar, linguist and statesman, laid the intellectual groundwork for Islam's great emotional appeal for Afro-Americans in the twentieth century. . . . Although he was a Presbyterian minister, [his] experience [during visits to Egypt and Palestine] led him to believe that what he perceived as Islam's lack of racism and emphasis on brotherhood made it a more appropriate religion for Africans than Christianity.[32]

The Reverend Blyden felt that Christianity, by and large, had become a white European religion, racist in content, which debased African-Americans and stripped them of their racial heritage. In contrast Islam could unify "the darker races of the world" and serve as the basis for an internationalist sense of black identity and solidarity.[33]

The internationalist perspective slowly gained momentum throughout the Reconstruction era, as African-Americans witnessed both the trammeling of post-Civil-War gains in civil rights and the European partition of Africa. Then, between 1900 and 1930, the total black population in the northern and midwestern urban centers of the United States increased, fourfold as approximately 2.5 million African-Americans left the south to escape overt racism (the Ku Klux Klan and Jim Crow laws) and to look for higher wages in industrial jobs.[34] Many blacks were discouraged, however, when they encountered perhaps more subtle forms of discrimination in the north, especially in employment and housing. The limited freedom and color prejudice they experienced in the north, combined with the impact of visits to their former homes in the south, raised their awareness of the extreme subordination of blacks in the south and sharpened their frustration with the white power structure in America generally.[35] Thus, during the years between the two world wars, the ideological leadership provided by such black intellectuals as W. E. B. DuBois, George Washington Williams, and other Pan-Africanists coincided with the mounting pressures of a disillusioned, recently urbanized mass of black working people who sought a panacea.

It was in this context that black nationalism found fertile ground in twentieth century America. In the first quarter of this century, various leaders articulated strategies ranging from accommodation to separation. Christianity increasingly came under fire as a racist "clan" religion of the white people and such criticism exacerbated the religious needs of blacks for a new vision and eschatology. Marcus Garvey, the major proponent of separatism, founded the first extensive international "Back to Africa" movement, called the United Negro Improvement Association (UNIA), on the principles of reconciliation with Africa—black independence, black culture, and black power. The UNIA movement, identified as "the quintessence of the internationalist identity which had been growing among black Americans since the late nineteenth century,"[36] reached its height of popularity during the 1920s, when its message of black pride and self-help offered an attractive alternative and survival strategy for oppressed blacks.

"The conversion of African-Americans to Islam is a twentieth century phenomenon"[37] and must be understood, at one level, as a reaction to American racism. It is part of a larger effort to cohere in a new cultural vision seeking to define a viable alternative to Christianity. Some black Americans perceived Christianity "as the root of their oppression in its glorification of suffering and promise of redemption in the hereafter,"[38] a religion belonging to white people, and the proximate cause of their continued subordination. They sought ameliorative belief systems, which might offer a better understanding of, if not solutions to, the problems stemming from the dislocations of the northward migration. Many of the alternative belief systems which arose wholly negated the message of white supremacy that was seen as inherent to Christianity, and rendered their distinctiveness—i.e., their blackness—a virtue, rather than evidence of their inferiority.

Alongside Garveyism, another black nationalist movement arose to offer an alternative faith—the Moorish Science Temple, established by Noble Drew Ali in Newark, New Jersey, in 1913. Noble Drew Ali, the "Prophet," stressed the "oriental" identity of black Americans, calling them "Asiatic" or "Moorish," and claimed that Islam, the dominant religion in Morocco, is the original religion of the black race. The Moorish movement provided an aberrant or nominal variety of Islamic faith based more on Drew Ali's eclectic understanding of eastern philosophies than a normative or orthodox interpretation of Islam. What is important, however, is not the movement's failure to conform to the basic doctrines of Islam, but the function Islam served as the negation of Christianity and the focal point for the development of a new identity.

In essence, Drew Ali's movement was a religious nationalism that maintained an accommodationist position. Unlike Garveyism, the main objective of the Moorish movement was to provide a source of racial pride, destroying the dominant culture's claims about black inferiority while emphasizing obedience to, and membership in, the United States. The Moorish movement spread to several northern cities, including Philadelphia and Detroit, as well as to a few in the south. It survives today in some east coast locations.

By far the largest organization to generate mass appeal based on its identification with Islam and black nationalism, is the Nation of Islam which emerged out of the Depression of the 1930s. Its founder and spiritual leader, Elijah Muhammad, born Elijah Poole in Georgia in 1876, was influenced by the current of black nationalism represented by Garveyism and the Moorish movement. A follower of a rather mysterious figure in Detroit, who was called variously W. D. Fard, Wali Fard, Wallace Fard, W. F. Muhammad, and Fard Muhammad, Elijah Muhammad emerged by 1934 as the leader of a movement known as "The Lost-Found Nation of Islam in the Wilderness of North America" (a.k.a. the Nation of Islam). Elijah

Muhammad expounded the "unique body of myths and doctrines" associated with the Nation of Islam until his death in 1975.[39] Under Muhammad's leadership, Fard was deified and became identified as "Allah," and Muhammad became his "Prophet" or "the Messenger of Allah."[40] Islam was declared the natural religion of the Black Man; due to slavery, African-Americans had been separated from their true Muslim identity. They had been kept in "mental slavery" by the white man, estranged from their heritage and from each other.[41] Muhammad's role, then, was to reveal the truth about white men, called blue-eyed devils, to expose their "tricknology" by which the Black Man continued to be subjugated, and to reconstitute the Black Nation. Blackness became the ideal; self-respect, economic independence, and ethical integrity were vaunted as essential goals and necessary preconditions for freedom.

The Nation of Islam was never a "Back to Africa" movement, although Muhammad preached that "the white man's home is in Europe" and that "there will be no peace until every man is in his own country."[42] The Black Muslims under Muhammad's leadership sought self-determination in North America, not Africa. A sense of entitlement to a nation within a nation, ceded from white America and the authority of the white man, and earned through slavery, is evident. In every issue of the community's official newspaper, "Muhammad Speaks," it was stated that the Black Muslims "want our people in America, whose parents or grandparents were descendants from slaves, to be allowed to establish a separate state or territory of their own . . . ."[43] Accordingly, justice would be served only when there was a Black Nation in America "on some of the land our fathers and mothers paid for in 300 years of slavery . . . right here in America."[44] The goal of a Black Nation was of consuming importance and, until that was achieved, Black Muslims would oppose political discourse with the white man. Initially, at least, they opposed integration and excluded themselves from participation in a political system which they perceived to have denied them the political values they sought—justice, equality, and liberty.

Elijah Muhammad was successful in creating a tightly knit organization with established rituals and worship. The ritual requirements were defined as: prayer five times daily; before prayer, proper ablutions; total abstinence from the consumption of tobacco, alcohol, and pork; and attendance at temple twice a week.[45] Over the next few decades, the Nation of Islam spread to all the major cities of the United States and found its greatest numbers in urban black ghettoes. Its growth coincided with the increased popularity of black nationalism as a whole in an era of African independence and civil rights struggles at home. Its success has been attributed to its promise of "a new identity, a feeling of 'somebodiness' denied by the dominant culture . . . ."[46] In Lincoln's words, "the ultimate appeal of the movement . . . is in the chance to become identified with a power strong enough to overcome the domination of the white man—and perhaps even to subordinate him in return."[47]

Elijah Muhammad had "an ambitious program of recruitment."[48] He preached to the disaffected black masses and sought even "the most unregenerate and then set about to rehabilitate them."[49] A good deal of recruiting was done in jails and prisons, and the movement grew there throughout the 1950s and 1960s. Malcolm X, perhaps the most famous Black Muslim prison convert, describes the appeal of Muhammad's message in prison:

> You let this caged-up black man start thinking, the same way I did when I first heard Elijah Muhammad's teachings, let him start thinking how with better breaks when he was young and ambitious he might have been a lawyer, a doctor, a scientist, anything. You let this caged-up black man start realizing, as I did, how from the first landing of the first slave ship, the millions of black men in America have been like sheep in a den of wolves. That's why black prisoners become Muslims so fast when Elijah Muhammad's teaching filter into their cages by way of other Muslim convicts. "The white man is the devil" is a perfect echo of that black convict's lifelong experience.[50]

The Nation of Islam movement found ready-made and receptive audiences in penal institutions, "for the racial character of the law enforcement agencies, the courts, and the custodial personnel is a key factor in sharpening the black prisoner's resentments and his sense of persecution."[51]

While Black Muslim ministers found willing converts among restive prisoners, the rehabilitative effect on the convicts who became Muslims was remarkable. Muslims who joined the Nation of Islam while in prison were subject to stringent rules of conduct, devised by the movement's leadership, and "invariably improve[d] in behavior and outlook."[52] The movement's "emphasis upon courtesy, cleanliness, and morality challenges the early Puritans in its austerity and unrelenting enforcement."[53] The Nation of Islam operated "on the premise that 'knowledge of the self' and of the 'truth about the white man'—when tied in with a constructive program, such as building the Black Nation—is sufficient to reclaim the most corrigible."[54] Many Muslims, both inside prison walls and out, came into the movement from "various levels of extra-legal activity," but those who stayed were rehabilitated and put to work, in keeping with the movement's emphasis on industriousness and the creation of black economic independence.[55]

Connected with the outside organization, Black Muslim prisoners recruited other black prisoners into the movement and the growing Muslim population alarmed prison administrators. Prison wardens observed that Muslim inmates shaved their heads closely, kept a cleancut appearance, wore medallions, and sometimes marked their foreheads with the "seal of Islam."[56] They observed strict dietary rules excluding pork, and tended to "segregate themselves in prison dining halls and exercise yards."[57] Muslims were seen by prison wardens and chaplains alike as striving for separate status within the prison population based on the belief in black racial supremacy. From the point of view of these officials, Muslim activities in prison, especially in proselytizing other black prisoners, amounted to "agitation" which threatened to lead to outbreaks of violence and riots.[58]

Despite the Nation of Islam's separatist doctrines and prison administrators' apprehensions, very little evidence exists which links prison violence to Muslims' presence.[59] Nevertheless, in some prisons rules were adopted which prohibited prisoners from belonging to the Nation of Islam. Muslims "clashed with the administrations only over restrictions on their religious practices"[60] when they tried to subscribe to the Nation's newspaper, *Muhammad Speaks*, obtain copies of the Qur'an, hold meetings, meet with outside representatives of the movement, and receive pork-free diets. In many instances prison officials, seeing prison Muslims as a threat to prison peace and their own legitimacy, tried to suppress Muslim activities in prison and denied Muslims requests to be treated as a religious group, declaring that they are a "sham" religion. By the early 1960s, the Muslims turned to the judicial system to ask the courts to intervene on their behalf, and to recognize the Nation of Islam as a *bona fide* religious organization.

Several cases from Muslim prisoners' litigation will be examined below. First, though, it is worth pointing out two things. One, not all legal challenges to prison rules herein discussed were raised by members of the Nation of Islam. A few were raised by Black Muslims of differing orientations. While the Nation was the largest such organization, other smaller Islamic groups have emerged in the black American community. The Hanafi movement, the Ansaru

Allah movement, and the Islamic Party of North America are just three such groups which have also reached into the prison system. Also presented here is a case raised by a member of the Nation's antecedent, which still exists, the Moorish Science Temple movement. Together, all of these Black Muslim groups presented the courts with essentially the same difficult issues: whether and how to treat grievances, raised by adherents to a provocative mix of religious and racist doctrines, against prison administrators who refuse to grant recognition to Muslim inmates as a legitimate religious group.

The second noteworthy point, closely related, regards the timeliness of the issues. The Muslims asked the courts to depart from their hands-off policy and to intervene in prisons in matters conventionally under the supervision of prison administrators, to recognize Muslim inmates as a legitimate religious entity, and to protect those inmates from the abuses of their keepers. By framing their grievances as a matter of "free exercise," the Muslim petitioners placed themselves within the larger context of the contemporary civil rights struggle. At this point, then, it is useful to examine briefly the relevance of the Constitution and the definition of religion recognized by the courts at the time the Muslims raised their legal claims.

LEGAL TREATMENT OF RELIGION

Within the American judicial tradition the courts have struggled to construct a broad, "functional"[61] definition of religion which does not reflect any *a priori* judgment of the content of the beliefs in question. As a result, the courts have variously interpreted the meaning of "religion" to bring under the protection of the First Amendment[62] a variety of religious belief systems, many of which range far beyond any common understanding of a Judeo-Christian norm. From the anti-Mormon cases of the late nineteenth century[63] to cases involving the Jehovah's Witnesses (in general in the 1940s),[64] Seventh Day Adventists[65] and Native Americans (both especially during the 1960s),[66] the Amish (1970s and 1980s),[67] and most recently the Rastafarians,[68] the Krishna Consciousness,[69] MOVE,[70] and others,[71] the courts have consented to review the adherents' claims to constitutional protection. While not all claims have been accommodated, the courts by and large have been most willing to protect the preferred freedom of religious exercise when presented in cases involving minority religious groups.

As David Rothman concludes: "When Black Muslims in 1961 pressed the cause of religious freedom in prison, judges found the right too traditional, the request too reasonable, and the implications of intervention ostensibly so limited that they had to act."[72] He might also have stated that American social and legal thought was in the midst of a due process revolution, fueled by concerns for racial equality. Yet constitutional protection of Islam has not been automatic. Muslim organizations such as the Nation of Islam have been treated as cults, or suspect and dangerous groups, due in part to the perception that Muslims teach racial hatred.[73] It has been argued before the courts, by prison administrators among others,[74] that Muslim doctrine contains political aspirations and economic goals, as well as racial prejudice, and presents a clear and present danger of imminent violence, and, as such, should be suppressed in the interest of society. Recognition of Muslims as a *bona fide* religious group would present difficult security problems for wardens who fear that such acknowledgement "would have a tendency to set off racial hatred inside the walls" of prisons.[75] More often than not, however, the courts have found that Islam is principally a religious faith and Muslims a religious community despite any political teachings and, as such, are protected by the "free exercise" clause of the First Amendment.

Judicial definitions of religion, developed at the turn of the century for the purpose of determining when to extend First Amendment protection, were theistic. That is, the courts contemplated belief in a Supreme Being as an indispensable characteristic of religion. The view was that the term "religion" applied to any belief system based on the recognition of a divine being and a relation to that being which involved obligations superior to those arising from any human relation.[76] By the middle of this century, the Supreme Court began to shift its position, moving away from theism as a requisite feature and embracing what was, arguably, a less normative definition of religion.[77] The Court adopted the position that religious freedom includes "the right to maintain theories of life and death and of the hereafter which are rank heresy to followers of the orthodox faiths. . . . [and that] it is no business of courts to say that what is a religious practice or activity for one group is not religion under the protection of the First Amendment."[78] In the well-known *Cantwell* (1940) case involving Jehovah's Witnesses, the Court also held that public officials such as licensing authorities should not become involved in the task of determining what is a religious cause, lest questions about equal treatment and a possible violation of the "establishment" clause of the First Amendment be raised. However, the Court did not make a clean break with theism, and its decisions continued to reflect its roots in Western religious tradition. In *Zorach v Clauson* (1952) Justice Douglas wrote that "we are a religious people whose institutions presuppose a Supreme Being."[79]

The judicial conception of religion expanded to include doctrines that do not necessarily teach a belief in the existence of God. The Supreme Court adopted a position which scrutinized not the veracity of the doctrine at issue but the nature of the adherent's beliefs. As early as 1955 the Court held, in *Witmer v United States*,[80] that the principal issue in conscientious objector cases is the sincerity of the objector's beliefs. In a major draft-exemption case called *United States v Seeger* (1965), the Court proposed a test for determining when a belief constitutes a religious belief for purposes of constitutional protection:

> The test. . . is whether a given belief that is sincere and meaningful occupies a place in the life of its possessor parallel to that filled by the orthodox belief in God of one who clearly qualifies for the [conscientious objector] exemption.[81]

With this test, called the "ultimate concern" test, there is no inquiry into the content of an individual's beliefs. Rather, the courts are asked to focus on the importance and place of the beliefs in the individual's life.[82]

Islam has been recognized by the courts as a religion deserving First Amendment protection according to both the theistic and the "ultimate concern" standards. In *Fulwood v Clemmer*, the U.S. District Court for the District of Columbia held that it is not

> the function of the court to consider the merits or fallacies of a religion or to praise or condemn it. . . . It is sufficient here to say that one concept of religion calls for a belief in the existence of a supreme being controlling the destiny of man. That concept of religion is met by the Muslims in that they believe in Allah, as a supreme being and as the one true god. It follows, therefore, that the Muslim faith is a religion.[83]

The federal district court found in this case that Islam is a theistic belief system and thus worthy of constitutional protection. Yet there are other instances where the courts have refused to base their decisions on a review of Islamic tenets but have recognized Islam to be a religion because of the function it serves in the lives of its adherents. These cases will be reviewed below.

THE CASES

Black Americans, as compared to immigrant groups, have been active in pursuing legal claims to obtain equal rights and access to the resources of society in general.[84] The realm of prisoners' rights has been no exception. African-American Muslim inmates have been responsible in large part for establishing prisoners' constitutional rights to worship.[85] The responsiveness of the courts to Muslim inmates' claims for religious liberty has turned on a number of factors: the issue of equality of treatment of religious groups in prisons; the courts' reticence to reverse the decisions of prison officials; the degree to which the inmates' challenges would undermine the fundamental interests of the state (for example, prison security and administrative security are often cited); and the showing that Islam is similar to the conventional Protestant, Catholic, and Jewish faiths.

In many instances the courts have recognized African-American Muslim inmates as a religious group entitled to First Amendment protection.[86] Cases brought by Muslims have established that prisoners have the right to assemble for religious services;[87] to consult a cleric of their faith;[88] to possess religious publications and to subscribe to religious literature;[89] to wear unobtrusive religious symbols such as medallions;[90] to have prepared a special diet required by their religion;[91] and to correspond with their spiritual leaders.

While several court decisions during the 1960s and 1970s extended civil rights protection to Muslims in prison, judicial deference to prison officials' authority and expertise in issues of prison management never entirely disappeared. The struggle to define the proper role of the federal judiciary in holding such public institutions as prisons accountable to constitutional principles is evident in many of the cases discussed here. The U.S. Court of Appeals for the Fourth Circuit held in *Sewell v Pegelow* (1961) that "maintenance of discipline in prison is an executive function with which the judicial branch ordinarily will not interfere."[92] However, the redefinition of prison problems as free exercise ones—e.g., interference with religious freedom—cast the debate in terms of the First Amendment, which, according to the district court in *Pierce v LaVallee* (1961) placed the "ordinary problems of prison discipline . . . into quite a different category," with overt constitutional implications.[93]

The courts have recognized that the state, in some instances, may have an interest which is important enough to outweigh the individual's interest in religious expression. Not all burdens on religion are unconstitutional and the state has a preeminent obligation to promote security, order, and rehabilitation in its penal system. The Court of Appeals for the Seventh Circuit stated in *Madyun v Franzen* (1983), a case involving Muslim inmates, that: "the balance between [the prisoner's] right to free exercise and the state's interest in applying to him its prison rules and regulations tips toward the state."[94] Moreover, prison inmates, by virtue of incarceration, give up some of their constitutionally protected rights. Prisoners "cannot expect the same freedom from incidental infringement on the exercise of . . . religious practices that is enjoyed by those not incarcerated."[95]

This reasoning was used in *Wright v Wilkins* (1961), where the Supreme Court of New York upheld Attica Prison officials' denial of permission to a prisoner to take an Arabic grammar, needed for the prisoner's religious education, into the prison recreation yard. The court held that "materials which prisoners were permitted to take with them to [the] prison recreational yard or elsewhere in prison was a matter of prison discipline entrusted to the department of correction and warden of [the] prison," and pertinent regulations did not violate the prisoner's right to freedom of religion.[96]

In *Brown v McGinnis* (1962), where Muslim inmates claimed the right to constitutional protection of their religious activities, the New York Court of Appeals noted that "freedom of exercise of religious worship in prison is not absolute, but rather a preferred right, which cannot interfere with laws enacted for [the] preservation, safety, and welfare of the state."[97] According to this ruling, the rights to religious worship and expression are subject to reasonable rules and regulations designed to promote disciplinary and managerial interests of the penal system.

Similarly, in an oft-cited passage from a 1964 decision, *Fulwood v Clemmer*, which denied African-American Muslim inmates access to controversial religious literature, the court stated: "No romantic or sentimental view of constitutional rights or of religion should induce a court to interfere with the necessary disciplinary regime established by officials."[98] The Supreme Court of California, relying on judicial precedents set by prisoners' litigation making non-religion First Amendment claims, held in *In Re Ferguson* that "inmates of state prisons may not be allowed to assert the usual constitutional rights guaranteed to non-incarcerated citizens."[99] While the right to believe is absolute, the right to act on those beliefs—e.g., by assembling and discussing "inflammatory Muslim doctrines in a prison situation"[100]—is not.[101]

When a highly preferred interest such as the free exercise of religion is at issue, however, the courts have made a general attempt to place the burden on the state to prove a substantial governmental interest related to the suppression of religious liberty.[102] In *Sewell v Pegelow*, the court held that "prisoners lose certain rights and privileges, but are not entirely bereft of all civil rights or every protection of the law."[103] In *Brown v McGinnis*, the Court of Appeals of New York wrote, "speculation as to the dangers inherent in dissemination among prisoners of beliefs ... of ... Islamic faith ... did not warrant prison officials' alleged denial of [the] right to exercise [the] Islamic faith."[104] The Court of Appeals for the Fourth Circuit noted in *Brown v Peyton* (1971) that "a prisoner does not shed ... First Amendment rights at the prison portals," and held that the prisoner's desire to practice his religion could be restricted by prison officials only upon "a convincing showing that paramount state interests so require."[105]

In *Fulwood v Clemmer*, the U.S. District Court for the District of Columbia balanced the state's interest in prison security and the Muslim inmates' First Amendment claims, in a decision which found in favor of the prison officials in part and in favor of the Muslim inmates in part. On the one hand, the court condoned the prison officials' decision to discipline a Muslim inmate for inflammatory remarks at a prayer meeting on a baseball field where many non-Muslims were within earshot. In doing so, the court invoked the "fighting words" doctrine set out in *Chaplinsky v New Hampshire* (315 U.S. 568 [1942]), claiming that inflammatory words are not protected by the First Amendment. Additionally, the court held that the prison officials' refusal to allow Muslim inmates to correspond with their spiritual leader or to receive a newspaper containing a column written by that leader was a proper exercise of prison administrative discretion.

On the other hand, the court found other deprivations to be impermissible. The denial of rights to wear religious medals and to conduct prayer services, where the state not only allowed but encouraged and supported religious services and the distribution of medals of other religious faiths, was ascertained to be discriminatory. Also, the disciplinary measures against the inmate who spoke the allegedly inflammatory words were judged to be too severe. The punishment was determined to be excessive because it was imposed not only for the offense but for the improper "purpose of suppressing . . . the Muslim religion in the prison."[106]

Although judicial treatment of Muslim prisoners' claims under the free exercise clause has been far from consistent, a general trend toward recognition of these claims, when framed in the context of discrimination, emerged during the Warren Court and the first half of the Burger Court years. However, the impact of judicial decisions on various prison religious groups has differed, falling more harshly on Muslim inmates. A review of the major issues of discrimination, diet, grooming, and prayer will demonstrate the qualitative differences in treatment.

Discriminatory Treatment

In many cases, the courts have had to address allegations by Muslim inmates of religious persecution and discriminatory treatment. Islamic practices often have been prohibited in prison settings while the practices of other religious denominations have not. Instances of interference with religious freedom, discriminatory treatment, and punishment inflicted as a result of attempts to practice their religious faith[107] have sometimes been proven through the efforts of Muslim inmates to claim their constitutional rights to free expression and equal protection. Yet "Muslims have won most of the opportunities for religious worship enjoyed by members of conventional religions,"[108] through considerable struggle. When Muslim inmates have been able to demonstrate convincingly that they have not received the same treatment as other religious groups in prison, the courts generally have been inclined to protect their constitutional claims. Most courts have ruled that suppression of religious liberty—for instance, the prohibition of prayer meetings and other forms of discriminatory treatment—if applied unequally at the expense of Muslim inmates, results in an impermissible denial of the constitutional guarantee contained in the First Amendment.[109] In *Fulwood v Clemmer,* Muslim inmates alleged, and the U.S. District Court held, that the District of Columbia promoted and underwrote the religious services and activities of Protestants, Catholics, and Jews in its penal institutions while denying the same rights to Muslim inmates.[110] The court ordered prison officials to make religious facilities available in a nondiscriminatory manner. In *Brown v*

McGinnis, where Muslim inmates alleged that prison authorities discriminated against them by prohibiting Muslim religious services, the New York Court of Appeals ordered the Commissioner of Prisons to issue rules and regulations that would secure the rights guaranteed by the Constitution in a nondiscriminatory manner not severely compromising considerations of prison security and discipline. Similarly, in *SaMarion v McGinnis* the Supreme Court of New York held that prison rules and regulations:

> providing for opportunity for practice of religion of Black Muslimism in state prison system which limited attendance at Muslim services to inmates who were "presently affiliated" or "professed" the religion of Muslimism were too restrictive and denied free exercise of religion to prospective members of the Muslim faith.[111]

In *Brown v McGinnis,* an inmate of Green Haven State Prison in New York alleged that he "is of the Islamic faith by religious choice and profession and seeks spiritual advice, ministration, and religious services"[112] from the local temple of Islam and from its minister, Malcolm X. Further, inmate Brown charged that prison officials discriminated against him and his coreligionists by prohibiting religious services, spiritual advice, and ministration from recognized clergy of the Islamic faith. Specifically, the New York Commissioner of Correction did not allow Muslim inmates to communicate with or be ministered to by Malcolm X because of his criminal record. The court ruled that the fact that the temple from which Brown sought ministrations was headed by a person with a criminal record did not warrant the denial of his right to exercise the Islamic faith in a manner similar to that of inmates of other denominations.

In the landmark prisoners' rights case, *Cooper v Pate,* a Black Muslim prisoner in an Illinois state prison brought federal charges against his prison warden, alleging that he was being discriminated against because he was denied permission to obtain religious literature from the Nation of Islam, consult with ministers of his faith, and attend Muslim religious services and, further, was being punished because of the warden's hostility toward the Black Muslim movement.

The counsel for the state sought to show that the Muslims were a revolutionary movement not entitled to free exercise:

> [The] Black Muslim movement despite its pretext of a religious facade, is an organization that outside prison walls, has for its

object the overthrow of the white race, and inside prison walls, has an impressive history of inciting riots and violence.[113]

The state's effort, however, was unsuccessful. The U.S. Supreme Court held that the prisoner's complaint stated a "cause for action" in federal courts despite the lower courts' reticence to intervene in matters of prison discipline and regulations. When the case was remanded to the district court for a hearing on the merits, the Muslim inmate's request for relief was granted in part because the court found that prison authorities must not punish a prisoner or discriminate against him on account of his religion. While the prison's rules regarding receipt of religious publications were upheld by the court on the basis that such materials were not necessary for the practice of the inmate's religion, rules regarding minister visitations and attendance at religious services were applied in a discriminatory fashion, and were enjoined by the court.

In *Walker v Blackwell*, Black Muslims sought to extend their religious privileges in the following ways: (1) to be served a specified restricted diet after sunset during the month of December (observed as the fast of Ramadan by the Nation of Islam as taught by Elijah Muhammad); (2) to listen to the national weekly radio broadcast of their spiritual leader; (3) to receive the Nation of Islam's newspaper, *Muhammad Speaks*; and (4) to correspond directly with Elijah Muhammad. The Court of Appeals for the Fifth Circuit stated that when claims of religious discrimination and denial of religious liberty were at stake,

> the government must show some substantial and controlling interest which requires the subordination or limitation of these important constitutional rights, and which justifies their infringement; and in the absence of such compelling justification the government restrictions are impermissible infringements of these fundamental and preferred rights.[114]

Applying this rationale to the facts in this case, the court then found that considerations of security and administrative expense outweighed the Muslim inmates' claims regarding special meals, and that the omission of Elijah Muhammad's radio broadcast from the prison radio system was not a denial of equal protection since there was no programming available for any religious denomination. However, the appellate court found that the Muslims were entitled to receive *Muhammad Speaks* and to correspond with Elijah Muhammad because inmates of other religious persuasions were permitted to receive religious literature and correspond with their spiritual leaders.

The U.S. District Court, N. D. California, held in *Northern v Nelson*[115] that prison authorities were required to pay a Muslim minister to perform religious services in prison facilities at an hourly rate comparable to that paid to chaplains of Catholic, Jewish, and Protestant faiths. In *Finney v Hutto,*[116] the U.S. District Court for the Eastern District of Arkansas held that Muslim inmates of an Arkansas state prison were entitled to the same privileges of religious worship as were granted to inmates of other faiths. When Arkansas prison authorities appealed, they did not contest the court decision on religious worship, but chose to appeal only the part of the decision regarding the treatment of Muslim inmates. Inmates had alleged, and the district court held, that solitary confinement, daily meals of less than one thousand calories, overcrowding, and inadequate toilet facilities violated the ban on cruel and unusual punishment contained in the Eighth Amendment.

In a case rejecting a free exercise claim when combined with an equal protection claim, the Supreme Court of California took the position that Muslim religious practices could be prohibited. In *In Re Ferguson,*[117] Muslim inmates contended that their rights to religious freedom had been violated by prison officials. Unlike the Protestant, Catholic, Jewish, and Christian Science groups of Folsom State Prison, the members of the Muslim Religious Society were not allowed a place to worship. They were not allowed to discuss their religious doctrines nor to possess "an adequate amount" of their religious literature; their meetings were disbanded, often by force; and prison visits by their religious leaders were prohibited. The Muslim inmates asked the court to intervene either to accord them the status of a religious group with religious privileges equal to those allowed to other prison religious groups, or deny religious privileges to all prison religious groups across the board. Failing this, the inmates asserted, they should be released from prison so that they might practice the Islamic faith unencumbered by discriminatory prison regulations.[118]

The Supreme Court of California, however, held that the Director of Corrections had not acted unreasonably in refusing to allow Muslim convicts to pursue their religious activities in prison. Due to the alleged racist content of the Muslim Religious Society's doctrine of black supremacy, and its adherents' rejection of the authority of whites, the court took the position that Muslim activities may be prohibited:

In light of the potentially serious dangers to the established prison society presented by Muslim beliefs and actions, it cannot be said that the present, suppressive approach by the Director of Corrections is an abuse of his discretionary power to manage our prison system.[119]

More recently, in *Thompson v Kentucky*,[120] the Court of Appeals for the Sixth Circuit held that prison officials did not violate the free exercise of religion or the equal protection clauses of the First and Fourteenth Amendments by allocating six and one-half hours of chapel time per week to Muslim inmates while allocating twenty-three and one-half hours per week to Christian groups, or in failing to provide funds for a Muslim prison chaplain while providing for one part-time and two full-time Christian chaplains. Although the claims involved equality of treatment, the appellate court found that the prison's policies were justified because they reflected the different numbers of Christian and Muslim inmates, and thus were not discriminatory. Furthermore, the court opinion held: "The 'free exercise' clause guarantees a liberty interest, a substantive right; that clause does not insure that all sects will be treated alike in all respects."[121]

Diet

Judicial responses to prisoners' deprivations with respect to diet have dealt with the denial of inmates' requests to be served a pork-free diet[122] and the prisons' failure to accommodate the fast of Ramadan.[123] Islam, like Orthodox Judaism, prohibits the consumption of pork or pork derivatives. According to the testimony of one Black Muslim minister, even "if our lives depended on it . . . we can't eat pork."[124] However, because of the low cost of pork and pork by-products, they are served frequently in prison dining facilities, sometimes to the extent that abstaining inmates cannot get adequate nourishment. Additionally, prison regulations rarely permit inmates to keep food in their cells, which prevents those who do not eat pork from independently observing religious dietary restrictions.

Analogous claims made by Muslim and Jewish inmates have resulted in dissimilar court rulings.[125] In *Moorish Science Temple, Inc. v Smith* (1976), Muslim inmate Smallwood-El alleged that although Jewish inmates were provided with alternative diets consistent with their religious beliefs, prison officials refused to provide him with a suitable diet. The appellate court remanded the case to the lower court for additional proceedings on Smallwood-El's claims. The Court of Appeals for the Second Circuit, in its 1975 term, upheld Jewish Defense League leader Meir Kahane's claim that the denial of kosher food in prison was a violation of the First Amendment. The *Kahane v Carlson* decision noted that "the courts have properly recognized that prison authorities must accommodate the rights of prisoners to receive diets consistent with their religious scruples,"[126] and held that the denial of kosher food to a Jewish inmate was not justified by an important governmental objective and thus was unconstitutional.

The following year, in *Jihaad v Carlson*, Muslim inmate Jihaad claimed that his religious beliefs required him to wear a beard and that the prison's shaving requirement violated his right to freely exercise his religion. As punishment for his refusal to shave, prison officials placed Jihaad in disciplinary segregation, and fed him nothing but pork sandwiches and oranges while he was there. Since Islam prohibits the consumption of pork, Jihaad was reduced to eating only oranges. The same district court that had ruled in favor of Kahane's claims in *Kahane v Carlson* remanded this case for an investigation of the competing institutional and inmate interests.[127] The *Jihaad* court held that "it is clearly within the power of prison authorities to require appropriate attire and grooming of prison inmates,"[128] but also cited the precedent set in another Muslim prisoner's case, *Knuckles v Prasse*: "The prisoners are not entitled to a special dietary program. Of course they will not be forced to eat pork products."[129] On the basis of the facts before them, however, the court was unwilling to declare the prison officials' decision to deny Jihaad a Muslim diet while he was kept in disciplinary segregation an unconstitutional deprivation.

In a case involving Rastafarian as well as Muslim prisoners, *Barnes v Virgin Islands*,[130] the federal district court ordered prison authorities to provide the inmates with food complying with their religious dietary restrictions. In this decision, the court relied on *Barnett v Rodgers*, where the D.C. Circuit Court, in remanding the case to the lower courts to review the merits, suggested that "a modest degree of official deference to . . . religious obligations [was] . . . constitutionally required."[131] A reasonable effort to accommodate religiously sanctioned dietary needs was urged on prison authorities but, unlike the outcome in *Kahane v Carlson*, was not required by the courts.

Members of the Nation of Islam, while under Elijah Muhammad's leadership, observed the fast of Ramadan during December.[132] The fast consists of restricting the consumption of food to the period from before sunrise to after sunset. Special arrangements for the proper celebration of the fast in prisons are rarely made. Requests for special dining hours and foods have been denied by prison administrators on the grounds of cost, convenience, and security.[133]

The Court of Appeals for the Second Circuit, in *Barnett v Rodgers*, however, was more accommodating to Muslim inmates' claims. The court noted that the inmates' request for one pork-free meal a day "represents the bare minimum that jail authorities . . . are constitutionally required to do, not only for Muslim, but indeed for any group of inmates with religious restriction on diet."[134] In another decision, *Battle v Anderson*, a federal district court held that there is no justification for failing to identify foods prepared with pork in prison dining facilities, and ordered immediate implementation of such a practice on behalf of Muslim inmates.[135]

Grooming

Nearly all prisons have regulations concerning inmate appearance and grooming. The justifications for such regulations include hygiene and the fact that beards, hair, and clothing can conceal contraband and identity. Muslim inmates, on the other hand, have claimed in various court cases that the enforcement of prison regulations prohibiting facial hair and prayer caps and robes interferes with their free exercise rights. They have testified, for instance, that their religion requires them to "let their beards flow."[136]

The Court of Appeals for the Second Circuit, ruling in *Burgin v Henderson*, where Muslim inmates alleged that prison authorities were interfering with their free exercise of religion by compelling them to shave their facial hair, suggested that the personal appearance of a prisoner is a legitimate concern of the state.[137] The court states: "It may well be that the state's interest in hygiene and identification of inmates outweighs the prisoner's interest in growing a beard as required by his religion,"[138] but the evidence before the court did not provide an adequate basis upon which to rule. In this case the prison officials also prohibited the wearing of prayer caps, in accordance with regulations prohibiting hats, and the performance of prayers five times a day because it conflicted with the prison schedule. Rather than decide the case on the basis of the evidence before the court, the judge remanded the case to the district court for a factual hearing on the state's justification for the prison regulations under challenge as well as the sincerity of the religious belief which required the wearing of facial hair and prayer caps and extensive praying. In remanding the case to the lower court, the appeals court judge attempted to clarify a distinction he saw as important, between the desire to wear a beard for reasons of personal appearance versus religious reasons, and indicated that the latter would merit constitutional protection.

Burgin v Henderson has helped to guarantee the right of a prisoner to wear a beard if done for religious reasons. It has been cited as precedent in several subsequent cases involving both Muslims and non-Muslims.[139] In *Monroe v Bombard,*[140] a case citing *Burgin* as precedent, the district court held that Sunni Muslims had a constitutional right to grow beards as an aspect of religious freedom and that no governmental interest sufficient to overcome this had been shown.[141] Institutional requirements with respect to security and prisoner identification could be satisfied by other means less restrictive than a total ban on wearing beards.

Without scrutinizing the reasonableness of prison shaving regulations, the Supreme Court of New York ruled in *People ex rel.Rockey v Krueger*[142] that evidence of discriminatory application of the rules in question invalidated the requirement that a Muslim inmate shave off his beard. In this case, Muslim inmate Rockey was held in solitary confinement because of his refusal to shave his beard on religious grounds. The jail supervisory officer admitted in his testimony that he would not require an Orthodox Jew to shave, and that while the Jewish inmate who did not shave would be isolated from other prisoners, he would not be placed in solitary confinement. Since the regulation was applied admittedly in a discriminatory manner, the court required that the Muslim inmate be released from solitary confinement.

In *Shabazz v Barnauskas*[143] the Court of Appeals for the Fifth Circuit held that the lower court had erred in dismissing a Muslim prisoner's challenge to a Florida state prison's "no beard" regulation without conducting a hearing into the plaintiff's religious beliefs and the state's justification for its prison regulations.

An examination of the court records reveals that Muslim inmates have contributed substantially to the defense of a prisoner's right to wear facial hair for reasons of religious belief in spite of the state's claims of security, prisoner identification, and hygiene interests. However, the courts have been more reluctant to recognize Muslim prisoners' claims than the claims of adherents to other faiths. While the right of American Indians to wear their hair long has been protected against prison regulations concerning hygiene,[144] and the right of individuals who attach private religious significance to their hair length has been protected,[145] the right of Muslims to refuse to shave off their facial hair in accordance with religious prescriptions has not been upheld as readily. In cases involving Muslim inmates, the courts have often conceded that prison policies might be defensible, and have called for further examination into both the sincerity of beliefs of Muslim inmates and the legitimacy of the prison regulations in question.

Prayers

Muslims are required by their faith to perform prayers at prescribed hours five times a day. These are accompanied by prescribed ablutions and prostration; "without any one of these forms the prayers would be incomplete."[146] Prison schedules sometimes interfere with Muslim prayers. In *Bethea v Dagget*,[147] where a Muslim prisoner contended that the prison regime did not permit him to pray five times daily, the court held that there was no impingement on religious liberty by the prison schedule because it allowed ample opportunity for prayer, although not at Islamically prescribed hours.

After a July 27, 1973, riot at the McAlester facility of the Oklahoma State Penitentiary, prison officials imposed a total ban on group worship. In *Battle v Anderson* a prisoner held in McAlester brought suit on behalf of inmates, including Muslims, who claimed that the ban on corporate religious services was a violation of their First Amendment rights and was not justified by any legitimate security concerns. The federal district court averred that the prohibition:

> appears to have had a greater impact on the Muslims, because [corporate] services provide for their only opportunity for religious guidance. Protestants and Catholics at the penitentiary have at least the services of a civilian chaplain with whom individual consultations may be arranged however brief or unsatisfactory they may be.[148]

In effect, the court suggested that the ban on gathering for worship combined with the failure to provide a Muslim chaplain, placed a heavier burden on Muslims, and may be inherently discriminatory.

In a 1987 U.S. Supreme Court case, *O'Lone v Shabazz*, where Muslim inmates challenged New Jersey prison policies which prevented them from attending Friday services, the Court, with Justice Rehnquist writing for the majority, held in part that "prison officials had acted in a reasonable manner by precluding Islamic inmates from attending weekly Friday religious services and prison regulations to that effect thus did not violate the free exercise of religion clause of the First Amendment."[149] The Court found that the reasonableness of the policies in question was supported by the fact that, while some Muslims are prevented from attending Friday services due to work assignments, they do not deprive Muslim inmates of all forms of religious exercise. All Muslims who wish to may, at one time or another, participate in a number of Muslim religious ceremonies.[150]

Despite the fact that Friday prayer services are of paramount importance to the Islamic faith, which the Court acknowledged, it was still determined that "the very stringent requirements as to the time at which [Friday services] may be held may make it extraordinarily difficult for prison officials to assure that every Muslim prisoner is able to attend that service."[151] Since other means of religious worship are available, the Court held that the Constitution does not require prison officials to "sacrifice legitimate penological objectives"[152] to accommodate inconvenient Muslim religious practices. Further, it was held that prison officials need not demonstrate that the policies in question are imperative to further such an important interest as security, discipline, or rehabilitation, and are not more restrictive of prisoners' constitutional rights than is necessary to achieve prison objectives. Even where First Amendment rights are concerned, according to this decision the Supreme Court will not substitute its judgment for that of prison officials.[153] The Court essentially deferred to the discretion of prison authorities in the execution of their duties.

It is worth noting that in his dissent in this case, Justice Brennan cited the brief for Imam Jamil Abdullah Al-Amin et al., as *amici curiae*, to illustrate that attendance at Friday Muslim prayer services is obligatory.[154] The Friday services, Brennan argued, "cannot be regarded as one of several essentially fungible religious practices."[155] The opportunity to participate in other religious activities in prison does not compensate for the Muslims' forced absence at the central service in Islam. Brennan compared the situation of Muslims who were not allowed to attend Friday services to that of a Catholic prisoner denied the right to attend Mass on Sunday: "Few would regard [the latter] deprivation as anything but absolute, even if the prisoner were afforded other opportunities to pray, to discuss the Catholic faith with others, and even to avoid eating meat on Friday

if that were a preference."[156] The fact that other types of religious
worship are available in prison does not warrant the deprivation of
the opportunity to participate in the central religious ceremony of
one's faith, a time when adherents "assert their identity as a community covenanted to God."[157]

Other Religious Issues

In *Abdullah v Kinnison,*[158] inmates Abdullah and Akbar challenged
an Ohio state prison regulation restricting prisoners' use of white
Hanafi Muslim prayer robes to the prison chapel only. The Muslim
inmates asserted that under Islamic law, Hanafi Muslims should
wear white prayer robes at all times, if possible, and must wear
them while performing prayers five times a day.[159] Until November
1977, Southern Ohio Correctional Facility inmates of the Hanafi
Muslim faith were permitted to keep prayer robes in their cells. A
new directive restricted the use of white prayer robes to the chapel
only. Prison authorities imposed this restriction in response to an
incident in which a prison guard took one of the white robes from a
prisoner's cell and used it to frighten another black inmate by imi-
tating a Ku Klux Klan member. The restriction was thus justified as
a "control mechanism" to prevent similar incidents from occurring in
the future. Additionally, the robes were described by prison officials
as a security risk, since they were loose-fitting and could be used to
conceal weapons, contraband, and food, or to resemble civilian dress
to aid in escape.[160]

The Court of Appeals for the Sixth Circuit held in this case that
the burden imposed on Muslim inmates' right to free exercise was
minimal, because the new prison policy merely limits, and does not
forbid, the use of the Hanafi Muslims' white prayer robes. The fact
that the ban on white prayer robes outside the chapel impinges on
the right to perform prayers in the prescribed fashion outside the
chapel appears to have had no bearing on the court decision. Further, the court accepted without question the prison officials' assertion that their objectives in promulgating the restrictive regulations
were legitimate and justified an abridgement of the Muslim inmates'
First Amendment rights.

In *Madyen v Franzen,* a male Muslim inmate, held in the Pon-
tiac Correctional Center in Illinois, refused to comply with a female
security guard's order that he submit to a limited frisk search[161] on
the grounds that the Islamic religion forbade such physical contact
with a woman other than his wife or mother.[162] The Court of Appeals

for the Seventh Circuit held that, although a limited frisk search by a female security guard might be incompatible with Islamic tenets, it would not impermissibly violate a male Muslim inmate's First Amendment right of free exercise since it is justified by the important state interests in providing adequate prison security and equal opportunity for women to serve as prison guards.[163] Equal opportunity for women in employment is cited by the court as a legal obligation incumbent on the state.[164] To provide such opportunity in state prisons, female guards must be able to perform all the tasks associated with their positions, including limited frisk searches. The court found the equal opportunity in hiring interest to outweigh the Muslim inmate's free exercise interest.

CONCLUSION

The general judicial approach has been deference to the authority and expertise of prison administrators, resulting often in the uncritical acceptance of stated institutional needs and apprehensions about Black Muslims at the expense of Muslim prisoners' religious liberty. The matter of incarceration and, more specifically, its considerable diminution of the constitutional rights of prisoners, complicates the issue of free exercise guarantees. While many judicial decisions have recognized prisoners' rights to religious worship and expression, some rulings indicated that freedom of religion may permissibly be curtailed by prison authorities. Prisoners may suffer deprivations which are a necessary result of confinement and the institutional structure of prisons. The state can justify an infringement on the prisoners' right to free exercise of religion by showing that it is the least restrictive means to attain a compelling interest. The courts, when "activist," generally moved away from the hands-off doctrine but they have not abandoned it. Many decisions reviewed here marked the resurgence of this doctrine. Courts no longer deny jurisdiction in prison matters, nor that the Constitution does apply to prisoners; however, now they require only a showing that prison policies are reasonably related to a legitimate governmental objective before they can justify certain deprivations on the basis of the necessities of prison administration. Most often the judicial approach has meant the refusal on the part of the courts to substitute judicial supervision for the expert judgment of prison officials in matters of prison management, even when violations of constitutional rights are at issue. They accept conclusions and assessments made by prison officials as outweighing the charges of interference with religious practices brought by Muslim prisoners. Yet deference to prison officials, who are not disinterested persons in the resolution of prison problems, jeopardizes the free exercise rights of adherents of nonconventional faiths which are perceived to be threatening or subversive.

In *O'Lone v Shabazz* (1987), the Court did not use the compelling interest standard, which was enunciated in the free excercise cases of *Sherbert v Verner* (1963) and *Wisconsin v Yoder* (1972), to strike a balance between the religious liberty claims of the inmates and the compelling government interests of the New Jersey state prison. Instead, the *O'Lone* decision upheld a "rational basis" standard. That is, the prison administrators needed only to show that the challenged regulations were reasonably related to a legitimate governmental objective, which is much easier to prove than the stricter legal standard of the compelling interest test.[165] This standard is deferential to the authority and interpretation of the prison administrators, who enforce the prison policies under challenge.

Legislative action since the *O'Lone* decision has prohibited use of the rational basis standard in the courts when a question of religious liberty is at issue. In 1993, Congress passed a bill to reverse a 1990 Supreme Court decision, *Employment Division v Smith*,[166] in which the Court effectively eliminated the compelling interest test and made it easier for federal and state government to pass laws that restricted individuals' religious rights. In *Smith*, two Native American men were fired from their jobs at a drug rehabilitation clinic, and subsequently denied unemployment compensation benefits, because of their use of peyote in a religious ceremony. The men sued the state of Oregon, claiming that the state's interest in enforcing antidrug laws was not compelling enough to warrant infringement of their religious freedom. The U.S. Supreme Court ruled against them, and held that the state's antidrug laws were constitutionally valid because they advanced a valid purpose and were not enacted specifically to inhibit the free exercise of religion.

The *Smith* ruling provoked widespread protest from religious organizations and the ACLU, and Congress drafted a bill to overrule it. Called the Religious Freedom Restoration Act (RFRA), the bill was meant to restore the pre-*Smith* compelling interest standard. The bill had remarkable bipartisan support in Congress, with Minority Whip Newt Gingrich introducing the bill in the House of Representatives, and Edward Kennedy (D-MA) as lead sponsor in the Senate (where the bill had 58 cosponsors; 37 Democrats and 21 Republicans). The bill passed in the Senate, by a vote of 97 to 3, on

October 27, and was signed by President Clinton on November 16, 1993.

What RFRA will mean for Muslims in prison, who raise legal challenges to prison policies that inhibit free exercise of religion, however, remains to be seen. Senator Harry Reid, (D-NV), introduced an amendment to the bill to prohibit the application of RFRA's protections to prisoners. In discussion of the amendment, Senator Alan Simpson (R-WY) and several others voiced concern about whether RFRA would require prison administrators to accommodate dietary and other demands from inmates in the name of religious freedom. Reid's amendment was rejected in the Senate by a vote of 41–58, but this was considerably closer than the vote to pass RFRA.[167]

The preceding court record demonstrates that, through their use of law to claim particular rights, by asking the courts to intervene to resolve disputes with prison officials, Muslim inmates became engaged with a political system they had condemned as a matter of dogma. Essentially, the separatist doctrines of the Black Muslim movement eschewed integration and political participation because such involvement was a validation of the racially biased power structure of American society. Yet, as a means to an end, the Black Muslims in prison aspired to official recognition as a religious group, with attendant rights and privileges in captive society, so as to further their objectives in liberating the Black Nation. Key concepts of religious liberty, free exercise of religion, and minority group rights initially enticed Muslim inmates to build a legal strategy to gain legitimacy as a religious entity, an already established status within the prison system. The awareness of the availability of the courts as a legal forum through which inmates could challenge prison administration encouraged Muslim prisoners to reconceptualize themselves and their situation. It created the expectation that their grievances would be redressed by the legal system and led many to initiate litigation. While it is not clear that the expected results were achieved, namely, that the courts and the law liberated the Muslims from the despotic authority of prison wardens and gave them room to discuss their doctrines, the litigation did effectively mobilize support for an interest—the prisoners' right to religious liberty—which had previously been excluded to Black Muslims in the allocation of values and rights in prisons.

Such a step must have been difficult to make, for the use of law is not a reflex, especially for those who have run up against the criminal justice system already and may consider themselves to be victimized, marginalized, and/or powerless. But once the tensions between prisoners and prison officials were framed as a religious liberty controversy, and not simply an issue of institutional management, then judicial intervention on behalf of the Muslim inmates became not only possible but necessary.

To a large degree, Muslim prisoners' litigation was meant to modify the conditions of their confinement and to limit the absolute power of prison officials, and *not* to sue for release.[168] The challenge was directed at the manner in which prison rules were used to structure Black Muslims' lives and curtail their operations. By asking for judicial intervention in the management of prisons, the inmates sought not only a means to resist the unchecked authority of prison administrators, but, more importantly, to transform existing conditions. The resort to law, then, was a form of self-help invoked by prisoners who had changed the way they thought about their "discontent," a change which then "politicized" their need.[169]

The result of moderate successes in litigation is that the prisoners became attentive to the courts as institutions which legitimately define and protect their rights in prison, in organizing important relationships within the captive community, with representatives of outside organizations such as clerics, and with their keepers. The Muslim inmates moved from total disengagement from the political system as an ideal, to calling upon law as a basis for their corporate rights. Vindication of their claims against prison authorities meant recognition of the ability of the courts and the authority of the Constitution to do so. Prior to the 1960s, the rule of law was not accessible to prisoners who were, consequently, "left without enforceable rights."[170] Once the courtroom became accessible, the law worked a change in the mode of representation of the inmate to the institutions of power—from black convict to Black Muslim—and, ultimately, on the inmate's self-identification.

Of course none of these changes transpired in a vacuum. Already mentioned here is the confluence of the civil rights movement and evolving race relations in the larger society with the developing prisoners rights movement. But coinciding with these events, and extremely important in the redefinition of the Black Muslim, were the momentous changes happening in the Nation of Islam itself. Shortly after his expulsion from the movement in 1963 for saying about the assassination of John F. Kennedy that "the chickens have come home to roost," Malcolm X travelled to Mecca to perform the pilgrimage and found there "an Islam markedly different from that preached by Elijah."[171] Reflecting on the multinational, multiracial nature of the brotherhood of believers he saw in Mecca, Malcolm X reevaluated and ultimately contested the racist doctrines of Elijah Muhammad's movement. In 1965, he was assassinated himself, by members of the Nation of Islam, ostensibly for his transformed religious beliefs. This event, combined with revelations about sexual indiscretions by Elijah Muhammad, had serious repercussions within the Black Muslim community. Some Black Muslims broke away from the Nation of Islam, thus damaging the unity of the movement.

When Elijah Muhammad died in 1975, one of his sons, Warith Deen Muhammad, became the leader of the movement. Under his leadership several changes were introduced, with the objective of bringing Black Muslims into the "mainstream of Islam."[172] Racist doctrines were eschewed in favor of orthodox Islamic teachings. Warith Deen Muhammad had studied Arabic, the Qur'an and Islamic law, and sought to renew the faith in America. In accordance with the practices of the Islamic world, he adopted Arabic-language terms for Islamic constructs; ministers became *imams*, and temples became *masjids* or mosques.[173] The history of the Nation of Islam was revised so that the period of Elijah Muhammad's leadership, characterized by doctrines of separatism and black supremacy, became known as a necessary transitional stage, the crucial period of the Nation's establishment and growth when the African-American was liberated from the mentality of subjugation. The influence of Malcolm X, who had been a close friend of Warith Deen Muhammad, was evident in these changes.[174]

The name of the movement went through various changes: from the Nation of Islam to the American Bilalian Community, then the World Community of Islam in the West, and the American Muslim Mission. By 1985, the movement "was officially integrated into the general Muslim community in the United States,"[175] and its adherents are known no longer as Black Muslims, but simply as Muslims.

Parallel changes were happening within the prison Muslim community as well. The former militant dicta of the organization were mitigated behind prison walls. By 1979, a survey conducted by the Federal Bureau of Prisons indicated that while membership in Islamic groups was growing in prisons at the close of the 1970s, the tenor of the movement had changed. Norman A. Carlson, the director of the Federal Bureau of Prisons, said that Muslims were "no longer considered a threat to prison discipline" because they no longer taught racial hatred. Moreover, he admitted that "the image of the Black Muslims as a source of disruption was blown out of proportion."[176] Although the Black Muslims before 1975 preached hostile rhetoric, vilifying white America, they actually precipitated little violence.

Jacobs puts it this way:

> Ironically, after their religious grievances were redressed, the Muslims became a quiescent and stabilizing force in many prisons, which began to be rocked by new cohorts of violent and disorganized ghetto youth.[177]

Few prisons hire Muslim chaplains in numbers approaching the number of Catholic or Protestant ministers. However, as an outcome of litigation, in 1984 the Federal Bureau of Prisons hired its first full-time *imam* to serve as a prison chaplain. Responding to an increase of interest in Islam among African-American inmates, eight prison chaplains who are trained as Muslim *imams* have been hired to date to work in federal prisons.[178] These chaplains serve the religious needs of the entire inmate population on a full-time basis, including but not limited to Christians, Jews, and Muslims. Some of the hundreds of mosques in the United States exist behind prison walls.

5

Hate Crimes Legislation
and the Protection of Religious Property

The number of mosques and Islamic centers in the United States has been growing rapidly, increasing by more than one-third in just the last five years. Over 950[1] mosques serve the needs of an estimated 4.6 million Muslims across the U.S.[2] This trend signals a new stage in the assimilation and acculturation of the American Muslim community. By building mosques, Muslims are laying the foundations for their permanent stay. Undertaken largely by first and second generation American Muslims, this can be seen as a watershed in their thinking about identity and an active investment in their future here, which is reflected in the recent observation made by Ahmad Zaki Hammad, president of the Islamic Society of North America: "Over the last 30 years, the first instincts were self-preservation and maintaining Muslim identity as much as we could. . . . The prevailing climate among American Muslims now is that we cannot live in isolation."[3]

This study sets a framework for consideration of the American Muslim community's transformation from isolation to active involvement. The purpose of this chapter and the next is to view the setting in which Muslims now attempt to establish a place for themselves and their institutions in North America. The security of the American Muslim community and its institutions is affected by three important factors: (1) The immigrant status of a portion of the community, which is generalized in the public mind to characterize Islam as a "foreign creed"; (2) The dramatic rise in the incidence of hate crimes[4] in the United States, which often are directed against places of worship including mosques; (3) The prevailing climate of hostility toward Islam, fanned by American foreign policy, which has made "Muslim-bashing" and "Arab-bashing" a common form of discrimination and expression of xenophobia.[5] The first two of these factors fit within the general pattern of immigrant history in the United States and make the Muslim experience comprehensible within that context. The third factor, antipathy toward Islam, makes the situation of Muslims exceptional.[6] It may, in fact, lead to a recurrence of nativism, with the Muslim community experiencing the legal and social discrimination Japanese-Americans suffered during World War II when they were interned for the sake of "public safety."[7]

Mosques in the United States are subject to two parallel trends in the late twentieth century: the domestic economic pressures that have led to the increasing incidence of hate crimes; and, on the international front, a deepening divide between the Western powers and the Muslim world. Consequently, mosques suffer under a double burden of vulnerability. Along with churches and synagogues, they share the costs of vandalism, arson, and bombing. Particular to mosques, though, is the fact that they signal the presence of what many consider a suspect and exotic faith. Prejudice about Islam, fueled recently by such international flashpoints as the 1979 Islamic Revolution in Iran with its attendant hostage-taking, the 1991 Persian Gulf War, and the February 1993 World Trade Center bombing in New York, has led to some instances of retaliation against Muslim institutions in the United States.[8] Mosques have become the targets for animus directed at Islam in general. Muslims sometimes find themselves and their institutions misunderstood, and fear the backlash resulting from terrorism and conflagrations abroad.

This chapter focuses on the phenomenon of hate crimes, a category of criminal acts motivated by prejudice. The following chapter will discuss the politics of zoning in residential neighborhoods and how apprehensions about Islam are expressed when construction of a mosque is proposed. While the emphasis lies on showing how institutional mechanisms function in ways that produce a particular social and political order, these chapters also demonstrate how Muslims factor into the detailed processes of regulation, of spatial organization, supervision, and surveillance which comparativist Timothy Mitchell posits are defining characteristics of the modern state.[9] An important purpose is to trace the development of a response on the part of the affected Muslim community as they work to build more mosques and Islamic centers in the communities in which they live. How have Muslims responded to the challenges they encounter? How have they come to participate in the processes of regulation? In what follows, an attempt is made to answer these questions and to describe the particular circumstances of suburban life, including the threat to religious property and municipal zoning ordinances, which condition Muslims' efforts. Here, we look at how Muslims, as religious individuals, seek to construct meaningful lives through a commitment to regulative ends which, in effect, transform the "very individuality" of the Muslim participants involved.[10]

HISTORICAL GROWTH OF MOSQUES

Like many immigrants, Muslims did not come to North America initially to propagate their faith or settle permanently. Instead they came as individuals seeking opportunity. Their primary aspiration was economic success, and religious or cultural affiliations were not instrumental to this pursuit. Some Muslim immigrants stayed on, but many returned to their home countries. Gradually, over generations, a pattern of settlement emerged, and Muslims collectively began to create their own linguistic and social organizations and places of worship. This was done primarily to preserve their faith by providing religious and cultural instruction for their children, whom they feared would be absorbed into Western secularism. The emphasis of the initial efforts was on keeping cultural traditions, and not necessarily on deepening the spiritual commitment of those who were already Muslim, or spreading the faith by gaining North American converts.[11]

In recent years, the objectives of the Muslim community have begun to shift as its constituents have changed. Many of those who have arrived since the liberalization of American immigration laws in the 1960s have been professionals and generally are better educated than the earlier immigrants. More importantly, the latest arrivals have a different orientation toward Islam, seeking a more active religious leadership and guidance in how to maintain an Islamic lifestyle in a non-Muslim society.[12] Islam is seen as an ideology, a complete way of life, and the mosque functions not simply in service to the needs of the Muslim community, but as a means of outreach to create an ideal community. Priorities have evolved to the point where the spiritual growth of the universal Islamic community is of utmost importance. This has been manifested in part in an effort to build new mosques in America.[13]

A comparison of the credo of the first umbrella Muslim association formed in 1953, the Federation of Islamic Associations of the United States and Canada—the Qur'anic injunction, "Hold fast to the rope of God all together and do not disperse"—to the credo of the organization which in effect had succeeded it by 1982, the Islamic Society of North America—the Qur'anic injunction, "You are the best community raised up for humanity, enjoining what is right and forbidding what is wrong"—illustrates the changing perception of the appropriate role of Muslims and their institutions in American society. While the former reflects a concern for cultural survival the latter prescribes an active role, promoting the Muslim community as an exemplar. Hence, a mosque represents more than a newly developed sense of permanence; it also provides a basis for collective activity and representation to the non-Muslim society. Apart from its primary functions of offering religious and language instruction, regular prayer services, and the performance of important Islamic celebrations, a mosque creates a socio-political structure that can facilitate group solidarity by serving as a focal point for the Muslim community. Further, in both a concrete, structural, as well as a conceptual sense, the mosque performs a boundary-maintenance function, constructing a space within which intra-communal activities take place and from which inter-communal relations can be launched. This lends coherence and helps to give further definition to the community.

Mosques also provide greater visibility, reminding the faithful of their daily obligations according to Islamic strictures as well as announcing the presence of Muslims to the surrounding non-Muslim community. Mosques are a place where Muslim leaders can mobilize and instruct the laity regarding the responsibility of each individual to be involved in *da'wah. Da'wah*, or missionary activity, is a method of outreach to the non-Muslim community for the purpose of converting individuals to Islam, which is a priority of the current activist leadership of the American Muslim community. Whether through proselytization or the more indirect approach of "lifestyle" evangelism—based on the belief that non-Muslims will convert once they have observed the highly attractive lifestyle of pious Muslims living in their midst—*da'wah* relies on the existence and proliferation of mosques.[14] Social contact is crucial to the establishment and growth of Islam in any environment, and mosques allow that contact to happen. As Akbar Mohammad notes, in its formative period it was largely "through social intercourse and similarities in interest, especially in local areas, which substantially account for the early spread and reinforcement of Islam."[15] A mosque is in many respects a pivotal component in a strategy for outreach. It provides both the focal point for what sociologists call "group feeling" among Muslims in a local community, and a base from which to negotiate the terms of their relationship with the host society.

Religious expression is a valued aspect of social intercourse in the United States and is, in fact, considered protected speech. As part of an adaptive strategy, Muslims have already to some extent adopted the discourse of religious liberty and equal protection in the United States, to seek for Muslims the same status granted to other mainline religious adherents. Evidence of this can be seen in the fact that Muslims have raised statutory claims under Title VII of the Civil Rights Act of 1964 and have filed complaints of religious discrimination in employment.[16] As chapter 4 demonstrated, Muslims in prison have raised constitutional claims to the free exercise right and equal protection.[17] The language of legal practice has conditioned the complexity of negotiations currently underway between the Muslim community and the larger society.

This is no more apparent than at the municipal level where, promises of liberty and equality notwithstanding, Muslims have encountered problems. In their efforts to build mosques and perform religious observances they have found themselves to be at odds with their neighbors who have developed certain prejudices about Islam and Muslims. This opposition has been expressed through legal as well as extra-legal means. A review of the rising incidence of hate crimes, which can be seen as an extra-legal means of opposition, would be useful at this point.

HATE CRIMES LEGISLATION

In March 1990, the oldest and largest mosque in New England, located in Quincy, Massachusetts, a suburb of Boston, was burned in a suspicious fire on the first Friday of Ramadan. The fire prevented worshipers from sharing the *iftar*, or breakfast meal which follows evening prayer during the month of fasting.[18]

The deliberate destruction of religious property is a serious problem. Of all arson fires in the United States investigated annually, nearly one-half involve religious property.[19] By the late 1980s, the U.S. Congress passed legislation which designated such crimes, based on hatred, as a special category of crime requiring Federal interdiction.

The problem of hate crime, also known as "bias crime," is defined by Congress as crimes which "manifest prejudice based on race, religion, affectional or sexual orientation, or ethnicity." According to a 1987 study of hate crimes commissioned by the National

Institute of Justice (NIJ), words or actions which are designed to intimidate an individual because of her race, religion, national origin or sexual preference are "far more serious than comparable crimes that do not involve prejudice because they are intended to intimidate an entire group. The fear they generate can therefore victimize a whole class of people."[20]

Organizations that monitor hate crimes[21] attribute the increasing frequency and violence of this type of activity to aggravated economic conditions and the resulting radicalization of the groups that perpetrate a portion of these crimes.[22] Monitoring organizations report that membership in such groups as the Ku Klux Klan and neo-Nazi groups fluctuates in proportion to swings in the economy and, in regions that are especially economically hard-pressed, they experience increased acceptability, if not popularity.[23] Frustrations associated with economic decline surface and, as a consequence, the symbols of suburbia, as signs of material success, have increasingly come under attack. Religious property has not been exempt from this trend. So-called hate crime, which can involve vandalism, arson or bombing of religious property, is a growing problem.[24]

Yet a substantial portion of crimes against religious property is committed by others who do not identify with white supremacy.[25] Some observers believe that an increasing number of these incidents are being perpetrated by individuals or small groups acting on their own. However, the 1987 NIJ study suggests that many of these offenders may be encouraged by the lack of an adequate response to the rhetoric of white supremacists and bias crime on the part of police and most community and national leaders. The assertion is made that this failure to respond often reflects the attitudes of local residents who do not want minorities or "disliked groups" in their community.[26]

The rising incidence of what are defined as hate crimes in the U.S. has led Congress to legislate Federal criminal penalties for the destruction of religious property and the obstruction of religious practices.[27] The first version of the bill was introduced to the House of Representatives in January 1985, but made specific reference only to churches, synagogues and Buddhist temples as the types of religious property the legislation was designed to protect. In his testimony before the subcommittee on criminal justice in May 1985, Representative Dan Glickman of Kansas pointed out that hate crime targeted not only synagogues and Jewish cultural centers but Christian churches and Buddhist temples as well. Nowhere in his testimony did Rep. Glickman mention mosques.[28] This omission can be attributed in part to the absence of reporting of statistics about crimes against mosques on the part of the government, the news media, and the Muslims themselves. Until recently the U.S. Justice Department has not compiled records of crimes motivated specifically by hatred of religions and religious adherents as such. These crimes have not been differentiated from other forms of malicious mischief and no systematic collection of data about them has existed at the national level.[29] However, the legislation attaching particular criminal penalties to such activity was followed by a bill that required the Justice Department to begin recording hate crimes as a discrete category.[30] As a result, the pattern of violence against mosques as well as other religious institutions should begin to be evident in criminal records.

The hate crime bill was later revised to include reference to mosques among the protected types of religious property, due to the testimony of Representative Mervyn Dymally of California. Dymally argued that the bill before the House and Senate was "inadequate in addressing the problem in Los Angeles County, and other parts of the United States" because any mention of mosques was omitted.[31] He relied on a Los Angeles County Commission of Human Relations Report of 1985 to show that about 17 percent of religiously motivated violence in Los Angeles County was "directed against Islamic mosques, centers or individuals of the Islamic faith."[32] He also referred to violence on a national scale:

> In Houston, Tx, on June 22, 1985, the Eid al-Fitr celebration had to be canceled because of repeated death threats from anonymous callers against the Muslim community at the South-West Mosque. At 11:30 p.m., on the same day, two homemade pipe bombs were thrown from a truck through the window of the mosque causing $50,000 in damages. Other mosques received threats: "One down, three to go."
> In June and July 1985 mosques and Islamic centers in San Francisco; Orange County, CA; Denver; Quincy, MA; and Dearborn, MI, were vandalized or threatened. In Dearborn, mosque windows were broken. Threatening phone calls in Orange County stated: "You people are dead."[33]

In addition, former Senator Abourezk testified before the Senate Judiciary Committee considering passage of the Hate Crime Statistics Act about the rising incidence of anti-Arab hate crimes. In his opinion Arab- and Muslim-Americans are being scapegoated for events in the Middle East. Among the evidence he presented to substantiate this was the report of a menacing phone call on October 23 1987 to the Washington, D.C., office of Abourezk's organization, the American-Arab Anti-Discrimination Committee (ADC). The caller said that "Arabs and Muslims are not covered under the Constitution. . . . Allah is a demon spirit . . . Mohammed is a false spirit."[34] This, along with Dymally's allusion to violence against Muslims and mosques, is now a part of the Congressional record.

The Hate Crime Bill was signed into law in August 1988 with specific reference to mosques included as a class of religious real property protected by the criminal statute. In April 1990 the Hate Crime Statistics Act became law, requiring the Justice Department to collect and publish statistics on crimes motivated by hate.

To date, however, reporting of such crimes and data collection remain problematic. One of the hindrances is a fear among those who are victimized that police and community responses to the problem will not be adequate, and that they will be stigmatized for reporting hate crimes. Another is its novelty. Hate crime is a recent legal construction. Arson, theft, vandalism, assault, rape, murder, and threat that manifest prejudice based on race, religion, sexual orientation, or ethnicity is a newly defined category of offenses with particular criminal penalties attached, only recently distinguished from similar acts based on other (unexamined) motivations. Having created a new category of crime based on motive, the government has also to create a method of gathering information about such crimes. Where local incidences of such crimes were recorded only sporadically before, a national accounting is mandated. Now law enforcement agencies and other institutions concerned with public safety must encourage the reporting of crimes apparently motivated by hatred, and victims of hate crimes to identify themselves as such.[35]

Since 1930, the FBI has been collecting data on a wide variety of crimes on a nationwide basis via the Uniform Crime Report (UCR) program. With the passage of the hate crimes bills, the UCR program, recently redesigned,[36] has been called upon to identify, isolate, and document crimes motivated by hatred. The Justice Department, among others, has argued that identification of this type of crime is difficult because the intentions of the perpetrators are not always clear. Further, the causal relationship between prejudice and a criminal act is not always possible to establish.

Another criticism of the legislation focused on the anticipated cost. Data collection can be costly, and the rather imprecise estimate provided by the General Accounting Office—from $2 million to $10 million annually—weakened but failed to defeat the measure.[37]

The Community Relations Service, an agency of the U.S. Department of Justice, recently established a national 800 number telephone hotline to receive reports from anyone witnessing incidences of hate crime.[38] In addition, the agency set aside a modest sum of approximately $400,000 for 1991, to fund what it calls "collaborative efforts in the collection of data on hate incidents and documentation of community response models."[39] The money is available to organizations which are "solely devoted to work in the area of prejudice and bigotry-related crime," with "substantial involvement of the Federal Government" in the funded project.[40] Eligible organizations include those which

> compile data relative to such crimes; . . . provide training to law enforcement officers and other community workers concerning how best to respond to this kind of conduct; . . . provide outreach and counseling to communities threatened by such activity; and must be conducting research related to various components of this activity.[41]

The purpose of the funding is to "enhance the results" achieved in the accounting of prejudice-related crimes by enlisting such organizations to produce

> a series of materials (training curricula, guidelines, videotapes, bibliography, etc.) that assist groups such as law enforcement, human relations groups, neighborhood groups, church and other civic groups, and school groups, respond to the community-wide impact of hate incidents; [and identify] minimum common data elements that agencies which collect data on hate incidents can use for development of a joint annual report on hate incidents.[42]

To accomplish these objectives, and to further technical innovations in crime reporting, the agency requires that the funded project include a series of "no less than four workshops of groups involved in combatting hate incidents (e.g., lawyers, law enforcement, civil rights organizations, etc.) to foster the collaborative process" and to produce the informational materials defined above; and a national three- to four-day conference to disseminate the materials delivered.[43]

What the federal agency is recruiting, then, is the cooperation of established monitoring groups, such as those cited above as having produced statistics and reports on hate violence, in reorganizing, if not inventing, crime detection and community relations models.[44] It is in effect marshaling the existing resources of organizations which have shown their expertise in the area of prejudice-related crimes, in collecting and sharing reliable crime data. Further, by providing nominal monetary incentive, the agency is nudging their efforts in a particular direction, namely, toward the development of more effective crime-reporting methods and, ultimately, the dissemination of these methods to other communities of interpretation in the criminal justice field (e.g., lawyers, police, civil rights groups).[45]

The conditions for receiving federal assistance are stipulated in detail. Apart from the usual review criteria applied in the evaluation of project proposals, the means of achieving the agency's goals are also defined (i.e., a series of workshops to produce curricular materials and/or guidelines), the federal government is to be "substantially involved" during the conduct of the project and, finally, a time limit is set. Federal commitment is limited to a maximum of twelve months; the agency does not anticipate continuing its involvement or support beyond the first year.[46] In other words, the agency plans to withdraw from the arena once it has established the structure for ongoing discussions about the detection of bigotry-related violence and adequate community responses in mitigating ensuing tensions.

The arrangements stipulated by the funding program announcement—the limited time period, the "substantial involvement" of the state, the type of materials to be produced, and the manner in which they are produced—help to underscore the appearance that state power operates as an exterior constraint to methods of social organization and control. The language used implies a dyadic relationship between the state, which exists as a political subject or an autonomous, self-willed entity, and society. It conveys the sense that the state is an actor that intervenes in society, creating the image of a binary order, of state versus society. Further the temporary, perhaps ephemeral nature of the federal government's involvement is stipulated in the limitation of support to a maximum of twelve months, imparting the sense that the state operates outside of society as a *deus ex machina*.

However, this is misleading; state-society relations are more complex than that. It is more accurate to say that the evolution of methods of hate crimes surveillance is the result of the intersection of what might ordinarily be understood as state (i.e., official) authority and the efforts of private sector human rights groups as well as victims, whether collectively or as individuals, in the maintenance of social order. It provides a good example of what Timothy Mitchell identifies as the boundary problem in conceptualizing a state-society distinction.[47] The appearance of a "boundary" separating state and society, Mitchell argues, is an elusive "structural effect," more the result of complex power relations than an actual division or functional differentiation. For Mitchell, the state should not "be located apart from and opposed to another entity called society," giving a two-dimensional effect.[48] Yet Mitchell does not go so far as to say that there is no practical distinction at all, that the state and private organizations operate as an undifferentiated monolith, or together form "a single, totalized structure of power."[49] Rather, he argues that the line is uncertain, and the effect of a boundary's existence is a crucial shared construct that needs to be explored if the nature of the modern state—i.e., its apparent autonomy—is to be understood. Mitchell proposes not to take the appearance of a two-dimensional system for granted: "[T]he distinction between state and society should . . . be taken seriously, as the defining characteristic of the modern order."[50] How this distinction is maintained, arrogating certain functions to society while others are seen as belonging appropriately to the state, is the central question. The performance of such disciplinary functions as crime detection is a characteristic feature of the modern state yet one which is not imposed upon society from outside but produced—and reproduced—from within, in the ordinary practices of its citizens and in the shared understandings of right and wrong, of what is permissible and fair.

In this instance, by setting up a means to improve police methods, the funding program sponsored by the Community Relations Service of the U.S. Department of Justice helps to create the impression that the state stands apart from society as the author of policies on crime detection. It is communicating a policy change—defining acts as criminal not simply on the basis of their outcome but also, importantly, the perpetrators' motivation. This change is justified, then, in terms of the larger impact this category of crime has on society. The announcement reads,

> Prejudice-related crimes in the United States are continuing at an alarming rate. . . . The impact of a prejudice-related hate crime or act may extend far beyond the immediate victim. Such incidents of hate, whether rising to the level of crime or not, tear through the fabric of a community, endangering the network of

human relations that constitutes civil society. While the need for
a law enforcement response to hate crime is a given, there is a
comparable need for a community response to bring the pieces of
the community back together and to strengthen it so that the
potential for future hate incidents is diminished.[51]

This presents a vivid image of an imminent danger, a crisis of law
and order in terms which explicitly call for the mobilization of society,
to reorganize the community response, to police itself more effectively, and thus to prevent crime—i.e., future hate incidents—from
happening. The need for a "law enforcement response"—separate and
distinct from a societal response—is a given; a similar "community
response" is the desired outcome of the funding program. Again, the
implication of these arrangements is that the state is "a subjective
starting point"[52] of law enforcement and community relations, with
the ability to impose its will on society. It suggests that the state
stands apart from the community and provides a framework for its
collective life. Moreover, it enhances the apparent power of the state.

This produces the effect that law exists "as a sort of abstract,
formal framework, superimposed above social practices,"[53] rather
than arising from them, and that what is incumbent upon society is
compliance with the law. Law is accepted as an autonomous agent
which brings order and discipline to what is considered to be a chaotic
and potentially dangerous situation. The appearance of the state as
an authoritative structure is an elusive effect which obscures the
dependent, reciprocal nature of the power relationships that are at
the foundation of state-society relations. If, as Mitchell asserts, "the
essence of modern politics"[54] is the production and maintenance of
this structure and the illusion that the state acts autonomously, "with
coherence, agency, and subjectivity,"[55] then the political process will
continually camouflage the whole story, namely, the crediting of particular practices and actors involved in the evolution of such policy
as the hate crimes bills. It gives the impression that the state precedes
society in generating efforts at crime control, and imparts a certain
logic to such newspaper headlines as "Rules on 'Hate Crime' Set for
Police by State."[56] Such processes as these contribute to the construction of a binary world where the state exists as "an intrinsic object,"
and masks the real complexity of social practices.[57] As Mitchell points
out and this case illustrates,

> The power to regulate and control is not simply a capacity stored
> within the state, from where it extends out to society. The appar-

ent boundary of the state does not mark the limit of the processes of regulation. It is itself a product of those processes.[58]

Leading individuals of the communities protected by the hate crimes legislation supported the passage of the bills, and have been active in encouraging the reporting of hate crimes.[59] In a sermon delivered at the Islamic Center of Southern California just two days after the bombing of Baghdad began in the Persian Gulf War, Dr. Maher Hathout, an Egyptian-born cardiologist and prominent leader of the Muslim community in Southern California,[60] urged Muslims to guard against bigotry and abuse and to report such incidents as crimes.[61] In addition, *The Minaret,* a quarterly publication of the Islamic Center of Southern California, now prints a telephone number for a Southern California "Muslim Anti-Discrimination Hotline" through which people can report incidents of discrimination against Muslims. The copy reads, "Call . . . immediately if you or anyone you know become a victim of anti-Muslim slurs, racial attacks or remarks."[62]

An anticipated problem of the new laws was the potential overbreadth of the reporting of hate crimes and the use(s) to which such information might be put.[63] As a result, a provision was written in the legislation to protect the anonymity of the victims reporting the crimes. However, the question whether surveillance methods constituted unfair scrutiny (bordering on harassment) arose during the Persian Gulf War, when the FBI contacted and questioned several Americans of Arab descent. Arab-American organizations feared that FBI questions were perhaps a prelude to internment or deportation. In an interview with the *Los Angeles Times,* an Arab-American man reported an instance of the FBI putting the hate crime law to questionable use imbued with discriminatory overtones. He relates that an FBI agent who interrogated him about his knowledge of any "terrorists" tried to allay his suspicions about the line of questioning by assuring him that the FBI was merely "concerned about hate crimes against our people" and, presumably, was gathering information in the best interest of Arab-Americans. The FBI agent asked for names of members of the Arab-American Institute and whether this particular man was familiar with any dissident student groups, telling him that the FBI was "trying to get a handle on the [Arab-American] community."[64]

On a related point, another Arab-American contacted by the FBI in connection to the Gulf War, a San Diego city clerk named Charles Abdelnour, queried the *Los Angeles Times* reporter, "Why would they [i.e., the FBI] even want to talk to me? I was born in Brawley," a rural community in southern California where Abdelnour's father settled upon emigrating from Lebanon in 1917. "The closest I've come to terrorism," said Abdelnour, "is at City Council meetings when land use matters are discussed."[65]

While hate crime is a virulent offense, it is by no means the only threat to the safe operation of mosques. The processes of spatial organization in suburban communities have also had their effect. Zoning and land-use regulations, and the citizen groups which have evolved as suburban populations have swelled, have had a significant impact on the development and growth of mosques during the 1980s, and is the subject of the following chapter.

6

There Goes the Neighborhood
Mosques in American Suburbs

Everyone likes to live in the suburbs. Everyone pokes fun at the suburbs. That's fair enough. Everyone respects those who made the suburbs. Everyone despises the suburbs. Everyone's friends live in the suburbs. Everyone hates the kind of people who live in the suburbs. Everyone wants bigger and better suburbs. Everyone thinks there is just too much suburbs. The You and I live in the suburbs—it's lovely to have a home in the suburbs. The whole idea of the suburbs fills us with dismay, alarm, and frustration. Almost everyone's business is dedicated to making life in the suburbs more and more and more enjoyable. The suburbs are a crashing bore and desolating disappointment. The suburbs are exactly what we asked for. The suburbs are exactly what we've got.

—Humphrey Carver, *Cities in the Suburbs*

Suburbia is one of the most distinctive aspects of American society. The vast majority of the American population now live in suburbs, and the complexity that characterizes suburban life in the post-World War II era extends further to touch the lives of nearly everyone in society, including those who live in teeming inner cities and rural small towns. Not only suburban residents but "outsiders" who are kept out of most communities as a result of local housing policies and land-use control, play a significant role in shaping the social relations that constitute suburban life.[1] The pressures of metropolitan growth, including the influx of recent immigrants, have contributed to changing suburban patterns in the United States. Suburban policies, in turn, influence settlement patterns in the metropolitan region at large to such an extent that in the 1970s, these policies became the focal point of political activism designed to promote greater racial integration.

117

The position of blacks in suburbia in particular has received much attention. In the 1970s, the NAACP called the suburbs "the new civil rights battleground" and urged blacks "to do battle in townships and villages to lower zoning barriers and thereby create new opportunities for [blacks] seeking housing closer to today's jobs at prices they can afford to pay."[2] Despite laws barring discrimination in real estate, suburbs in large part remain segregated.[3]

Observers of suburbia in the United States analyze suburban patterns of land use and social class in order to understand better the connections between "abundant land, democratic ideals and exclusionary practices."[4] In the process, they reveal something of the political, social, and economic realities that both shape and result from the mosaic of differing ethnic and class cultures found in metropolitan areas, including suburbia. Land-use classifications, definitions, and standards that were developed in order to regulate the size, quality, and quantity of housing and commercial building available in a particular community, came under increasing scrutiny beginning in the 1970s, as concerns for "growth management" escalated. Pro-housing advocates clashed with environmentalists, city planners, and others who, for one reason or another, wanted to preserve the quality of suburban neighborhoods. Exclusionary politics in the suburbs had consequences for life in the central city—resulting in the persistence of urban poverty, de-facto segregation, and the restriction of economic opportunity. Much attention has been given to discrimination in housing and education, and planning analysts have accentuated the socio-economic impact of suburban policies on the urban poor. However, not much has been said about the *ideas* behind suburban policy decisions, and we still have much to learn about social perspectives— i.e., shared assumptions about society's structure—by examining anew the use of restrictive land-use regulations as mechanisms to exclude unwanted outsiders from the suburban community.

Ideas about the way society is and ought to be organized are reflected in suburban zoning and land-use decisions. Efforts to decipher the implications of categories used to define and regulate land use primarily have focused on the role and impact of economic interests.[5] According to this view, land-use and zoning decisions reflect the impact of socio-economic forces at play in a community. They create and rely on land-use categories, and define what are believed to be the correct relationships among them. The putative aim in regulating land use is economic. That is to say that a framework of categories is created and maintained by suburban city councils and planning boards in order to protect property values and preserve economic relationships that at least implicitly are recognized as being valid and vital to the community's well-being. It has been a long-standing principle in the United States that zoning should be used to protect and preserve property values.[6] The nature of one category affects the potential land-use value—and thus the market value—of land that is located nearby.

However, a land-use classification system that defines zoning districts in terms of their permitted and forbidden buildings and activities[7] attaches differing values to the land it regulates, and, in the process, to those who *use* the land. In this way, the classification system creates not just economic categories but social categories, and it regulates not just economic but social relationships as well. Exclusionary policies about land use in the suburbs are not motivated strictly by economic interests, but by extra-rational motivations such as racial prejudice, the fear of crime, and the desire to maintain community character, including appearance. Suburban decisions to restrict or exclude altogether certain land uses (e.g., multifamily dwellings, mobile homes) in effect excludes certain people (e.g., low- and moderate-income people) from the community, and reinforces an economically and racially segregated society. Such decisions reflect conceptions about the desirability of potential land *users* and the appropriate relationships among them. They are the product of the penetration of wider social forces into the particular realm of zoning.

Suburban life in America has a number of visible symbols, such as the single-family detached house surrounded by lawn, the commuter car, and the freeway system.[8] Readily recognized among these symbols are the church and, increasingly with the large-scale suburbanization of Jews beginning in the 1950s, the synagogue.[9] To the suburban American public, however, mosques symbolize outsiderhood at two levels. Mosques represent the presence of Islam, a "foreign creed" that is perceived to be inherently violent and at odds with the Judeo-Christian tradition; and the proximity of immigrants, a class whose transition to the suburbs traditionally has been resisted. Immigrants are "interstitial,"[10] at least at the initial stages, meaning that they are caught between living in the inner city and the suburban outskirts. Immigrants typically arrive and initially settle in large port-of-entry cities but tend to move up and out of the inner city and into the more affluent suburb as their incomes increase and they acquire the means to escape city problems—e.g., gangs, smog, and congestion.[11] Yet the impulse on the part of suburbanites is to confine these outsiders to the inner city, because they are viewed as not being "one of us." Institutions of immigrant groups, such as mosques, present a visible sign of the proximity and material success of outsiders, and are often perceived to threaten the character, if not the security, of the suburb.

Victims of hate crimes—including vandalism, arson, and bombing of religious property—now would appear to have legal recourse by virtue of the hate crime laws discussed in chapter 5. People who are victimized by more subtle forms of discrimination such as exclusionary practices in zoning, however, have a more difficult obstacle to overcome. This chapter examines the Muslims' experiences in applying for the necessary approvals to build new mosques. What follows focuses on the politics of zoning in residential neighborhoods where Muslims proposed to build places of worship, and how apprehensions about Islam were expressed when construction of a mosque was proposed. The data is drawn largely from interviews with people in two places where Muslims have successfully negotiated the approval process: Rochester, New York, and Fremont, California. Their experiences show that the project of building a mosque also entails a simultaneous process of politicization. In other words, as Muslims proceeded through the stages of organization, land purchase, and public hearings, they were drawn into the local practices governing property. Further, their chances for success improved as they became familiar with the social conventions and administrative procedures that are important structural determinants of municipal politics.

ZONING

From 1926, when the U.S. Supreme Court upheld the use of municipal zoning as a legitimate "police power," cities and towns have relied on zoning and land use regulations, in conjunction with a general plan, to guide development.[12] An examination of the history of land use regulations shows that, over time, they have become increasingly complicated, rigorous, and demanding, requiring environmental impact assessment, permits, and review procedures to protect neighborhoods from the negative impact of encroaching urban sprawl. As David Dowall points out in his study of land conversion and regulation in the San Francisco Bay area, growth management techniques beginning chiefly in the 1970s have effectively curtailed suburban growth, ostensibly to minimize traffic congestion, protect the natural environment, and avoid overtaxing the existing infrastructure. They have also helped to keep down local taxes.[13]

While in the early post-World War II period, suburbanites were generally passive about accepting new development, or even in some cases aggressively pursued it, by the 1970s they had adopted a different attitude. They took on an active and vocal role in local planning to advocate limited growth.[14] This can be seen as part of the "gangplank" syndrome, which in effect closed off opportunities to build as a way of preserving the quality of life that local residents felt was jeopardized by rapid development. As concerns for environmental protection intensified and land use controls became more complex, local citizen groups (from small neighborhood associations to broadly based environmentalist coalitions) formed and became assertive in local decision making. Pressure groups formed because it was felt that city councils and planning commissions represented a progrowth position and that that tendency had to be countered. Consequently, suburban citizen groups have become familiar with and influential in shaping city regulations. They have had a say in determining the rate and type of development permitted within the communities in which they live. Suburbanites have used such devices as restrictive zoning, traffic planning, and architectural review boards to establish and maintain a comfortable community for themselves through the instrumentality of local government.

In terms of religious institutions, many cities and towns have sought to exclude churches and other religious property from residential neighborhoods by law, arguing that from a traffic and safety standpoint such property is unsuited or harmful to the neighborhood. Where such regulations have been challenged in court, judicial opinions have varied. Many courts have found that exclusion is an infringement on the freedom to worship. Others have sought to balance interests, arguing that if exclusion is an *undue* infringement— in other words, if exclusion overburdens religion to a degree exceeding the "general welfare"—then it should not be allowed.[15] The prevailing standard has developed that zoning regulations which effectively ban churches from certain neighborhoods are constitutional, provided that a means of requesting exemptions exists. As land-use regulation has evolved, many cities and towns have paid attention to the assorted and sometimes divergent court rulings on this issue, and have allowed churches special or conditional exemptions from governing ordinances in residential neighborhoods on an *ad hoc* basis.

In some places, zoning ordinances have also regulated land use on the basis of aesthetic considerations, architectural appeal, and functions, on the theory that protection of property values is a legitimate interest of the state. Again, many appellate courts have upheld this. In *Berman v Parker* (1954), the U.S. Supreme Court held that the public welfare was defined broadly enough to include aesthetics.[16] The Missouri Supreme Judicial Court, in *State ex. rel. Stoyanoff v Berkeley* (1970), upheld an ordinance in a St. Louis suburb which required that a review board approve plans for structures in order to promote conformity to "minimal architectural standards" and prevent "unsightly, grotesque and unsuitable structures," on the basis that it promoted the general welfare and protected property values.[17] In 1963, a leading court case in New York, *People v Stover*, held that land-use regulations based on aesthetic considerations alone performed a valid "police power" objective.[18] Architectural review boards have become an authoritative part of the zoning approval procedures.

Efforts to block all but the most desirable developments are nothing new, and the citizen's role in local planning is predicated on the individual's private property rights.[19] This principle, along with the fact that citizen groups and architectural review boards are now an authoritative part of the municipal land use decision-making process, are factors which affect the character of the Muslims' experiences as they build new mosques in the suburbs in which they work and live. Those experiences will be examined below.

MOSQUES

Throughout the 1980s, Muslims have tried to build new mosques and convert existing property into places of worship at an increasing rate that may be expected to continue. In many places, they have encountered indifference and, at worst, hostility from non-Muslim residents. For example, in December 1980, in Burnaby, a suburb of Vancouver, British Columbia, "300 residents . . . booed and stamped their feet at the very thought of allowing a Moslem mosque in their neighborhood."[20] The ostensible objection to the planned $500 million mosque was "traffic congestion," although a Burnaby planner said that such an objection was "unfounded."[21] Many residents said that "the mosque would affect their quality of life."[22] With regard to zoning regulations, the president of the North Central Burnaby Retailers Association "said a mosque is not a church and could not be built as it did not fall within the guidelines of the municipal bylaw."[23]

CASE STUDIES

Rochester, New York

In the Rochester, New York, area, the Muslim community decided in the early 1980s to build a new mosque to meet the growing needs of

Muslims in the greater metropolitan area.[24] Two mosques already existed, both in older properties converted into mosques. One serves primarily the Turkish community in the Rochester area and the other—known as the "local *masjid,*"[25] located in downtown Rochester—serves primarily African-Americans. However, there are no firm rules about ethnic divisions. Anyone can attend the two mosques, but in practice they serve primarily these two respective communities.

The proposed new mosque was planned primarily by Pakistani Muslims in the Rochester area. Since the early 1970s, the Pakistani community in the Rochester metropolitan area has grown steadily, so that now the community is comprised of over one hundred families. However, the new mosque was not built to serve the Pakistani Muslim community only. It was intended to bridge ethnic cleavages and to provide the foundation for an overarching Islamic identity. The envisioned constituency included Muslims of all national origins. This is in keeping with the recent rise in Islamic consciousness and the tenet of Islamic ideology which stresses the universal nature of the religion. The final selection of the site for the new mosque was, in fact, determined in part by its convenience to the various Muslim communities scattered throughout the metropolitan area, and the hope that this location would accommodate as many Muslims as possible. Its present location is roughly equidistant from the Pakistani, Turkish, and African-American neighborhoods, and is accessible by bus from the downtown area. It is close to a major highway, giving ease of access to the Muslim students at the local university and community college. The new mosque was not meant to supplant the other mosques in the Rochester area but to augment them as the demand for religious and cultural services exceeded the existing resources. This is clear in the words of a founder of the new mosque, that we "can't have [only] one *masjid* in a metropolitan area."[26]

The foundation stone for the mosque/Islamic center, located in Brighton, a suburb on the East side of Rochester, was laid in 1983. The first prayers were said in the unfinished building in 1984, and construction was completed in 1985. However, the process of selecting the site and getting the necessary building permits was a lengthy one. Two unsuccessful attempts were made before the Brighton location was picked. The first attempt was in Henrietta, on a three-acre parcel on the western side of the Rochester Institute of Technology. The Muslims bought the land outright and then began to make construction plans. According to Professor M., a founding member of the Islamic center who was involved in the conception and implementation of the mosque project, the neighbors immediately expressed their opposition to the proposed mosque. They "were not comfortable" with the idea of having this type of religious property (as opposed to a church or synagogue) in the vicinity; they "didn't like us there." "Indifference and hostile" sentiments were conveyed in "unofficial ways."[27] At this site the mosque project never reached the stage of a public hearing before the city planning commission. Feeling unwelcome, the Muslims eventually decided to sell the property in Henrietta and try elsewhere.

The decision to abandon the Henrietta location was based not simply on the neighbors' opposition, but on internal dissent within the Muslim community as well. Some of the African-American Muslims reportedly did not support the plans to build in Henrietta, because the site was not convenient for those who would be traveling by bus from downtown Rochester. The closest bus stop to the proposed site was three-quarters of a mile away. Professor M. admitted that he also had opposed the proposed site in Henrietta on the grounds that it would take too much time and effort to allay the neighbors' fears about the mosque and thereby gain community acceptance. He felt that there was no guarantee that such efforts would succeed. He explained his position by saying, "Islam means submission, total submission to God's pleasure." Therefore, from his perspective it would have been futile for the Muslims to direct their energies to gain the understanding of an indifferent neighborhood. Rather, they should accept the inhospitable reception as a sign of God's will and look to build elsewhere.

The second attempt was across town on the northwest side of Rochester, in a "blue collar" suburb. Professor M. characterizes this attempt as having benefited from the Henrietta experience. First, the Muslims did not buy the land outright and then try to gain zoning approval and building permits. Instead, they made a purchase offer pending zoning and construction approvals. The parcel was next door to a Catholic church, so that it would appear that the question of zoning for religious land use was already settled. All that was necessary were approvals from the city planning commission, the architectural review board, and any other forums with the authority of review.[28]

However, once again neighbors had reservations about the proposed mosque. The congregation of the church adjacent to the property resisted the plans for a mosque and the church officials initially refused to grant the necessary right of way over the easement connecting the two properties. The Muslims saw this as unfair, for as Professor M. understands it, the church had already granted the right of way for construction on the lot before there was a purchaser for the property. Once it became clear that the Muslims intended to buy the lot and build a mosque there, however, the church refused to cede the right of way. At a public hearing to review the application for site review, the city planning commission refused to force the issue by exercising its authority to take the easement, as the Muslim buyers urged it to do.

The planning commission's denial of the right of way is not surprising given what David Dowall observed in California: city planners and elected officials reflect the interests of their constituents or they risk losing their jobs. "When there is strong and vocal opposition to a residential project at planning commission or city council hearings, local officials see little choice but to deny a permit. . . ."[29] If this is applied to the case at hand, the resistance of the Catholic church to cede the right of way for construction of a mosque on the adjacent lot would carry considerable weight. The existence of a powerful public interest in opposition to the Muslims' plans was in fact persuasive in determining the outcome.

The sense that the neighbors were hostile or indifferent to Islam was manifested in this second attempt to build a new mosque in the Rochester area. There was a "lack of reception" or a "lack of at home feeling" perceived on the part of the Muslims. The purchase offer for the land was "on hold" for approximately one year while the Muslim buyers made attempts to win the necessary approvals. In the meantime, they looked for other possible sites where they might find "a more welcome reception."[30]

An alternative site was found in Brighton, an upper-middle class suburb on the east side of Rochester. Here the Muslims were pleasantly surprised by the warm reception they received and the level of friendly interest and support, especially at city board meetings. Once the Muslims made a purchase offer pending zoning approval, the city sent out a notice announcing a zoning board hearing to consider their application for site approval. Approximately twenty to twenty-five people from the neighborhood responded to the notice by attending the hearing. In this initial hearing for site review, the neighbors and city officials asked, "Will you have the call to prayer?" According to the architectural sketches of the proposed mosque, a minaret was planned for construction without a set of stairs visible. In effect, they were "policing" the quality of the residential neighborhood by voicing concern over the possible noise level introduced by a mosque and the prayer call. The Muslims responded by explaining that while the function of the minaret in mosques in the Middle East is to announce the call to prayer, this would not be the case in Brighton, New York. According to Professor M., the nearest Muslim household was over three miles away so the call to prayer probably would not be heard by Muslims. The minaret was simply a part of the design because it is an integral part of Islamic architecture and represents the purpose of a mosque, which is to remind the faithful of their duty to pray to God. It is a part of every mosque.[31]

Approvals of the building plans for the mosque proceeded without many problems. The entire process took between five and six months. The general feeling the Muslims had of Brighton residents was that they welcomed the addition of a mosque. Professor M. attributes this to two factors: (1) The Muslims were well prepared to answer questions as a result of their earlier attempts to find a site. They were more experienced, knew what would be required of them, and had developed architectural sketches and other supporting materials. (2) The fact that Brighton is an upper-middle class professional city. Professor M. felt that there was a "meeting of the minds" between the Muslims who were planning the mosque, many of whom are professionals, and the local community. Pakistanis in the Rochester area are in large part middle to upper-middle class professionals, physicians, engineers, scientists, professors, pharmacists, and businesspersons. In essence, a class-based explanation is given: educated people are more tolerant as a function of their education and knowledge. This is true not simply of the Rochester area, in Professor M.'s words, but "true of America—indifference [toward Muslims] is based on ignorance." Even highly educated people are subject to ignorance and misinformation, though, because, in the words of Professor M., they are "hostage to prejudiced writings on Islam." In his opinion, this is slowly changing, mainly because people are curious to know more about Islam and are seeking to educate themselves on the subject, and the available materials are improving. As a consequence of the process of seeking approvals to build a new mosque, and the greater visibility it gave to the local Muslim community, members of the Islamic Center of Rochester have been invited to speak at a growing number of public forums on Islamic topics. They have addressed a number of church congregations and high school classes over the last three years or so, thus performing the function of informing the public about Islam.

Fremont, California

Fremont is located in the East Bay-San Francisco area in Alameda County. It is a growing suburb of over 150,000 residents which has grown tremendously since the 1960s as major transportation corridors in the San Francisco and San Jose area have opened up. Residents of Fremont can commute easily to Silicon Valley, San Francisco, and Oakland.

The process of rapid growth and urbanization of the East Bay region and Fremont in particular have shaped land use policies. Increasing awareness of the environmental impact of urban sprawl—traffic congestion, air pollution, and dwindling open space—has led to efforts to limit residential growth which were increasingly effective during the 1970s. Concerns for neighborhood and environmental quality have meant that local citizen groups have become much more influential in shaping land use policy. With the expanding population of Fremont in the 1970s, Fremont city planners reported "rising attendance at public meetings where residential projects are discussed, and new homeowner and citizen groups continue to spring up."[32]

The project approval process in Fremont involves five separate steps, several reviewing agencies, and numerous submittals of plans.[33] The steps involve rezoning, preliminary site review, precise development plan review, preliminary approval, and final permit approval. The average length of the entire project approval process ranges from six to eighteen months. Those who plan construction must appear before the city planning commission, the SPARB committee (city Site Planning Architectural Review Board), and the city council. Any of these review boards may stipulate a design change which the others in earlier reviews did not require. The change then means that the party seeking approval must return to each review board to gain approval of the altered plan, lengthening the approval process. Once the proposal reaches the final public hearing, neighborhood groups could ultimately undermine the entire project if they voice opposition to the plan.

In 1985, the Islamic Society of East Bay-San Francisco bought a 2.2 acre parcel of land at public auction with the intention of building a Grand Masjid (mosque and Islamic center estimated to cost $1.2 million).[34] There were two adjacent parcels offered at auction which were zoned for religious property. Many church groups bid on the property and the city of Fremont sold the parcels to the Islamic Society and the United Methodist Church. At the time of purchase, the land was already zoned for religious use, so the Islamic Society did not have to go through the process of rezoning before they proceeded to plan construction of a mosque. The problems came later, according to Rifaat, a key member of the mosque planning committee, from "the shock wave in the neighborhood" once residents realized that the Islamic Society had bought one of the lots.[35] Rifaat felt that "the reaction [was] shocking in the neighborhood." To him the sentiment seemed to be disbelief—"Where are the Muslims coming from?"—when the Muslims had been living in Fremont for years and were "very integral to the community." Several Muslim professionals live in Fremont and the surrounding cities and work in Silicon Valley corporations. The plans to build the mosque gave the Muslims sudden visibility and, as a consequence, their presence was felt and recognized by the non-Muslim community.[36]

Once the members of the Islamic Society realized that the residents were somewhat alarmed by their plans for a mosque, they organized a meeting with the homeowners association in Fremont. Ten to fifteen members of the association and about seven or eight members of the Islamic Society attended the first meeting, where everyone tried to get to know each other and the Muslims answered general questions about Islam and specific questions about the mosque project. In sum, Rifaat expressed this observation: "People are uneducated about Islam—and they showed an ignorance about their own neighborhood" as well because they had been unaware of the presence of Muslims in their city.[37]

The Islamic Society worked closely with the architectural review board (SPARB) to make sure that the size and height of the dome and minaret were within the city's statutory guidelines. The members of the SPARB review board, in Rifaat's words, were Fremont residents, not city officials. They included an architect, a landscape architect, and an engineer, among others. At the first meeting of the review board, the discussion centered on Islamic architecture. Board members said that the proposed mosque "looked like a cathedral" due to its dome and minaret. Their conception of religious architecture led them to prefer a structure that was more modest and resembled a church. The Muslims explained that "a mosque cannot look like a church" and that there were certain details that were integral to the design of a mosque, such as the minaret. After two or three more meetings the architectural review board accepted the Muslims' explanations for the architectural design.[38]

In the process, the review board members and the members of the Islamic Society became better acquainted. According to Rifaat the successful completion of the reviews was the product of better information. The Muslims also established good relations with the city mayor, the city council, and the review board in the approval process. Like the residents, the city officials initially seemed to be unaware of the Muslims' presence in Fremont before the purchase of the land for the proposed mosque, but Rifaat credits them with having had a "broader view" than the residents from the outset. Their support, which came once the public officials understood the nature of the project, was crucial at the public hearings for approval of the preliminary plans, which took only about fifteen minutes. All objections to the mosque, from the city and residents, were anticipated and handled beforehand.

The preliminary approval process was "a task in educating not only the City Staff, but also the public" about the functions of a mosque and the intention of the prospective worshipers.[39] Representatives of the Islamic Society tried to allay potential apprehensions about the mosque by publicizing their plans broadly. Plans for the mosque were published in such newspapers as the Fremont *Argus,* the San Jose *Mercury,* the Oakland *Tribune,* and the San Francisco *Chronicle.*

The Fremont mosque was built on a site adjacent to the United Methodist Church lot, where construction of St. Paul's Methodist Church was also underway. The Islamic Society has cultivated amicable relations with the Methodists, and the two groups went together for approvals. The church and mosque will share parking and landscaping, an arrangement which the city favored. Rifaat felt that the city was especially cooperative because of the shared relations between the church and mosque, something which was symbolized by a placard at the site which announced the future site of the church and mosque.

On the other boundary of the Islamic Society property, the city of Fremont has built a park. The Islamic Society paid the city approximately $25,000 for their share in improvements that included street widening, sidewalks, and the extension of utilities to the mosque building site.[40]

In February 1990, the city council gave its final approval of the site plans, and construction planning and fund raising are in progress. Construction began October 1991.

Rifaat advises others who plan to build a mosque to get involved with local politics. "If you have political strength you can achieve your objectives."[41] In fact, he is, personally, deeply involved in state Republican politics, and believes that better organization and mobilization of Muslim-American political interests at all levels, local, state, and national, is necessary. Also central to better relations, in his opinion, is interfaith involvement.

STRATEGIES OF ASSIMILATION

With these two cases, we have examples of different modes of representation, both coming from professional, middle-class Muslim communities where substantial material success had already been
achieved and a stronger religious and cultural identification was
sought. In the Rochester case, Professor M. related the outcomes of
a strategy exhibiting conflict avoidance, offering little resistance to
the alienating reactions of non-Muslim neighbors. His story is one of
isolation, choosing to relocate when local prejudices became overwhelming, until a suitable neighborhood with adequate, if not ideal,
conditions for the establishment of an Islamic center was found.
Once the critical formative period had been successfully negotiated,
though, and the mosque was functioning, lay volunteers from the
Islamic center such as Professor M. proceeded in outreach efforts to
represent the Muslims to the surrounding communities. They
became engaged in projects of community education about their culture, current events, and religion, seeking to dispel the negative
image of the Islamic world presented by the American media. Their
purpose in addressing church congregations, high school classes,
and the like was one of offering enlightenment and an Islamic witness while at the same time preserving their religious culture from
the potentially corrosive effects of accommodation with the larger
non-Muslim society. The emphasis was placed on maintaining a discrete corporate life, safe from cultural accretions, through Islamic
observances and institutions.

In the case of the Fremont *masjid,* Rifaat suggested that
greater participation and engagement in the political life of the non-
Muslim society was the preferred alternative for negotiating a niche
for Muslim corporate life. Yet as in Rochester, a preference for the
distinctive aspects of Islamic life—what sets it apart from the larger
society—was indicated in the Fremont experience. This was
expressed in the assertion of the right to preserve external form, to
perpetuate an Islamic architecture in the design of the mosque,
keeping the dome and minaret even though it reportedly raised con-
sternation. The remark, made by members of the Fremont architectural review board, that the plans for the proposed mosque "looked
like a cathedral" was received, at least by Rifaat, as a suggestion
that Christian forms were more appropriate and should be adopted.
Pressures for this type of accommodation in design were resisted by
the Muslims who argued that "a mosque cannot look like a church,"
and that such details as a minaret were integral to the mosque.

Through persistence, the Muslims in Fremont succeeded in winning approval of their plans with these design features intact. A cultural aspiration, then, to maintain a visible element of their religion, gives rise to political expression.

The Fremont strategy differs from the Rochester case because of the level of engagement with the non-Muslim residents of the city. Involvement in politics, both local and state, in conversation with the home owners' association and municipal officials, and in sharing access to resources with the Methodists, all show a willingness to cooperate in the social processes incumbent in the organization of city life and to learn how things get done. Rifaat responded to the same dynamics encountered in the Rochester case by increasing efforts to be effective in the political process, and recommended that other Muslims renounce isolation and join in politics.

Important in this process of establishing mosques in residential communities has been the role of non-Muslims in supporting Muslims' efforts. Many who have been involved in interfaith dialogue have long observed and encouraged Muslim activity in the political and social life of the general community. For instance in Harrison, a suburb of New York City, the Muslims asked Dr. Marston Speight, Director for Christian-Muslim Relations for the National Council of Churches, to speak in support of their petition to acquire the necessary approvals to build a mosque. A United Methodist minister and a strong proponent of interfaith dialogue, Dr. Speight was invited to speak before a city council hearing where the Muslims of Harrison sought approval of construction plans for an Islamic center and mosque. Some of the residents of Harrison objected to the Muslims' project. Complaints were that the center/mosque would be disruptive to the neighborhood and would cause property values to decline. In Dr. Speight's opinion these objections were possibly contrary to what they would say had the proposed structure been a church; people "are suspicious of things they don't understand."[42]

The proposed site for the mosque was on the edge of a residential neighborhood, across the street from an office building. The State University of New York campus at Purchase is not far away. Opposition to the proposed mosque prolonged the approval process considerably. Finally, the city council convened a public hearing on the matter. The hearing was packed. At this hearing Dr. Speight, among others, spoke in support of the Muslims' project.[43] He told the gathering that the mosque and Islamic center would be an asset to community life and they "shouldn't pass up the opportunity" for cultural enrichment.[44] When asked by a council member how much the Muslims paid him to attend the hearing and speak on their behalf, he pointedly answered that he was not paid anything, "not even reimbursement for mileage."[45] The Muslims eventually gained the requisite approvals to build their mosque and Islamic center in Harrison.

Dearborn, Michigan, is home for the largest concentration of Middle Easterners in the United States. The city hosts five Islamic centers, all but one in converted properties. Of the converted properties, one Muslim group converted an old bank building, another a former public school, and a third an electric company's abandoned offices. These sites were selected because of the relative affordability of the properties—conversion is less costly than construction—and their convenience to the Muslims who would use the services of the mosques. The principal public concerns addressed in the approval process were the ease of public access (preventing traffic congestion), adequate parking, and rezoning for religious use.[46]

In September 1979, neighbors of a mosque in the city's heavily Arab, blue-collar southeastern section asked the courts to stop the mosque from broadcasting the Islamic call to prayer over outdoor speakers, charging that the mosque officials were violating the city's noise ordinance.[47] The legal battle continued into the early 1980s, and eventually was resolved when the court placed a limit on the decibel level of the prayer call similar to limits placed on church bells.

Observing these changes has been the Reverend William Gepford of the Presbytery of Detroit Interfaith Ministry, the rector of the Littlefield Presbyterian Church in Dearborn. Rev. Gepford has worked in interfaith ministry in Dearborn for the last thirteen years. Like Rifaat in Fremont and Professor M. in greater Rochester, Rev. Gepford stresses the importance of education as a means to allay fears and overcome prejudice. While he asserts that the primary responsibility for good community relations and a "warm reception" rests with the host community, the non-Muslim residents who "have power," he advises Muslims to take an active role in contributing to the life of the community. His recommendation to Muslims is "to get to be known, [to] come out and set the tone."[48] He points to the service projects in the southeastern section of Dearborn associated with the Islamic center there, helping in translation, health care, and networking, as positive examples of this kind of activity. These, he says, are "active and involved" especially among the immigrant population.[49]

CONCLUSION

In the process of creating and enforcing zoning restrictions, suburbanites display their hopes, fears, and prejudices. A look at suburban zoning decisions indicates the kinds of things that can happen when subjective fears about newcomers infect powerful actors in the local community, and will, presumably, enlarge our understanding of the mood of this era. It provides an important insight into the suburban setting as well as a special perspective on how national and global trends affect the quality of Muslims' lives in the United States. More importantly, it illustrates how ordinary practices in determining particular spatial arrangements govern residential communities and influence the character of those communities.

The increased involvement of Muslims in the political life of suburban communities has resulted from their efforts to create places of worship for themselves. The politics of municipal zoning has had a significant role in the change in position of the American Muslim community, from a state of relative isolation from the general community to active involvement in it. The consequences of this transformation for their religious mission, and specifically the current debates within the Muslim community concerning whether they should remain marginal to secular power relations or adopt a strategy of assimilation, continues to be a subject of discussion within the community, as Muslims reflect on their status as a minority in the modern world.

7

Reaching a Crossroad

In the preceding pages, I have studied the Muslim experience in the United States historically, hoping to shed some light on the complex interactions of law and politics: how law functions as a social control mechanism, how court decisions are products of historical conditions, and how the daily concerns of people are influenced by legal norms. As Jim Thomas notes, law "does not exist independently of other forms of social action. . . . [Rather,] legal concepts, theories, and principles emerge, are modified, or pass out of existence as a response to changing social factors and interpretations of order, right, and obligation."[1] The approach I have adopted, then, historicizes law to examine how ideas about law are continually redefined and transmitted.

Central to these processes is the pattern of events that shapes particular responses, which "make sense" in their own given context. At the core of this common "sense" lies a unity of shared assumptions—about social arrangements, etc.—which are often unexamined and always mutable. What roles do such categories as race, ethnicity, and citizenship play in expressions of collective identity and tolerance over time? How has law functioned in constructing these categories and, through them, in conveying an "image of social relations and shaping popular consciousness in accordance with that image?"[2] This study has been an attempt to address these questions, deriving insights from the specific circumstances of Muslims in the United States. The focus has been on the Muslims' recognition and adoption of law as a legitimate means of social control, manifested in their efforts to temper an increasing attentiveness to American legal institutions with a sense of cultural and religious "outsiderhood." By examining this process, and the attendant tensions it produces, we can begin to advance our understanding of the intersection

135

of law and social processes, and the impact this has on the corporate life of the involved community.

Acceptance of law as a legitimate institution of social control, which allocates values, resolves disputes, and guides how things get done, both suggests and inhibits behavior. This study began with an investigation of modes of representation, how immigrants from the Muslim world characterized themselves before the court officials who determined whether they made admissible citizens at the turn of the century. Lengthy efforts at documentation ensued, as these applicants for membership in the polity tried to show that they approached the white, rather than the colored, end of the spectrum in accordance with contemporary legal standards. In the case of John Mohammed Ali, we have an instance where the applicant for naturalization had acquiesced in the court's characterization of him as a "high-caste Hindu" until his certificate of naturalization was placed in jeopardy some years later, when Congress changed the standards for citizenship so as to exclude those of South Asian origin. When the government challenged Ali's citizenship he altered his self-representation before the court by insisting that he was of "Arabian," not "Hindu," background and thus was a fit citizen. His efforts failed.

In many other instances, immigrants from the Muslim world also had to master and manipulate the elusive elements which defined ethnicity or race at the turn of the century, as ties between race and moral character were extremely relevant to the construction of a peculiarly American identity. There was no apparent consistency in the legal outcome of this mastery; many courts granted citizenship but others did not. However, one result seems clear: as the applicants mobilized to comprehend and respond to the fickle standards, to discern a coherence in the judicial approach, they argued in kind. The aspiring citizens relied on whatever legal and social principles appeared in the pattern of judicial rulings, and cohered in those standards. This adoption of governing norms not only altered the mode of representation to the larger society and its legal institutions but also, inevitably, had an impact on their self-definition.

Minow points out that interpretation of the law takes place through acts of resistance as well as compliance, and in the "investment of old forms with new meaning."[3] Membership in a minority religion can be an important source of identity and experience that lends meaning to existence[4] in a pluralistic society. Religious groups in the United States sometimes make "a virtue of their perceived roles as outsiders,"[5] and offer innovative interpretations of legal concepts through action—by avoiding, resisting, or complying with standard practices. At the same time, by invoking rights within the polity, a religious individual or group "claims the attention of the larger community and its authorities."[6] The very act of stating a claim "acknowledges the claimant's membership in the larger group, participation in its traditions, and observation of its forms."[7] Further, Minow contends that stating a claim "in a form devised by those who are powerful in the community expresses a willingness to take part in the community, as well as a tactical decision to play by the rules of the only game recognized by those in charge."[8] In particular, this can be seen here in the instance of hate crimes legislation, where the leadership of the affected communities, including Muslims, urged their constituencies to report incidents of discrimination as crimes; and again in the case of the Fremont, California, *masjid*, where a high level of engagement with the life of the larger (non-Muslim) community is apparent.

The enduring debates within the global Muslim community about minority status and the appropriate model for living in a non-Muslim society continue to move between two poles: accommodationism, seeking religious equality and equal access to society's resources, versus isolationism, which emphasizes the distinctiveness of Islam and seeks to preserve Islamic cultural modes of representation.[9] Those who approximate the isolationist paradigm have advocated maintaining a separate existence as a discrete, insular entity which can serve as an Islamic witness in the midst of an unenlightened society until such time that return to the Islamic world is possible. This model allows no cultural adaptations in a non-Islamic setting, as Islam alone, in its unadulterated form, stands as the governing norm for the religiously observant Muslim. Islam is seen as a comprehensive and inherently superior and self-sufficient mode of existence, set forth for the global community of believers, whether living within the "domain of Islam" or beyond. As Haddad characterizes it, according to this position, "Muslims therefore must not accept minority status as a permanent condition in which they accommodate and acquiesce to those in power."[10]

This position is heard somewhat in the words of Sher Ali, presented here in chapter 3, when he objects to the American ban on polygamy, and the preaching of polygamy, held against Mr. Sadiq of the Ahmadiya movement during the second decade of this century. Sher Ali, in protest, writes from England decrying the treatment of the Ahmadiya missionary in America whose prosyletizing efforts are

constrained by the necessary concession to "America's intolerance."
Preaching Islam without reference to the Islamic laws on polygamy
is seen as an abridgement of Islamic tenets.

However, the preponderance of Muslim settlers in the United
States have approximated the accommodationist model. Promises of
religious liberty and the entitlement to equal treatment and access
have led Muslims to think about and assert rights in the predominant legal idiom. For instance, in Dearborn, when neighbors challenged a mosque's use of loudspeakers to broadcast the call to
prayer, mentioned in chapter 6, the mosque officials saw the complaint as an infringement of their constitutional guarantee to the
free exercise of religion, citing the Constitution to maximize their
religious freedom and protect a practice which they consider to be
"inviolable."[11] The court decided in this case to impose the same
restrictions on the mosque as were imposed on churches in Dearborn
with regard to the decibel level. The result, then, of what must have
seemed like a liberating paradigm—the notion of *absolute* freedom
to worship—turned out to be parity. The mosque became subject to
the same restrictions placed on Christian worship.

Changes wrought by the civil rights struggle of the middle
decades of the twentieth century had a profound effect on the prevailing social and legal principles. Late nineteenth-century concerns
for color distinctions and their connections with morality gave way
to beliefs about equality and discrimination as the basis for legal
claims. These changes redirected the conceptualization of needs,
rights, and obligations within the Muslim community as well.

The story of the Black Muslims in prison best illustrates this
tendency. Beginning in the 1960s, Muslims in prison called for recognition as a distinct religious group. Once they achieved moderate
success, they moved from "outsiderhood" toward claiming a minority
status. They gained, through federal court intervention, greater
access to such resources as law libraries, and some relief from the
restrictions of prison life which were judged to interfere with religious worship. Other inmates followed suit, with street gangs organizing themselves as religious groups making religious liberty
claims, leading to the Balkanization of prison society.[12] This transformation from the status of someone outside the system, to identification as a religious minority, has been shaped by using the law to
assert and protect particular rights.

When immigrants from the Muslim world who aspired to citizenship and prison Muslims raised legal claims, the categories they
desired already existed. What they sought was inclusion in what

appeared to be a liberating process, staking a claim to the entitlements that attached to official recognition as particular legal categories—citizen and religion. However, in the cases of the hate crimes legislation and municipal zoning, active participation in the innovation of change was required, a process which irrevocably altered the nature of the Muslim experience in America and understandings about social order.

Over the past two decades, mosques have been especially pivotal in the Muslims' corporate life, in forming the basis for representation to the non-Muslim society and stronger identification internally. By virtue of the legislation of federal hate crimes statutes, the interests and rights of Muslims, including the security of religious property, have become a protected category. Presumably, the state is empowered to safeguard mosques and Muslim practices from the inherent risks raised by their increased visibility, in becoming targets of animus directed toward the Islamic world, and Muslims who report the incidence of such crimes acquiesce in the recognition of the capability of the state to do so. Similarly, increased contact with neighborhood groups and municipal politics has been part of the Muslim experience in establishing mosques, and has brought out the human factor in the social processes of determining important spatial relationships.

Such legal practices, deciding how things get done, serve as a mediating and transformative link. As Muslims have moved from isolationism and religious exclusivity to an enhanced consciousness of their status as a religious minority in America, their identity has evolved.

NOTES

INTRODUCTION

1. See Hans Wehr, *A Dictionary of Modern Written Arabic, Arabic-English*, ed. J. Milton Cowan, Third Printing (Beirut: Librairie du Liban; and London: MacDonald & Evans, Ltd., 1980), p. 668.

2. 8 Johns. (N.Y.) 290 (1811). Leonard W. Levy asserts that *"People v Ruggles*, decided by the New York Supreme Court of Judicature in 1811, remains to this day one of the most important blasphemy cases in our history." *Blasphemy: Verbal Offense Against the Sacred, From Moses to Salman Rushdie.* New York: Alfred A. Knopf, 1993, 401. While the case was not about Islam or Muslims, Judge Kent, in writing the court opinion, ruled that only Christianity could be blasphemed because "the religion of Mohammed" is an "imposter" religion, a superstition, "equally false and unknown." Kent argued that Americans are "a christian people, and that the morality of the country is deeply ingrafted upon christianity. . . ." (Ibid.: 403).

3. For scholarly accounts, see especially the provocative article by Samuel P. Huntington, "The Clash of Civilizations?" in *Foreign Affairs* Summer 1993, and responses published in *Foreign Affairs* September/October 1993. Huntington argues that "[c]ivilizational identity will be increasingly important in the future, and . . . the most important conflicts of the future will occur along the cultural fault lines separating these civilizations from one another. . . . The people of different civilizations have different views on the relations between God and man, the individual and the group, the citizen and the state . . . as well as differing views of the relative importance of rights and responsibilities, liberty and authority, equality and hierarchy." (p. 25) See also Bernard Lewis, "The Roots of Muslim Rage," in *The Atlantic Monthly*, September 1990.

4. R. Lawrence Moore, *Religious Outsiders and the Making of Americans.* New York: Oxford University Press, 1986, p. viii. Moore claims that tolerance of the outsider status of religious groups is typically American, a tradition that allows religious groups to maintain a sense of separation from secular society.

141

5. Lewis, p. 60.

6. See *The New York Times* 2–7 May 1993.

7. *Providence Journal Bulletin* 8 May 1993, A–11.

8. "Keep out the Fundamentalists," in *Providence Journal Bulletin* 12 July 1993, A–14.

9. For information about immigration to the United States see Yvonne Yazbeck Haddad and Adair T. Lummis, *Islamic Values in the United States: A Comparative Study.* New York: Oxford University Press, 1987.

10. Jim Thomas, *Prisoner Litigation: The Paradox of the Jailhouse Lawyer* (Totowa, New Jersey: Rowman and Littlefield, 1988), p. 5.

11. "Federal Prisons Giving Considerations to Muslims," *The New York Times,* 18 November 1989, p. 57.

12. Martha Minow, *Making All the Difference: Inclusion, Exclusion, and American Law* (Ithaca: Cornell Univerity Press, 1990), p. 294.

CHAPTER 1: SYMBOLISM AND LEGAL INSTITUTIONS

1. Arthur A. Cohen, *The Myth of the Judeo-Christian Tradition and Other Dissenting Essays* (New York: Schocken Books, 1971), p. xiii. Cohen writes, "We can learn much from the history of Jewish-Christian relations, but one thing we cannot make of it is a discourse of community, fellowship, and understanding. How, then, do we make of it a tradition?" (Ibid.) See also Martin E. Marty, "A Judeo Christian Looks at the Judeo Christian Tradition," *The Christian Century,* 8 October 1986, p. 858. For a different analysis and an example of consensus history which praises the Judeo-Christian tradition, see Will Herberg, *Protestant, Catholic, Jew: An Essay in American Religious Sociology* (Garden City, N.Y.: Doubleday Anchor, 1960). See also discussion in Mark Silk, "Notes on the Judeo-Christian Tradition in America," *American Quarterly* 36 (1984), pp. 74–77, and, for comments on the fortunes of consensus historians, p. 84; and *Spiritual Politics, Religion and America Since World War II* (New York: Simon and Schuster, 1988), in which Silk points out that the term "Judeo-Christian" first appeared in the *Literary Guide* in 1899: "a 'Judeo-Christian continuity theory' postulated the development of Church ritual out of the practices of the Second Temple" (41).

2. At the forefront of this response has been Allan David Bloom's book, *The Closing of the American Mind: How Higher Education Has Failed Democracy and Impoverished the Souls of Today's Students* (New York: Simon & Schuster, 1987). See also Dinesh D'Souza, *Illiberal Education: the Politics of Race and Sex on Campus* (New York: Free Press, 1991), and E. D. Hirsch, *Cultural Literacy: What Every American Needs to Know* (New York: Vintage Books, 1988).

3. Proclamation 6514 of December 9 1992, Religious Freedom Day, 1993, in *Federal Register* Vol. 57, No. 239 (Friday, December 11 1992), pp. 58697–8.

4. Presidential Proclamation 6646 of January 14, 1994 as Religious Freedom Day, 1994, in *Federal Register* Vol. 59, No. 13 (January 20 1994), p. 2925.

5. Between 1971 and 1979, approximately 1,350,000 Asians were admitted legally into the United States as immigrants, accounting for more than 44 percent of the total of all Asian immigration between 1820 and 1980 (Jeff H. Lesser, "Always 'Outsiders': Asians, Naturalization and the Supreme Court," *Amerasia* 12 (1985/6), p. 95, n. 45.)

6. One source estimates conservatively that the nonconventional faiths (e.g., Muslims as well as Orthodox Christians, Buddhists, and Hindus) now comprise four percent of the total United States population, an increase from one percent in the 1950s (Roof and McKinney, pp. 17, 235).

7. According to Yvonne Y. Haddad, if the American Muslim community continues to grow at the present rate, it will exceed six million and become the second largest religion—smaller than Christianity but larger than Judaism—by the year 2015 ("A Century of Islam in America" [The Muslim World Today]) Occasional Paper No. 4 (Washington, D.C.: Washington Institute for Islamic Affairs, 1986), p. 1).

8. See Carol Stone, "Estimate of Muslims Living in America," in *The Muslims of America*, ed. Yvonne Yazbeck Haddad (New York: Oxford University Press, 1991), pp. 25–36.

9. Ibid., pp. 28 and 34.

10. See Isma'il Raji al-Faruqi, ed., *Trialogue of the Abrahamic Faiths, Second Edition* [Issues of Islamic Thought no. 1] (Herndon, Virginia: International Institute of Islamic Thought, 1986). This volume is a collection of essays emanating from the "Trialogue of Abrahamic Faiths" meetings cosponsored by the Islamic Studies Committee of the American Academy of Religion (New York) and the Muslim-Christian-Jewish Conference. A professor of religion at Temple University, Al-Faruqi was pivotal in establishing Islamic Studies programs in North American universities and scholarly associations, and in organizing Muslims in America. He contributed to the contemporary interpretation and understanding of Islam among Muslims by, among other things, creating an Islamic think tank, the International Institute for Islamic Thought (Virginia), and promoting the Islamization of knowledge. For more information, see John L. Esposito, "Isma'il R. al-Faruqi: Muslim Scholar-Activist," in *The Muslims of America*, pp. 65–79, esp. pp. 73–74.

11. See Ronald Takaki, *Iron Cages, Race and Culture in Nineteenth-Century America* (New York: Oxford University Press, 1989).

12. Cited in Ibid., p. xiv.

13. See Timothy Mitchell and Roger Owen, "Defining the State in the Middle East: A Workshop Report," *Middle East Studies Association Bulletin* 24 (1990), pp. 179–184, for a brief discussion of this idea. In part, the authors argue against relying on the conventional distinction between state and society, suggesting that the antithesis of state and society is a discursively produced effect. The challenge, then, is to understand how that effect is created.

14. Clifford Geertz, *The Interpretation of Cultures: Selected Essays* (New York: Basic Books, 1973), p. 89.

15. Ibid., p. 91.

16. Haddad, "A Century of Islam in America," 1986, p. 9.

17. See especially *Discipline and Punish: the Birth of the Prison* (translated from the French by Alan Sheridan) (New York: Vintage Books, 1979).

18. Timothy Mitchell, "Everyday Metaphors of Power," *Theory and Society* 19 (1990), p. 572.

19. Ibid., p. 561.

20. Ibid., p. 573.

21. Mitchell and Owen.

22. Mitchell, p. 573.

23. Minow, p. 236.

24. See Michel Foucault, *Discipline and Punish.*

25. John Brigham, *The Cult of the Court* (Philadelphia: Temple University Press, 1987), p. 24.

26. Ibid., p. 3.

27. Ibid., p. 17.

28. Ibid., p. 25.

29. As legal anthropologist Carol Greenhouse notes, "the plural form [of ideolo*gies*] is significant" ("Courting Difference: Issues of Interpretation and Comparison in the Study of Legal Ideologies," in *Law and Society Review* 22 (1988), p. 688). Sally Engle Merry, in reviewing the literature on legal pluralism, suggests that multiple normative orders co-exist in society,

and that pluralism is a condition found to a greater or lesser degree in most societies ("Legal Pluralism," in *Law and Society Review* 22 (1988), pp. 873, 879).

30. See "From the Special Issue Editors," *Law and Society Review* 22, p. 632, where the works of Clifford Geertz (*The Interpretation of Cultures*) and Susan Silbey ("Ideals and Practices in the Study of Law," *Legal Studies Forum* 9 [1985]) are cited in connection with ideologies and legal behavior and institutions. Carol Greenhouse identifies courts as well as law itself as places where ideologies are formed and articulated.

31. "From the Special Issue Editors," *Law and Society Review* 22 (1988), p. 631.

32. Haddad, "A Century of Islam in America," 1986, p. 1.

33. Stone, pp. 28 and 34.

34. For a brief discussion of the transition of the Black Muslim movement from a revolutionary movement to one seeking recognition as an institutionalized faith community in the context of the American constitutional order, see Oliver Jones, Jr., "The Black Muslim Movement and the American Constitutional System," *Journal of Black Studies* 13 (1983), pp. 417–437. See also V. DuWayne Battle, "The Influence of Al-Islam in America on the Black Community," *The Black Scholar* (Jan/Feb 1988), pp. 33–41.

35. The estimate of African American Muslims living in the U.S. in 1980 puts the number at 1 million. See Stone, p. 27.

36. Haddad and Lummis, p. 14.

37. For details on the causes of chain migration of the Arabic-speaking community, see generally Eric J. Hooglund, ed., *Crossing the Waters, Arabic Speaking Immigrants to the United States Before 1940* (Washington, D.C.: Smithsonian Institution Press, 1987) and George Tumeh, *Al-Mughtaribūn al-Arab fi Amrika al-Shamaliyyah (The Arab Immigrants in North America)* (Damascus: *Wizarat al-Thaqafah wa al-Irshad al-Qawmi*, 1965), pp. 10–13.

38. "How the U.S. and Islam Can Work Together," *Arabia: The Islamic World Review* (June 1982), p. 36. Cited in Larry Allan Poston, *Islamic 'Da'wah' in North America and the Dynamics of Conversion to Islam in Western Societies (Vols. I and II)* (PhD diss., Northwestern University, 1988), p. 55.

39. Haddad and Lummis, p. 14.

40. Stone, p. 31.

41. In one year alone—1960—seventeen African nation-states achieved independence.

42. C. Eric Lincoln, *The Black Muslims in America*, rev. ed. (Boston: Beacon Press, 1973) (originally published, 1961).

43. Ibid., p. xxvii.

44. See Clifton E. Marsh, *From Black Muslims to Muslims: The Transition from Separatism to Islam, 1930–1980* (Methuchen, New Jersey: The Scarecrow Press, 1984). See also Jones; Battle; and the writings of Warith Deen Muhammed, son and successor of Elijah Muhammed, especially *An African American Genesis* (Calumet City, Illinois: MACA Publication Fund, 1986).

45. However, not all members of the Nation of Islam agreed with the changes following Elijah Muhammed's death. A significant schism developed within the movement. Minister Louis Farrakhan continues to preach Elijah Muhammed's doctrines and still maintains an organization called the Nation of Islam.

46. See Don Terry, "Black Muslims Enter Islamic Mainstream," *New York Times*, 3 May 1993, p. 1. Splinter groups, such as the Five Percenters, the Nation of Islam, and the Moorish Science Temple, continue to exist and occasionally capture media attention, but in no way represent the view of the majority of African-American Muslims.

47. In its publication *al-Mashriq*, the Islamic Society of East Bay-San Francisco touts this event to be "the beginning of a Muslim action that will change America."

48. The Islamic Society of North America (ISNA), founded in 1982/83, developed from the Muslim Students' Association of U.S. and Canada. It is the most inclusive organization that provides services to individuals and Muslim communities in the United States and Canada, including a Zakah Fund, which collects and administers donations for the needy and orphans; educational workshops; a speakers bureau; a film library; a publishing house; and a credit union.

49. This last point is in reference to the Qur'anic injunction to the community of believers to fulfill God's will on earth by living in complete accordance with Islamic principles ("enjoining the good and forbidding the evil"). See Qur'an 3:110, "You are the best of peoples, evolved for mankind, enjoining what is right, forbidding what is wrong, and believing in Allah."

50. For evidence that Islam was the faith of Africans brought to the United States as slaves, see Allan D. Austin, *African Muslim in Antebellum America: A Sourcebook* (New York: Garland Publishing, 1984). In addition, immigration of significant numbers of Syrians and Lebanese to the U.S. and Canada by the 1880s helped establish Islam in North America. For information about the African-American movements in the U.S., see E. U. Essien-

Udom, *Black Nationalism: A Search for Identity in America* (New York: Dell Publishing, 1962); and Lincoln. A bibliography of the literature on indigenous Islam is provided in Yvonne Y. Haddad, "Muslims in America: A Select Bibliography," *The Muslim World* 76 (1986): pp. 93–122.

51. Jeffrey L. Sheler, "Islam in America," *U.S. News and World Report,* 8 October 1990, p. 69.

52. See *New York Times,* 2–7 May 1993.

53. Bernard Lewis, *Islam and the West* (New York: Oxford University Press, 1993), p. 40.

54. Haddad, *The Muslims of America,* pp. 4–5. For figures of Middle East students admitted to the United States from 1960 to 1973, see Hossein G. Askari and John Thomas Cummings, "The Middle East and the United States: A Problem of 'Brain Drain'," *International Journal of Middle East Studies* 8 (1977), pp. 65–90.

55. Ibid., p. 4.

56. The Egyptian Sayyid Qutb was one of the most influential ideologues of the contemporary Islamic revival. His interpretations of Islam and politics continue to circulate.

57. Yvonne Y. Haddad, "Sayyid Qutb, Ideologue of Islamic Revival," in *Voices of Resurgent Islam,* ed. John L. Esposito (New York: Oxford University Press, 1983), p. 69.

58. For instance, Haddad has reported Sayyid Qutb's observations about American life in the following passage from his book, *Nahwa Mujtama' Islami* (*We are an Islamic Society*): "I do not know how people live in America, the country of the great production, extreme wealth, and indulgent pleasure. . . . I saw them there as nervous tension devoured their lives despite all the evidence of wealth, plenty, and gadgets that they have. Their enjoyment is nervous excitement, animal merriment. One gets the image that they are constantly running from ghosts that are pursuing them. They are as machines that move with madness, speed, and convulsion that does not cease. Many times I thought it was as though the people were in a grinding machine that does not stop day or night, morning or evening. It grinds them and they are devoured without a moment's rest. They have no faith in themselves or in the life around them. . ." (cited in Haddad, *Contemporary Islam,* p. 90). His aim in this and other writing is to condemn the American obsession with the material aspects of life, and denounce the Western path as anti-spiritual and destructive.

59. A good guideline for what is likely to happen to the Muslim community in transition may be found in the North American experience of the Jewish community and the development of a Jewish strategy (or strategies) for survival in the United States. Several books have been written about the

transformation of the Jewish community in America; for reference to this literature, see R. Lawrence Moore, Chapter Three. Not mentioned there, but also noteworthy, is Chaim I. Waxman, *America's Jews in Transition* (Philadelphia: Temple University Press, 1983). For discussion of the transformative nature of relations between nineteenth-century religiously based American utopian communities and the legal system, see Carol Weisbrod, *The Boundaries of Utopia* (New York: Pantheon Books, 1980).

60. See the ISNA membership handbook, P.O. Box 38, Plainfield, IN. 46168.

61. The project began when land was purchased in April 1987. In February 1990, the Fremont City Council approved the site plans. As of July 1990, fund raising efforts continued and building permits remained to be obtained before construction could begin. For information, see the Islamic Society of East Bay-San Francisco publication, *al-Mashriq* (August 1989), p. 6, and *al-Mashriq* (July 1990), p. 7.

62. Khalid Abdullah, the Chairman of the Masjid Planning and Development Committee (i.e., the mosque project), writes that "[i]t took a tremendous amount of effort to obtain final approvals from the City of Fremont," and the "Masjid Project looked more feasible after negotiating a joint parking arrangement with the St. Paul Methodist Church" (*al-Mashriq*, July 1990, p. 7).

63. *al-Mashriq* (July 1990), p. 7.

64. For reference to the literature on Muslims in North America, see Yvonne Y. Haddad, "Muslims in America: A Select Bibliography." *The Muslim World* 76 (1986), pp. 93–122. See also Haddad and Jane Idleman Smith, *Mission to America: Five Islamic Sectarian Communities in North America* (Gainesville: Univeristy of Florida Press, 1993).

65. Selim Abou, "Ethnical History and Migration," *Cultures* 7 (1980), p. 84.

66. See, for instance, Michael W. Suleiman, "Early Arab Americans, the Search for Identity," in Hooglund, pp. 37–54 and "Arab-Americans: Community Profile," in *Journal Institute of Muslim Minority Affairs (JIMMA)* 5 (1983/4), pp. 29–35; Adele L. Younis, "The First Muslims in America: Impressions and Reminiscences," in *JIMMA* 5 (1983/4), pp. 17–28; Philip M. Kayal and Joseph M. Kayal, *The Syrian-Lebanese in America, A Study of Religion and Assimilation* (Boston: Twayne Publishers, 1975); Alixa Naff, *Becoming American, The Early Arab Immigrant Experience* (Carbondale and Edwardsville, Illinois: Southern Illinois University Press, 1985); Harry A. Sweeney, Jr., *A. Joseph Howar, the Life of Muhammed Issa Abu Al-Hawa* (Washington, D.C.: the Howar Family, 1987); and Gregory Orfalea, *Before the Flames, A Quest for the History of Arab-Americans* (Austin, Texas: University of Texas Press, 1988).

67. See, for instance, Raymond Brady Williams, *Religions of Immigrants from India and Pakistan* (Cambridge and New York: Cambridge University Press, 1988); Salim Khan, "Pakistanis in the Western United States," in *JIMMA* 5 (1983/4), pp. 43–46, and "A Brief History of Pakistanis in the Western United States" (M.A. thesis, California State University at Sacramento, 1981).

68. See, for instance, *Muhammad Speaks* (publication of the Nation of Islam) and Malcolm Little and Alex Haley, *Autobiography of Malcolm X* (New York: Ballantine Books, 1964).

69. See especially Edward W. Said, *Covering Islam, How the Media and the Experts Determine How We See the Rest of the World* (New York: Pantheon Books, 1981), and *Orientalism* (New York: Vintage Books, 1978); Michael C. Hudson and Ronald G. Wolfe, eds. *The American Media and the Arabs* (Washington, D.C.: Center for Contemporary Arab Studies, 1980); the 1979 International Press Seminar, *The Arab Image in Western Mass Media* (London: Morris International Ltd., 1980); Laurence Michalak, "The Arab in American Cinema: A Century of Otherness," in *Cineaste* 17 (1989, pp. 3–9, and *Cruel and Unusual: Negative Images of Arabs in American Popular Culture*, Second Edition [Issue Paper no. 15, ADC Issues] (Washington, D.C.: American-Arab Anti-Discrimination Committee, n.d.); and Janice J. Terry, *Mistaken Identity: Arab Stereotypes in Popular Writing* (Washington, D.C.: American-Arab Affairs Council, 1985).

70. In May 1986 the U.S. Justice Department's Immigration and Naturalization Service (INS) prepared a 31-page document called "Alien Terrorists and Undesirables: A Contingency Plan," in which details for surveillance and detention of people are developed. Only Iranians and Arabs are mentioned explicitly as possible suspects. The plan states that the government would "concentrate its counter-terrorism efforts against particular nationalities or groups known to be composed of certain nationalities [i.e., Muslims], most probably those citizens of states known to support terrorism" (cited in "Aliens face jail in plan," *Detroit Free Press*, July 7, 1987).

71. The one notable exception, which deals with Islam and Muslims rather than Arabs, is Said, *Covering Islam*.

CHAPTER 2: IMMIGRATION AND CITIZENSHIP
IN TURN-OF-THE-CENTURY UNITED STATES

1. Haddad and Lummis, p. 13. For details see also Naff; and Orfalea. This is not to overlook the presence of Muslims among the slave population in America, which antedates the recorded arrival of Muslim immigrants from Asia, North Africa and Eastern Europe. An estimated 30 percent of Africans enslaved in the U.S. were Muslim, while a small number of Muslim African slaves were transported to Canada. For details see Y. N.

Kly, "The African-American Muslim Minority: 1776–1900," *Journal Institute of Muslim Minority Affairs* 10 (1989), pp. 152–160. However, Muslim African slaves were brought to America by force and were not subject to the immigration and naturalization regulations that other Muslims were. Moreover, Muslim-African slaves, severed from their religious and cultural origins, lost knowledge of Islam, to be reconstituted only in the 1930s as a result of the Garveyite movement. See Austin; Lincoln; Beverlee Turner Mehdi, *The Arabs in America 1492–1977* (New York: Oceana Publications, Inc., 1978); and E. U. Essien-Udom, *Black Nationalism*. For information about Muslims in Canada see Earle Waugh, Baha Abu-Laban, and Regula Qureishi, eds., *The Muslim Community in North America* (Edmonton: University of Alberta Press, 1983), and Abu-Laban, "The Arab-Canadian Community," in *The Arab-Americans: Studies in Assimilation*, Elaine C. Hagopian and Ann Paden, ed. (Wilmette, Illinois: Medina University Press, 1969).

2. For example, they receive no attention at all in Oscar Handlin, *Race and Nationality in American Life* (New York: Doubleday Anchor Books, 1957); John Higham, *Send These to Me, Immigrants in Urban America* Revised Edition (Baltimore and London: Johns Hopkins University Press, 1984); Maldwyn Allen Jones, *American Immigration* (Chicago: University of Chicago Press, 1960); and Carl Wittke, *We Who Built America, The Saga of the Immigrant* (2nd. ed. rev.; Cleveland, 1964).

3. Seymour Martin Lipset, "Historical Traditions and National Characteristics: a Comparative Analysis of Canada and the United States," *Canadian Journal of Sociology* 11 (1986), p. 124.

4. See especially Samuel Huntington, *American Politics: The Promise of Disharmony* (New York: Belknap Press, 1981); and discussion of it in Rogers M. Smith, "The 'American Creed' and American Identity: The Limits of Liberal Citizenship in the United States," *Western Political Quarterly* 41 (1988), pp. 225–251. See also Higham.

5. T. Alexander Aleinikoff, "Citizens, Aliens, Membership and the Constitution," *Constitutional Commentary* 7 (1990), p. 13.

6. Stephen Thernstrom, ed. *Harvard Encyclopedia of American Ethnic Groups* (Cambridge, Massachusetts: Harvard University Press, 1980), s.v. "Naturalization and Citizenship," by Reed Ueda, p. 734.

7. Rogers M. Smith posits that the ethnocentric perspective is but one among multiple conceptions of citizenship which still compete in American political thought, and that no single conception has ever won exclusive sway. He argues that the ethnocultural perspective runs counter to and has been obscured by Enlightenment philosophy. For details see Smith.

8. Aleinikoff, pp. 9–10.

9. Ibid., pp. 10 and 15.

10. Aliens can be naturalized after a probationary period, during which they are free to return home and the government has the power to deport them.

11. Aleinikoff, pp. 15–16.

12. *Minor v Happersett*, 88 U.S. (21 Wall.) 162, 165–66 (1874) (Chief Justice Waite).

13. Aleinikoff, p. 14.

14. Ibid.

15. Higham, p. 30.

16. Ibid., pp. 40 and 47.

17. See also Peter H. Schuck and Rogers M. Smith, *Citizenship Without Consent, Illegal Aliens in the American Polity* (New Haven and London: Yale University Press, 1985), which tries to show historically how "consensual" and "ascriptive" models of citizenship have competed for dominance in American law.

18. Ronald T. Takaki, *Iron Cages*, p. xiv.

19. For discussion of racialist thought in nineteenth-century America, see especially Reginald Horsman, *Race and Manifest Destiny, The Origins of American Racial Anglo-Saxonism* (Cambridge, Massachusetts: Harvard University Press, 1981); and Takaki.

20. Horsman, p. 99.

21. Ibid., p. 61.

22. In the oft-cited *Dred Scott* decision, the Supreme Court declared that Dred Scott was not a citizen but a "Negro" of African descent whose ancestors were slaves. He was thus prohibited from filing suit in court to obtain recognition of his freedom once he entered and resided in free territory. See *Scott v Sanford*, 60 U.S. 393 (1856).

23. The Citizenship Clause of the Fourteenth Amendment was intended to guarantee the rights of black people to citizenship. Proponents of the amendment argued that the Emancipation Proclamation had freed the enslaved, but was not sufficient to confer citizenship. That would require an amendment to the Constitution.

24. *Plessy v Ferguson*, 163 U.S. 537 (1896). Jim Thomas points out that, in writing the majority opinion in the *Plessy* decision, Justice Brown argued that races cannot be "put on the same plane" by judicial command:

"Legislation is powerless to eradicate racial instincts, or to abolish distinctions based on physical differences, and the attempt to do so can only result in accentuating the difficulties of the present situation. If the civil and political rights of both races be equal, one cannot be inferior to the other civilly or politically" (cited in Thomas, p. 41).

25. See Sheldon Goldman and Thomas P. Jahnige's description of American political history, which states that the Second Republican political era (1896–1932) "was marked by the almost complete halt to all attempts to protect black Americans . . ." (*The Federal Courts as a Political System*, 3rd ed. [New York: Harper and Row, 1985], p. 231). For a "black perspective" of this era and the national retreat from civil rights, see the *Messenger* magazine, published from World War I to 1928 and edited by African American intellectuals Chandler Owen and A. Philip Randolph.

26. See Higham, p. 47.

27. Thernstrom, "Naturalization and Citizenship:" p. 748.

28. Myron Weiner, *Sons of the Soil: Migration and Ethnic Conflict in India* (Princeton: Princeton University Press, 1978), p. 17.

29. Ibid., p. 11.

30. Myron Weiner, "Immigration: Perspectives from Receiving Countries," *Third World Quarterly* 12 (1990), p. 140.

31. Ibid.: 160.

32. Ibid.,p. 154.

33. Lincoln, pp. 36–37.

34. Cited in *The Alien in Our Midst*, ed. Madison Grant and Charles Stewart Davison (New York: Galton Publishing, 1930), p. 188.

35. Weiner, "Immigration," pp. 153–4.

36. W. Peter Ward, *White Canada Forever: Popular Attitudes and Public Policy Toward Orientals in British Columbia* (Montreal: McGill-Queen's University Press, 1978), p. x.

37. Ibid., p. 22. For further discussion of pluralism and the development of the dominant group's self-perception founded upon race, see Ibid., pp. 19–22. While Takaki posits that racism has cultural and economic bases, and results from the "interaction among psychological needs, ideology, and economic interests," (Takaki, p. 11) and Horsman explores the intellectual origins of racism that came to influence popular attitudes, Ward argues that racism is primarily a problem of social psychology in race relations.

38. Weiner, "Immigration," p. 154.

39. According to Weiner, nativism "became a respectable attitude" among American social scientists, theorists, and humanists certainly by the end of the nineteenth century ("Immigration," p. 152). Social Darwinism, eugenics, and a concern for cultural preservation did not come from fringe elements alone, but shaped the American intellectual tradition.

40. Stuart C. Gilman, "Degeneracy and Race in the Nineteenth Century: The Impact of Clinical Medicine," *Journal of Ethnic Studies* 10 (1983), p. 29.

41. Higham, p. 47.

42. Gilman, p. 34.

43. Ibid., p. 35.

44. Handlin, p. 67.

45. Ibid.

46. Ibid.

47. Ibid., p. 70.

48. Horsman, p. 140.

49. Horsman writes that phrenology, popular by mid-century, promoted the concept of inferior and superior races. "They found in skulls and heads what they wanted to find. . . . Whites were inventive, creative, powerful; blacks were docile and ignorant; Indians were savage and intractable" (Ibid., p. 145).

50. Higham, p. 47.

51. Ward, p. 47.

52. Gilman, p. 35.

53. Milton R. Konvitz, *The Alien and the Asiatic in American Law* (Ithaca, New York: Cornell University Press, 1946), 31; see also Ward, pp. 84–85.

54. The Commissioner-General of the U.S. Bureau of Naturalization acknowledged this line of reasoning when he wrote in 1909, "From one point of view, at least, heterogeneousness [of race] is undesirable, homogeneousness desirable. There can be but little homogeneity between the people of southern and eastern Europe and the real American."

55. Horsman, p. 298.

56. Congress, House, Committee on Immigration and Naturalization, *Hearing on Immigration,* 61st Cong., 2d. sess., 25 January 1910, p. 87.

57. This legislation was passed in the wake of a steady increase in the number of Chinese immigrants in the United States. Takaki writes that "between 1850 and 1880, the Chinese population in the United States shot up from 7,520 to 105,465, a fifteenfold increase; in 1870 the Chinese constituted 8.6 percent of the total population of California and an impressive 25 percent of the wage-earning force. Significantly, in their descriptions of these new immigrants, whites tended to identify them with groups they had historically set apart from themselves—blacks and Indians" (Takaki, p. 216). The Chinese were subjected to a process of "Negroization" which depicted them, like emancipated blacks, as threats to republicanism and made their exclusion by law possible (Ibid.). South Asians were subjected to the same process, which rendered their exclusion via the Barred Zone provision of the 1917 Immigration Act intellectually reasonable. Details will be discussed below.

58. Thernstrom, "Naturalization and Citizenship," p. 739. The impact of the statutory phrase "aliens ineligible for citizenship" will be discussed below in connection with the situation of South Asians and *United States v Baghat Singh Thind*, 261 U.S. 204 (1922).

59. See *Chae Chan Ping v United States*, 130 U.S. 581 (1889) (Chinese Exclusion Case); *Fong Yue Ting v United States*, 149 U.S. 698 (1893).

60. Gary R. Hess, "The 'Hindu' in America: Immigration and Naturalization Policies and India, 1917–1946," *Pacific Historical Review* 38 (1969), p. 63. For details see also Karen Leonard, "The Pakhar Singh Murders: A Punjabi Response to California's Alien Land Law," *Amerasia* 11 (1984), pp. 75–87; and Dhan Gopal Mukerji, *Caste and Outcast* (New York: E.P. Dutton & Co., 1923).

61. See Congress, House, Committee on Immigration and Naturalization, *Hearings on Hindu Immigration* (Restriction of Immigration of Hindu Laborers), 63rd Cong., 2d. sess., 13 February 1914.

62. Ward, p. 38.

63. Ibid., pp. 40–41.

64. Ibid., p. 38.

65. Barbara Roberts, "Doctors and Deports: The Role of the Medical Profession in Canadian deportation, 1900–1920," *Canadian Ethnic Studies* 18 (1986), p. 18.

66. Ibid., p. 20.

67. Ibid.

68. Ibid., p. 21.

69. In 1899 and 1900 as many as 20,000 Asians entered British Columbia. See Ward, p. 55.

70. *Industrial World* (Rossland), 28 April 1900, cited in Ward, p. 56.

71. Cited in Ibid., p. 84.

72. Ibid.

73. Report by W. L. MacKenzie King, deputy minister of labor on mission to England to confer with the British authorities on the subject of immigration to Canada from the Orient and immigration from India in particular; cited in (U.S.) Congress, Senate, Commission on Immigration, *Immigrant in Industries; Japanese and Other Immigrant Races in Pacific Coast and Rocky Mountain States*, 3 Vols., 61st Cong., 2d. sess., 1909–1910, p. 329.

74. Ward, p. 76. The term "continuous journey and on through tickets" was later entrenched in Canadian law (*Statutes*, 7–8 Ed. VII, c. 33, cited in Ward, p. 183, n. 66).

75. The League was founded in 1894 with the express purpose to warn of the social and economic dangers inherent in the "new" immigration.

76. Higham, p. 41.

77. Congress, House, Commission on Immigration, *Statements and Recommendations by Societies*, 61st Cong., 3rd sess., 1910–1911, p. 106.

78. Higham, p. 42.

79. Ibid., p. 43.

80. Ibid., p. 44.

81. Handlin, p. 78.

82. Higham, p. 45.

83. There were five distinct classifications. For a discussion of the Dictionary of Races and the entire report, see Handlin, pp. 80–110.

84. Handlin, pp. 77–78.

85. Congress, House, Commission on Immigration, *Statements and Recommendations by Societies*, 61st Cong., 3rd sess., 1910–1911, pp. 106–107.

86. Henry Cabot Lodge of Massachusetts, prominent proponent of isolationism in American foreign policy, was among the first and most influential congressional advocates of immigration restriction.

87. Congress, House, Commission on Immigration, *Statements and Recommendations by Societies*, 61st Cong. 3rd sess., 1910–1911, p. 127.

88. Ibid., pp. 130–131.

89. Congress, House, *Hearing on Immigration Bills* (Statement of Hon. John L. Burnett, Rep. from State of Alabama, in support of literacy test), 61st Cong., 2d. sess., 29 March 1910, p. 393.

90. Ibid., p. 386.

91. Cited in Kemal H. Karpat, "The Ottoman Emigration to America, 1860–1914," *International Journal of Middle East Studies* 17 (1985), p. 186.

92. Gilman, p. 27.

93. Thernstrom, ed. *Harvard Encyclopedia of American Ethnic Groups* (Cambridge, Massachusetts: Harvard University Press, 1980), s.v. "Mormons," by Dean L. May, p. 727.

94. Thernstrom, p. vi.

95. Cited in Thernstrom, "Mormons," p. 720.

96. Congress, House, Commission on Immigration, *Abstracts of Reports, Vol. II*, 61st Cong., 3rd sess., 1910–1911, pp. 569–70.

97. Immigration Act of 1891, 26 Stat. 1084.

98. Congress, House, Committee on the Judiciary, *Hearing on Polygamy*, 25 February 1902, p. 8.

99. Ibid., p. 9.

100. From 1862 to 1887 Congress passed a series of anti-polygamy statutes. In the 1887 Edmunds-Tucker Act, Congress disincorporated the Mormon Church, and the Supreme Court upheld the constitutionality of the Act in 1890. In August 1890 Wilford Woodruff, the president of the Mormon Church, officially denounced polygamy. See Thernstrom, "Mormons," pp. 720–731.

101. Sanford Levinson, *Constitutional Faith* (Princeton: Princeton University Press, 1988), p. 55.

102. Ibid.

103. The oath was upheld by the Supreme Court in *Davis v Beason*, 133 U.S. 333 (1890).

104. Lothrop Stoddard was a Harvard-educated specialist of eugenics and racialist theories in the early twentieth century. His best-known work, *The Rising Tide of Color Against White World Supremacy*, is a lengthy tract defending the Anglo-Saxon "race" against the overwhelming deluge of inferior "races," which calls upon scientific evidence to support his case. Stod-

dard also authored *The New World of Islam* (1921), which was republished in London and translated in Arabic and French.

105. Congress, House, Committee on Immigration and Naturalization, *Hearings on Admission of Near East Refugees*, 67th Cong., 4th sess., Sec. 15, 16, and 19, 1922, p. 13.

106. Ibid., p. 17.

107. Ibid.

108. 42 Stat. 5.

109. 43 Stat. 153.

110. The origins of fears about these "isms" in American political thought date back to the eighteenth century, when Thomas Jefferson warned that the new republic had to protect itself from monarchical principles by keeping out immigrants "potentially capable of corrupting government in America" (Takaki, 39). Jefferson identified British corruption, monarchical ideas, the passions, etc., as threats to republican society which had to be purged. See Takaki, p. 65.

111. John Brigham, "Judicial Impact Upon Social Practices: A Perspective on Ideology," *Legal Studies Forum* 9 (1985), p. 52.

112. Ibid., pp. 51–52.

113. Takaki, p. 136.

114. Joan M. Jensen, *Passage from India: Asian Indian Immigrants in North America* (New Haven: Yale University Press, 1988), p. 55.

CHAPTER 3: OTHER ASIAN: IMMIGRANTS FROM THE MUSLIM WORLD

1. Many Muslim immigrants are from Pakistan, Iran, Afghanistan, Turkey, and the Arab world in general. Thernstrom's *Harvard Encyclopedia of American Ethnic Groups* has essays on various Muslim groups, including Arabs, Afghans, Albanians, Azerbaijanis, Bangladeshis, Bosnians, Fijians, Indonesians, Iranians, Kurds, Pakistanis, Tatars, North Caucasians, Polish and Lithuanian Tatars, Turkestanis, and Turks. Stephen Thernstrom, ed., *Harvard Encyclopedia of American Ethnic Groups* (Cambridge, Massachusetts: Harvard University Press, 1980).

2. Karen Leonard, p. 76.

3. Abdo A. Elkholy, *The Arab Moslems in the United States, Religion and Assimilation* (New Haven: College and University Press, 1966), pp. 81–84.

4. For details on this migration, see Kemal H. Karpat, "The Ottoman Migration to America, 1860–1914," *International Journal of Middle East Studies* 17 (1985): pp. 176–180.

5. Akbar Muhammad, "Muslims in the United States: An Overview of Organizations, Doctrines, and Problems," in *The Islamic Impact*, ed. Yvonne Yazbeck Haddad, Byron Haines, and Ellison Findly (Syracuse: Syracuse University Press, 1984), p. 196.

6. Yvonne Y. Haddad, "Muslims in Canada: A Preliminary Study," in *Religion and Ethnicity*, ed. H. Coward and L. Kawamura (Waterloo, Ontario: Wilfrid Laurier University, 1978), p. 71.

7. Yvonne Haddad, "Muslims in the U.S.," in *Islam: The Religious and Political Life of a World Community*, ed. Marjorie Kelley (New York: Praeger Press, 1984), p. 261.

8. Baha Abu-Laban, "The Arab-Canadian Community," *The Arab Americans, Studies in Assimilation*, ed. Elaine C. Hagopian and Ann Paden (Wilmette, Illinois: Medina University Press), p. 31.

9. Samir Khalaf, "The Background and Causes of Lebanese/Syrian Immigration to the United States Before World War I," in *Crossing the Waters: Arabic-Speaking Immigrants to the United States Before 1940*, ed. Eric J. Hooglund (Washington, D.C.: Smithsonian Institution Press, 1987), p. 21.

10. Orfalea (94) and Naff (84) rely on the following passage from Elkholy: "'In 1885,' says an elderly Moslem woman, 'my father planned to accompany some Christian friends to America. He bought the ticket and boarded the boat. Shortly before sailing he asked the captain whether America had mosques. Told that it had none, he feared that America was *bilad kufr* [a land of unbelief]. He immediately got off the boat.'" (17) Since Elkholy relates this from one of the interviews he conducted among Arab-American Muslims in Toldeo, Ohio and Detroit, Michigan it seems that either the woman relating the story or her parent(s) eventually chose to immigrate to the United States despite her father's initial reticence.

11. Sweeney, p. 18.

12. John Brigham, "Judicial Impact Upon Social Practices: A Perspective on Ideology" p. 55.

13. 1 Stat. 103.

14. 18 Stat. 318.

15. *Harvard Encyclopedia*, s.v. "Naturalization and Citizenship," by Reed Ueda, p. 739.

16. Ibid., p. 741.

17. Ibid.

18. Karpat shows that Ottoman emigrants from areas outside of Syria under Ottoman rule were sometimes also mistakenly included in immigration and census figures as Syrians. Well-kept statistics about immigration at the turn of the century are lacking (Karpat: p. 176).

19. Hugh Johnston, "The Development of the Punjabi Community in Vancouver Since 1961," *Canadian Ethnic Studies* 20 (1988): p. 2.

20. "Turkey in Asia"—Syria, Anatolia, and northern Iraq—is distinguished from "Turkey in Europe"—the Balkans, Crimea, and the Mediterranean islands.

21. Naff, p. 110.

22. E. P. Hutchinson, "Notes on Emigration Statistics of the United States," *American Statistical Association Journal* 53 (1958): p. 963, cited in Karpat: p. 181.

23. Gregory Orfalea, p. 73.

24. 43 Stat. 153.

25. Abu-Laban, p. 21.

26. Philip K. Hitti, *The Syrians in America* (New York: George H. Doran Co., 1924), p. 89.

27. Ibid., p. 88.

28. Michael W. Suleiman, "Early Arab-Americans: The Search for Identity," *Crossing the Waters, Arabic-Speaking Immigrants To the United States Before 1940*, ed. Eric J. Hooglund (Washington, D.C.: Smithsonian Institution Press, 1987), p. 44.

29. Although this is the Library of Congress translation of the title, it would be more accurate to translate "*al-mughtaribūn*" as "emigrants" rather than "immigrants" since, according to Hans Wehr, the verb from which it is derived, *ightaraba* (Form VIII), means "to go to a foreign country; emigrate; to be (far) away from one's homeland." Furthermore, etymologically speaking, for our purposes it is interesting to note that this verb is closely related to two other verbs derived from the same root: *tagharaba* (Form V) and *istaghraba* (Form X), which mean "to assimilate o.s. to the Western way of life" (Hans Wehr, *A Dictionary of Modern Written Arabic, Arabic-English*. J. Milton Cowan, ed. Third Printing. [Beirut: Librairie du Liban; and London: MacDonald & Evans Ltd., 1980], p. 668).

By paying closer attention to etymology and the multiple meanings of this word, we get a better understanding of the nature of Tumeh's work:

namely, as a description of the ways in which the "Americanization" process affected the Arabic-speaking community in North America. It is noteworthy that he did not choose to use *muhajirūn*, which also means "emigrant" but without the implied Westernization. *Muhajirūn* also has a religious connotation, since it is derived from the same root as *hijra*, the emigration of the prophet Mohammed from Mecca to Medina, or the event which marks the beginning of the Muslim era.

30. Tumeh, pp. 66–67.

31. Ibid., pp. 68–69.

32. Suleiman, p. 44.

33. Cited in Suleiman, p. 45.

34. Ibid.

35. 174 Fed. 834 (Circuit Court, D. Massachusetts, 1909).

36. 180 Fed. 694 (Circuit Court of Appeals, Second Circuit, 1910).

37. 205 Fed. 812 (District Court, E.D. South Carolina, 1913).

38. 213 Fed. 355 (District Court, E.D. South Carolina, 1914).

39. 226 Fed. 145 (Circuit Court of Appeals, Fourth Circuit, 1915).

40. 205 Fed. at 812.

41. In re Najour, 174 Fed. at 736.

42. See *Reynolds v United States*, 98 U.S. 145 (1878)(prohibition of polygamy applies to Mormons); *Church of Jesus Christ of Latter Day Saints v United States*, 136 U.S. 1 (1890); and *Davis v Beason*, 133 U.S. 333 (1890). After these decisions, Mormon leaders rewrote church bylaws to remove polygamy as an accepted practice. Also, immigration officers had to be satisfied that immigrants from the Muslim world did not practice polygamy before letting them enter.

43. The Immigration Act of 1891 (26 Stat. 1084) specifically excluded polygamists.

44. 205 Fed. at 814.

45. 205 Fed. at 814–15.

46. 205 Fed. at 816, 813.

47. 205 Fed. at 815.

48. 205 Fed. at 816.

49. 213 Fed. at 356.

50. Ibid.

51. 213 Fed. at 357.

52. 213 Fed. at 360.

53. 213 Fed. at 366.

54. 226 Fed. at 148.

55. Ibid.

56. See *In re Najour*, 174 F. Rep. 735 (Circuit Court, N.D. Georgia, 1909); and *In re Mudarri*, 176 F. Rep. 465 (Circuit Court, D. Massachusetts, 1910) for further discussion whether Syrians are "white persons."

57. Minow, p. 214.

58. See Ibid., especially pp. 121–145.

59. Ibid., p. 235.

60. Ibid.

61. Hess, p. 60.

62. Leonard, p. 76.

63. Jensen, p. 39. The process of "Negroization," which Ronald Takaki describes happening to Chinese laborers at the close of the nineteenth century (*Iron Cages*, pp. 216–219), is at work in this statement about South Asians.

64. Jensen, p. 38.

65. Mukerji, pp. 277–282.

66. Cheng Tien-Fang, *Oriental Immigration in Canada* (Shanghai: The Commercial Press, Inc., 1931), p. 140.

67. Ibid., p. 139.

68. According to Hess, "Fear of labor competition, the seeming impossibility of assimilation, and racial antagonism led to demands for exclusion" of South Asian immigrants on the part of Canadians. (Hess: p. 60) Similar nativist sentiments existed in Canada and the United States simultaneously.

69. Hess, p. 61.

70. The total number of South Asians in the United States, concen-

trated on the Pacific Coast, was under 6,000 before 1950 (Hess: p. 62; Leonard: p. 75).

71. Hess, p. 62.

72. Ibid.

73. Ibid.

74. Ibid.

75. Tien-Fang, p. 141.

76. Ibid.

77. Leonard, p. 76.

78. Hess, p. 61.

79. Jacoby, p. 1–2; Konvitz, p. 88. One scholar notes that between 1908 and 1923 at least sixty-nine "natives of India acquired citizenship by action of no less than thirty-two courts in seventeen different states. How many applications were denied during this same period is not known—and probably there were a great many—. . . ." (Jacoby: 1)

80. Jacoby, p. 1.

81. The "Barred Zone" provision of the Immigration Act of 1917 (39 Stat. 874) prohibited immigration from India, Siam, Arabia, Indo-China, the Malay Peninsula, Afghanistan, New Guinea, Borneo, Java, Ceylon, Sumatra, Celebes, and parts of Russian Turkestan and Siberia.

82. 261 U.S. at 204.

83. For discussion of the Thind case see also Hess: pp. 65–67; Konvitz: pp. 88–97; and Lesser: pp. 88–89.

The Japanese exclusion case, *Ozawa v United States*, 260 U.S. 178 (1922), was decided by the Supreme Court in the same term as the Thind case. The Ozawa case turned on the issue of race rather than color.

84. 261 U.S. at 215.

85. Hess, p. 66.

86. Ibid.

87. Ibid., p. 67.

88. Ibid., p. 69.

89. Ibid., p. 65.

90. 7 F.2d 728 (D. Michigan, 1925).

91. 7 F.2d at 731.

92. Cited in Ibid.

93. 7 F.2d at 732.

94. Ibid.

95. Ibid.

96. 27 F. 2d. 568 (1928).

97. Ibid.

98. As Goldman and Jahnige note, *stare decisis* "was emphasized as *the legal norm* [Emphasis in original]" at that time, and Supreme Court decisions were vehicles by which lower court judges—"and other interested persons, for that matter"—could know what the law was (p. 193).

99. Richard Brent Turner, *Islam in the United States in the 1920s: The Quest for a New Vision in Afro-American Religion* (PhD diss., Princeton University, 1986), p. 129.

100. Ibid., p. 133.

101. *The Review of Religions* 19 (July 1920): p. 240.

102. Turner, p. 142.

103. *The Moslem Sunrise* 1 (July 1921): p. 9.

104. Ibid.

105. *The Review of Religions* 19 (July 1920): pp. 240–241; *The Review of Religions* 19 (April/May 1920): p. 158.

106. Turner, p. 142. He reports that the converts were from Jamaica, British Guiana, Poland, Russia, Germany, the Azores, Belgium, Portugal, Italy, and France.

107. Headlines included: "Picturesque Sadiq," "Hopes to Convert U.S.," "Speaks Seven Tongues," "Optimistic in Detention," and "East Indian Here With New Religion," *The Review of Religions* 19 (July 1920): p. 242.

108. Turner, p. 150.

109. Ibid., p. 152.

110. Mufti Mohammad Sadiq, "No Polygamy," *The Moslem Sunrise* 1 (July 1920): pp. 9–10.

111. Ibid., p. 9.

112. Ibid., p. 10.

113. Ibid.

114. Sher Ali, "America's Intolerance, Our Missionary in the Detention House," *The Review of Religions* 19 (April/May 1920): pp. 158–160.

115. Turner, p. 2.

116. Yvonne Yazbeck Haddad, "Arab Muslims and Islamic Institutions in America, Adaptations and Reform," in *Arabs in the New World: Studies on Arab American Communities*, ed. Sameer Y. Abraham and Nabeel Abraham (Detroit: Wayne State University Press, 1983), pp. 67–68.

117. Orfalea, pp. 94–95.

118. Haddad, "Muslims in Canada," p. 73.

119. For instance, in Ross, North Dakota, a mosque was built in 1920, only to be abandoned by 1948 as the Muslims of Ross became integrated, adopted Christian names, and married Christians (Haddad, "Arab Muslims and Islamic Institutions," p. 68). According to Karpat, membership of the first Muslim communities dwindled because of conversion, death, and return to their home countries (Karpat: p. 183).

120. *The Moslem Sunrise* 1 (July 1921): 1; cited in Turner, p. 150, n. 81.

121. Larry Allan Poston, *Islamic Da'wah in North America and the Dynamics of Conversion to Islam in Western Societies* (PhD diss., Northwestern University, 1988), p. 56.

122. See Karpat, pp. 182–183.

123. Elkholy, p. 17.

124. Said, *Orientalism*.

125. Today some writers make the case for *ijtihad*, the practice of individual interpretation of Islamic legal tenets to apply to contemporary concerns. *Ijtihad*, allowed in early Islamic history, it is argued, could be revived and used as a strategy to reconcile Islamic norms with the North American context and as an adaptive mechanism (see Waugh, et al.). Essentially Muslims today are concerned about the free exercise of religion: whether the demands of the workplace and secular institutions, such as schools, hospitals, prisons, and the military, will allow Muslims to observe religious dietary laws, dress code, Friday sabbath and holidays, and daily prayers.

126. Myron Weiner, "Immigration: Prespectives from Receiving Countries," *Third World Quarterly* 12 (1990): p. 154.

CHAPTER 4: MUSLIMS IN PRISON:
CONSTITUTIONAL PROTECTION OF RELIGIOUS LIBERTY

1. Malcolm M. Feeley and Roger A. Hanson, "The Impact of Judicial Intervention on Prisons and Jails: A Framework for Analysis and a Review of the Literature," in *Courts, Corrections, and the Constitution*, John J. DiIulio, Jr., ed. (New York and Oxford: Oxford University Press, 1990), p. 12.

2. See *Banning v Looney*, 213 F. 2d 771 (10th Cir., 1954), *cert denied*, 348 U.S. 266 (1954), which states that "courts are without power to supervise prison administration or to interfere with the ordinary prison rules or regulations." See also Note, *Beyond the Ken of the Courts: A Critique of Judicial Refusal to Review the Complaints of Convicts*, Yale Law Journal 72 (1963). The federal courts adhered to the "hands-off" policy generally "out of concern for federalism and separation of powers and a fear that judicial review of administrative decisions would undermine prison security and discipline" (James B. Jacobs, *New Perspectives on Prisons and Imprisonment* [Ithaca: Cornell University Press, 1983], p. 35).

3. *Ruffin v Commonwealth*, 62 Va. 790 (1871).

4. See John Irwin where he cites the following from "typical" decisions illustrating the "hands-off" doctrine: "The problem is moreover one which involves administrative discretion . . . which as an independent and abstract question is not within the jurisdiction of this court" [1948, citation omitted]; "It is not the province of the courts to supervise prison discipline" [1948, citation omitted]; "Courts do not have the power and it is not their function or responsibility to supervise prisons [1954, citation omitted]" *(Prisons in Turmoil* [Boston: Little, Brown and Co., 1980], p. 102).

5. See David J. Rothman, *Conscience and Convenience, The Asylum and its Alternatives in Progressive America* (Boston: Little, Brown & Co., 1980).

6. Ibid., p. 31.

7. See Ibid., which describes the "Auburn system," named for a nineteenth century penitentiary in Auburn, Massachusetts, where absolute silence was maintained during the regular day and prisoners spent their nights in solitary cells with nothing to read but the Bible. Mandatory religious services were held with a prison guard standing next to a loaded cannon pointing toward the inmates.

8. 365 U.S. 167 (1961).

9. Title 42 U.S.C. Section 1983, the Civil Rights Act of 1871 (a.k.a. the "Ku Klux Klan Act"), allows for "civil cause of action enforceable in federal courts against any state official found to be violating rights 'under color of law'" (Thomas, p. 37). It provides: "Every person, who, under color of any statute, ordinance, regulation, custom, or usage, of any State or Territory, subjects, or causes to be subjected, any citizen of the United States or any person within the jurisdiction thereof to the deprivation of any rights, privileges, or immunities secured by the Constitution and laws, shall be liable to the party injured in an action at law. . . ."

10. Ibid., p. 84.

11. Ibid.

12. Ibid., p. 85.

13. *ex rel Morris v Radio Station WENR*, 209 F. 2d 105 (1953), cited in Thomas, p. 85.

14. Ibid., p. 92.

15. Jacobs, p. 35. See also Irwin; Feeley; DiIulio; Note, "Beyond the Ken of the Courts; and Comment, "The Religious Rights of the Incarcerated," *University of Pennsylvania Law Review* 125 (1977).

16. Jacobs, p. 36.

17. Ibid.

18. Feeley and Hanson, p. 13.

19. 378 U.S. 546 (1964). The Cooper case held that Muslim prisoners have standing to challenge religious discrimination in prisons under Section 1983 of the Civil Rights Act of 1871.

20. Jacobs, p. 41.

21. 418 U.S. 539 (1974). In Wolff the Court also addressed some right-to-counsel issues. Although this is not a case directly involving Muslim inmates, several cases that do are cited as legal precedents.

22. Ibid., p. 556.

23. Feeley and Hanson, p. 36.

24. *Annual Report*, U.S. Courts, 1970 and 1989.

25. Feeley and Hanson, p. 26.

26. Ibid., pp. 31–32.

27. Ibid., p. 27.

28. Ibid., p. 15.

29. Ibid.

30. Stuart A. Scheingold, *The Politics of Rights* (New Haven: Yale University Press, 1974), p. 131.

31. See Beverly Thomas McCloud, "African-American Muslim Women," in *The Muslims of America*, ed. Yvonne Y. Haddad (New York: Oxford University Press, 1991), pp. 177–187; Y. N. Kly: pp. 152–160; Austin; Mehdi; Essien-Udom; Turner; and Lincoln, *The Black Muslims in America*, rev. ed. (Boston: Beacon Press, 1973).

32. Turner, p. 11.

33. Ibid., p. 12.

34. Lincoln, pp. xxiv, 23.

35. Ibid., p. 23. See also W. Haywood Burns, "The Black Muslims in America: A Reinterpretation," *Race* 5 (1963): pp. 26–27.

36. Turner, pp. 16–17.

37. McCloud, p. 177.

38. Ibid., p. 178.

39. Lincoln, p. 70.

40. Ibid., p. 18.

41. Ibid., p. 81.

42. Ibid., pp. xxvii, 74.

43. Cited in Ibid.

44. Cited in Ibid., p. 74.

45. Ibid., pp. 83–85.

46. McCloud, p. 178.

47. Lincoln, p. 29.

48. Ibid., p. 116.

49. Ibid., p. 31.

50. Malcolm Little and Alex Haley, *The Autobiography of Malcolm X* (New York: Ballantine Press, 1964), p. 183.

51. Lincoln, p. xxvii.

52. Ibid., p. 119.

53. Burns, p. 34.

54. Lincoln, p. 120.

55. Ibid., p. 26.

56. Wallace F. Caldwell, "A Survey of Attitudes Toward Black Muslims in Prison," *Journal of Human Relations* 16 (1968): p. 223. The "seal of Islam" is a symbol of piety, ostensibly the result of frequent prostrations in prayer, placing head to ground repeatedly. Black Muslim converts are reported to have made the mark by various means, including cigarettes and caustic soap, to signify their newfound faith.

57. Ibid.

58. Ibid.

59. Irwin, p. 69.

60. Irwin, p. 68.

61. See Laurence Tribe, *American Constitutional Law* (Mineola, New York: The Foundation Press, 1978), p. 830. Also, the Court states in *Thomas v Review Board of Indiana Employment Security Division* (450 U.S. 707, 1981): "The resolution of that question [what constitutes religion] is not to turn upon a judicial perception of the particular belief or practice in question; religious beliefs need not be acceptable, logical, consistent or comprehensible to others in order to merit first amendment protection."

62. U.S. Constitution amendment I: "Congress shall make no law respecting an establishment of religion, or prohibiting the free exercise thereof."

63. *Reynolds v United States*, 98 U.S. 145 (1878) (prohibition of polygamy applied to Mormons); *Church of Jesus Christ of Latter Day Saints v United States*, 136 U.S. 1 (1890); *Davis v Beason*, 133 U.S. 333 (1890). "The term 'religion' has reference to one's view of his relations to his Creator, and to the obligations they impose of reverence for his being and character, and of obedience to his will" (Reynolds at 342).

64. *Cantwell v Connecticut*, 310 U.S. 296 (1940); *Cox v New Hampshire*, 312 U.S. 569 (1941); *Prince v Massachusetts*, 321 U.S. 158 (1944); *Thomas v Review Board of Indiana Employment Security Division*, 450 U.S. 707 (1981).

65. *Sherbert v Verner*, 374 U.S. 398 (1963).

66. *People v Woody*, 394 P.2d 813 (Sup. Ct. of Ca. 1964).

67. *United States v Lee,* 102 S.Ct. 1051 (1982); *Wisconsin v Yoder,* 406 U.S. 206 (1972).

68. *Robinson v Foti,* 527 F. Supp. 1111 (E.D. La., 1981).

69. *International Society for Krishna Consciousness, Inc. v Barber,* 650 F.2d 430 (2d Cir. 1981).

70. *Africa v Commonwealth of Pennsylvania,* 662 F.2d 1025 (3d Cir. 1981), *cert. denied* 456 U.S. 908 (1982). In this case, the Appeals Court rejected the claim that MOVE was a religious organization because "it is not structurally analogous to those 'traditional' organizations that have been recognized as religions under the first amendment" (*Africa* at 1036). This conclusion was reached after the court found that MOVE conducts no regular services, observes no religious holidays of its own, and has nothing which passes for scripture.

71. See George C. Freeman, III, *The Misguided Search for the Constitutional Definition of 'Religion',* Georgetown Law Journal 71 (1983): pp. 1519–1565, in which the author cites seven cases and twelve articles that deal with the elusive definition of religion. See also Note, *Soul Rebels: The Rastafarians and the Free Exercise Clause,* Georgetown Law Journal 72 (1984).

72. David Rothman, "Decarcerating Prisoners and Patients," *Civil Liberties Review* 1 (1973): pp. 14–15; cited in Jacobs, p. 67.

73. As W. Haywood Burns points out, "much of the comment upon and analysis of the Black Muslims in America in both academic and popular accounts has tended to emphasize the racist aspects of the movement" ("The Black Muslims in America: A Reinterpretation," *Race* 5 (1963): p. 26).

74. For the prison administrators' point of view, see Caldwell: pp. 220–238, in which a random sample of 71 wardens and superintendents of Federal and State correctional institutions and 142 prison chaplains is studied. In some responses Muslims are depicted as "a cult, not a religion"; "a militant organization"; and "not a legitimate religious denomination or group" (228).

75. Ibid., p. 228.

76. *Davis v Beason,* 133 U.S. 333, 345–48 (1890); *United States v Macintosh,* 283 U.S. 605, 633–34 (1931).

77. Freeman, p. 1525.

78. *United States v Ballard,* 322 U.S. 69–70, 78, 86–87 (1944).

79. 343 U.S. 306, 313 (1952). What sociologists call the "civil religion"—Christian categories appropriated by the secular world—is captured

in American legal institutions. See Robert Bellah, *The Broken Covenant: American Civil Religion in Times of Trial* (New York: Seabury Press, 1975).

80. 75 S.Ct. 392 (1955).

81. 380 U.S. 163 (1965) at 165–66.

82. See Note, *Soul Rebels*, p. 1612.

83. "Muslim faith is 'religion' within the constitutional provisions as to the freedom of religion" (*Fulwood v Clemmer*, 206 F.Supp. 370 [1962] at 373).

84. For a discussion of African-American Muslims legal claims, see Oliver Jones, Jr., "The Black Muslim Movement and the American Constitutional System," *Journal of Black Studies* 13 (1983): pp. 417–437.

85. William Bennet Turner, *Establishing the Rule of Law in Prisons: A Manual for Prisoners' Rights Litigation*, Black Law Journal 1 (1971): p. 106.

86. *Walker v Blackwell*, 411 F.2d 23 (5th Cir. 1969) (Black Muslims' religious interests recognized under the First Amendment); *Barnett v Rodgers*, 410 F.2d 985 (D.C. Cir. 1969); *Cooper v Pate*, 382 F.2d 518 (7th Cir. 1967) (a determination that beliefs of Black Muslims do not constitute religion would require a comparative evaluation of religions, which is beyond the powers of the courts); *Sostre v McGinnis*, 334 F.2d 905 (2d Cir. 1964), *cert. denied*, 378 U.S. 892 (1964) (accommodation of Black Muslim religious practices in prison settings); *Knuckles v Prasse*, 302 F.Supp. 1036 (E.D. Pa. 1969), *cert. denied*, 403 U.S. 936 (1971); *Bryant v Wilkins*, 265 N.Y.S. 2d 995 ("Islamic group known as Muslims, followers of sect led by Elijah Muhammad constitutes a 'religion'"); *Banks v Havener*, 234 F.Supp. 27 (1964) ("Black Muslim movement as here taught and followed is a religion").

87. *Battle v Anderson*, 376 F. Supp. 402 (1974); *Knuckles v Prasse;* and *Walker v Blackwell*.

88. *Northern v Nelson*, 315 F.Supp. 687 (1970); In the Matter of *Brown v McGinnis*, N.Y.S. 2d 497 (1962); *Finney v Hutto*, 57 L.Ed. 2d 522 (1976).

89. *Northern v Nelson; Brown v McGinnis;* and *Finney v Hutto*. Also, *Cooper v Pate; Battle v Anderson;* and *Rowland v Sigler*, 327 F. Supp. 821 (D. Neb.), *aff'd. sub nom. Rowland v Jones* 452 F.2d 1005 (8th Cir. 1971).

90. State *ex rel. Tate v Cubbage*, 210 A.2d 555 (Del. Super. Ct. 1965); and *Fulwood v Clemmer*.

91. The court decision in *SaMarion v McGinnis*, 284 N.Y.S. 2d at 508 (1967), reads in part: "Diet of inmates shall be left to the discretion of the

Wardens but where reasonable and practicable and consistent with the ability to do so, religious dietary habits should be accommodated." See also *Battle v Anderson* at 427; *Waddell v Aldredge,* 480 F.2d 1078 (1973); *Long v Parker,* 455 F.2d 466 (3d Cir. 1972); and *Barnett v Rodgers.*

92. 291 F.2d at 196 (1961).

93. *Pierce v LaVallee,* 203 F.2d 233 (1961).

94. *Madyun v Franzen,* 704 F.2d 954 (1983) at 958.

95. Ibid.

96. *Wright v Wilkins,* 26 Misc. 2d 1090, N.Y.S. 2d 309 (Sup. Ct. 1961).

97. *Brown v McGinnis* at 497.

98. *Fulwood v Clemmer* at 370.

99. *In Re Ferguson,* 361 P.2d 417 (1961) at 421.

100. Ibid. at 422.

101. For a discussion of the distinction between the two concepts—freedom to believe and freedom to act—see *Cantwell v Connecticut* at 296. While the *Cantwell* case does not address the issue of religious liberty in prisons, it is often cited in cases that do. Essentially it is argued that the right to practice one's religious beliefs is subject only to regulation for the protection of society.

102. The recent Supreme Court decision in *O'Lone v Shabazz,* 107 S.Ct. 2400 (1987), is a noteworthy exception. The Court, Rehnquist writing, held that the appellate court erred in placing the burden on the prison officials to prove that no reasonable method existed by which inmates' religious rights could be accommodated without creating a *bona fide* security problem.

103. *Sewell v Pegelow* at 196.

104. *Brown v McGinnis* at 497.

105. *Brown v Peyton,* 437 F.2d 1228 (1971). In this case, Black Muslim inmates alleged that prison officials' denial of permission to subscribe to *Muhammad Speaks,* to order religious buttons, and to hold prayer meetings violated their rights to free exercise of religion.

106. *Fulwood v Clemmer* at 379.

107. See Note, *Beyond the Ken of the Courts,* pp. 540–544.

108. Jacobs, p. 66.

109. In *Pierce v LaVallee* and *Sewell v Pegelow,* two federal courts held that discriminatory treatment on the basis of religion is prohibited by the Civil Rights Act and cannot be justified merely for the sake of efficient prison administration. In *Cooper v Pate,* the Supreme Court held that claims of Black Muslims of religious suppression and discrimination stated a federal cause of action.

110. *Fulwood v Clemmer* at 373.

111. *SaMarion v McGinnis* at 505.

112. *Brown v McGinnis* at 498.

113. *Cooper v Pate* at 518.

114. *Walker v Blackwell* at 23.

115. 315 F. Supp. 687 (1970).

116. 57 L.Ed. 2d 522 (1976).

117. 361 P. 2d 417 (1961).

118. *In Re Ferguson* at 420.

119. Ibid. at 422.

120. 712 F.2d 1078 (1983).

121. Ibid. at 1081.

122. For example, *Moorish Science Temple of America, Inc. v Smith,* 693 F.2d 987 (1982); *Battle v Anderson; Elam v Anderson; Walker v Blackwell* (citing administrative expense as the prevailing concern); *Knuckles v Prasse; Barnett v Rodgers; Waddell v Aldredge; Long v Parker; Abernathy v Cunningham,* 393 F.2d 775 (1968).

123. For example, *Cochran v Sielaff,* 405 F. Supp. 1126 (S.D. Ill. 1976); *Walker v Blackwell; Barnett v Rodgers.*

124. *Barnett v Rodgers* at 998.

125. See *Moorish Science Temple, Inc. v Smith; Jihaad v Carlson,* 410 F. Supp. 1132 (1976); *United States v Kahane,* 396 F. Supp. 687, aff'd sub. nom. *Kahane v Carlson,* 527 F.2d 492 (2d Cir. 1975).

126. *Kahane v Carlson* at 495, citing *Chapman v Kleindienst,* 507 F.2d 1246 (7th Cir. 1974) at 1251; *Ross v Blackledge,* 477 F.2d 616 (4th Cir. 1973); and *Barnett v Rodgers.*

127. *Jihaad v Carlson* at 1134.

128. Ibid.

129. Ibid., citing *Knuckles v Prasse,* 302 F. Supp. at 1059.

130. 415 F. Supp. 1218 (D.V.I. 1976).

131. *Walker v Blackwell* at 23.

132. However, after Muhammad's death in 1975 and the subsequent "restoration" of the Nation of Islam, African-American Muslims have observed Ramadan in accordance with the world Islamic lunar calendar.

133. See *Cochran v Sielaff; Elam v Henderson*, 472 F. 2d 582 (5th Cir.), *cert. denied*, 414 U.S. 868 (1973); *Walker v Blackwell;* and *Barnett v Rodgers*.

134. *Barnett v Rodgers* at 1101.

135. *Battle v Anderson* at 402.

136. *Shabazz v Barnauskas*, 598 F.2d 345 (1979).

137. *Burgin v Henderson*, 536 F.2d 501 (2d Cir. 1976).

138. Ibid. at 504. Also, Black Muslims believed that "it is against the nature of the creation of Allah, that one should shave the hair off his face and thus resemble women, defacing the nature of man" (M. Sayed Adly, "About the Beard of Muslims 1 (sermon) (1976)," cited in Comment, *The Religious Rights of the Incarcerated*, University of Pennsylvania Law Review 125 (1977): p. 814.

139. For example see *Wright v Raines*, 457 F. Supp. 1082 (1977), where Sikhs in prison filed a challenge to prison regulations that interfered with their free exercise of religion.

140. 422 F. Supp. 211 (S.D.N.Y. 1977).

141. Ibid. at 211.

142. 306 N.Y.S. 2d 359 (1969).

143. 598 F.2d 345 (1979).

144. *Teterud v Gillman*, 385 F. Supp. 153 (5th Cir. 1976).

145. For example, *Brooks v Wainwright*, 428 F.2d 652 (5th Circ. 1970) (divine revelation commanded plaintiff inmate not to shave); *Brown v Wainwright*, 419 F.2d 1376 (5th Cir. 1970) (prisoner alleged that he was "an offspring of God and a mortal," and that moustache was a gift from God). See also Comment, *The Religious Rights of the Incarcerated*, University of Pennsylvania Law Review 125 (1977): p. 812.

146. *Burgin v Henderson* at 501.

147. 329 F. Supp. 796 (N.D.Ga. 1970).

148. *Battle v Anderson* at 419.

149. *O'Lone v Shabazz,* 107 S.Ct. 2400 (1987).

150. Ibid. at 2401–2402.

151. Ibid. at 2406.

152. Ibid.

153. Ibid. at 2400.

154. Ibid. at 2410.

155. Ibid.

156. Ibid.

157. Ibid., citing Brief for Imam Jamil Abdullah Al-Amin et al., as *amici curiae,* at 32.

158. 769 F.2d 345 (1985).

159. Ibid. at 347.

160. Ibid. at 346, 347, and 349.

161. The standard limited frisk search entails contact along most of the body excluding the genital-anal area. See *Madyun v Franzen* at 956, n. 1 and 2.

162. Ibid. at 956.

163. Ibid. at 954.

164. Ibid. at 960.

165. The compelling interest test requires that the policy in question serve a compelling government interest in a way that poses the least possible burden on religious freedom.

166. 494 U.S. 872, 1990.

167. See Reid Amendment No. 1083, in *Congressional Record Daily Digest* (Tues., Oct. 26 1993), 103rd Congress, 1st Session.

168. Thomas, pp. 15–16.

169. Scheingold, p. 131.

170. Note, "Beyond the Ken of the Courts," p. 508.

171. Haddad, "A Century of Islam in America," p. 4.

172. Ibid.

173. Ibid.

174. Ibid.

175. Ibid.

176. "Federal Prisons Giving Considerations to Muslims," *New York Times* 18 November 1979, p. 57.

177. Jacobs, p. 67.

178. Janet Rae-Dupree, "Sermons on the Island, Muslim Chaplain Gives Guidance to All Faiths at Prison," *Los Angeles Times* 13 December 1991, Sec. B, pp. 1, 8.

CHAPTER 5: HATE CRIMES LEGISLATION
AND THE PROTECTION OF RELIGIOUS PROPERTY

1. "Muslims a Growing U.S. Force," *Los Angeles Times*, 24 January 1991.

2. Estimates of the size of the American Muslim population vary considerably. The estimate used here is based on Stone, pp. 25–38. See also Yvonne Y. Haddad, "Muslims in America: A Select Bibliography": p. 93; and U.S. Representative Mervyn M. Dymally's remarks in Congress, House, "Religious Hate Violence Targets Islamic Mosques." 100th Cong., 1st sess. *Congressional Record* 133, no. 206 (22 December 1987), E4990. However it should be noted that other estimates place the figure higher. For instance, forty-four representatives of various American Muslim organizations, assembled 14–16 December 1990 to discuss the Persian Gulf Crisis, stated in a letter to President Bush that American Muslims are a significant minority of six to eight million citizens, almost double the estimate used here (cited in *Al-Mashriq*, Magazine of the Islamic Society of San Francisco-East Bay, Jan./Feb. 1991, p. 17). Also the *Boston Globe* reported in "US Moslems say Crisis Distorts Peaceful Faith" (22 September 1990) that the figure is five million.

3. Cited in "Muslims a Growing U.S. Force," *Los Angeles Times.*

4. "Hate crime" is defined as any criminal act which is motivated by prejudice based on race, religion, affectional or sexual orientation, or ethnicity. As a result of recent legislation arson, theft, vandalism, and any form of assault which has a bias motive is now classified as hate crime with additional criminal penalties attached.

5. Daniel Pipes raised the subject of "muslimphobia" in the west in his article in the *National Review*, "The Muslims are Coming! The Muslims are Coming!" (19 November 1990, pp. 28–31). Rather than dispel pejorative myths about the threat Muslims and Islam represent for the west, Pipes reaffirms deep anxieties by arguing that "the fear of Islam has some basis in

reality. . . . Muslim countries have the most terrorists and the fewest democracies in the world" (29). Further, Muslims have the highest birth rate in the world and are immigrating in record numbers to Western Europe and North America, where "Muslim immigrants bring with them a chauvinism that augurs badly for their integration into the mainstream. . ." (31). And, most importantly for Pipes, "[t]he key issue is whether the Muslims will modernize" (31).

6. Several writers have addressed the centuries-old enmity between the Christian West and the Muslim East. See especially Norman Daniel, *Islam and the West, the Making of an Image* (Edinburgh: University Press, 1960); Bernard Lewis, *Islam and the West* (New York: Oxford University Press, 1993); and Said, *Orientalism*.

7. For example, one American Muslim expressed his fear by saying, "When the bodies of American youth come back, [people] are going to blame the Muslims" (quoted in "Muslims a Growing U.S. Force," *Los Angeles Times*). For more information about the Muslims' worries about a possible backlash, see "A Call to Prayer," *Los Angeles Times*, 24 January 1991; and "Middle Eastern Enclave Fears Reprisals in U.S.," *Washington Post*, 11 January 1991. Concerns about internment and other forms of war-related discrimination are reflected in "FBI Quest Leaves Many Arab-Americans Fearful," *Los Angeles Times*, 24 January 1991; "Inquiries on Arab-Americans by FBI Raise Concern," *New York Times*, 12 January 1991; "U.S. Moslems Say Crisis Distorts Peaceful Faith," *Boston Globe*, 22 September 1990.

On a related point, in the wake of the Persian Gulf war many American Muslims are quick to point out that Saddam Hussein did not represent Islam and that Muslims did not support his invasion of Kuwait. See Mathis Chazanov, "Mosque has a U.S. Flavor," *Los Angeles Times*, 25 January 1991; and *al-Mashriq*, (Dec./Jan. 1991), (Jan./Feb. 1991), and (Feb./Mar. 1991).

8. See, for example, "Anti-Iran Feelings Reach US Moslems," *New York Times*, 25 November 1979, p. 18, where harassment and vandalism are reported by Middle Easterners and blacks who practice the Islamic faith in America.

9. See Timothy Mitchell, "The Limits of the State: Beyond Statist Approaches and Their Critics," *American Political Science Review* 85 (March 1991): pp. 77–96, where he discusses the shortcomings of systems theory and the statist approach in comparative politics and offers a third alternative for the comparative study of state-society relations, based on a historical perspective.

10. This part of the analysis is indebted to Mitchell's points in his brief review of Foucault's thesis about the disciplinary effects, and Mitchell's own related point about the structural effect, of particular "authoritative" practices. Mitchell writes that "[t]he apparent boundary of the state does not

mark the limit of the processes of regulation." Various means of social control, e.g., culture, provide both the constraints and inducements to action which are crucial to the maintenance of order in society. See Mitchell, especially pp. 92–94; quotation on p. 90. See also Michel Foucault, *Discipline and Punish: the Birth of the Prison* (trans. Alan Sheridan) (New York: Vintage Books, 1979) and *The History of Sexuality* (New York: Vintage Books, 1978); and the writing of Jean Comaroff, an anthropologist who studies how Europeans colonized Africa (see Jean Comaroff and John Comaroff, *Of Revelation and Revolution: Christianity, Colonialism, and Consciousness in South Africa* [Chicago: University of Chicago Press, 1991]; and Jean Comaroff, *Body and Power, Spirit of Resistance: the Culture and History of a South African People* [Chicago: University of Chicago Press, 1985]).

11. For information on early settlement patterns, see Akbar Muhammad, "Muslims in the United States: An Overview of Organizations, Doctrines, and Problems," in *The Islamic Impact*, ed. Yvonne Yazbeck Haddad, Byron Haines, and Ellison Findly (Syracuse, New York: Syracuse University Press, 1984), pp. 195–217; and Yvonne Y. Haddad and Adair T. Lummis, *Islamic Values in the United States, A Comparative Study* (New York: Oxford University Press, 1987), pp. 13–16, 155–158. See also Gutbi Mahdi Ahmed, "Muslim Organizations in the United States," in *The Muslims of America*, ed. Yvonne Yazbeck Haddad (New York and Oxford: Oxford University Press, 1991), pp. 11–24.

12. Haddad and Lummis, pp. 5–6. Strict adherence to the teachings of Islam has been advocated and supported by the Islamic Society of North America (ISNA), currently the central organization which, by 1982, evolved from the Muslim Student Association. Gutbi Mahdi Ahmed also characterizes the immigrants since the 1960s as "more radical" and "well-educated." He argues that the Muslim Student Association, founded in 1963, differed from earlier organizations in North America in that it identified Islam (rather than ethnic affiliations) as the focal point: "Commitment to Islam overrode every other affiliation.... [Further] Islam was seen as an ideology, a way of life, and a mission, and the organization was not considered simply as a way to serve the community but as a means to create an ideal community and serve Islam" (Ahmed, p. 14).

13. There has been a steady increase in the number of mosques and Muslim organizations since the early 1970s, with the most rapid growth rate currently underway. In 1986 the number of American mosques/Islamic centers was 598; today it is over 950.

14. The proponents of the indirect "lifestyle" approach contend that the witness of the Muslim way of life is sufficiently persuasive to win converts and is in fact the only acceptable method of conversion, given the Qur'anic injunction "let there be no compulsion in religion." (2:256) For discussion of different approaches to *da'wah*, see Poston, especially pp. 270–311.

15. Akbar Mohammad, "Some Factors Which Promote and Restrict Islamization in America," *American Journal of Islamic Studies* (August 1984), pp. 41–43. Cited in Poston, p. 281.

16. See Gloria T. Beckley and Paul Burstein, "Religious Pluralism, Equal Opportunity, and the State," *Western Political Quarterly* 44 (March 1991): pp. 185–208. According to this article, Muslims filed eleven percent of the sample of 207 religious discrimination complaints the authors examined.

17. See also Kathleen Moore, "Muslims in Prison: Claims to Constitutional Protection of Religious Liberty," in *The Muslims of America*, ed. Yvonne Yazbeck Haddad (New York: Oxford University Press, 1991), pp. 136–156.

18. "Mosque Damage Hinders Holy Observance," *Boston Globe*, 3 April 1990.

19. Congress, House, Committee on the Judiciary, Subcommittee on Criminal Justice, *Crimes Against Religious Practices and Property*, 99th Cong., 1st sess., 16 May and 19 June 1985.

20. Cited in Congress, Senate, Committee on the Judiciary, Subcommittee on the Constitution, *Hate Crime Statistics Act of 1988*, 100th Cong., 2nd sess., 21 June 1988, p. 125. Records of the committee hearings include the study authored by Peter Finn and Taylor McNeil of Abt. Associates, Inc., entitled "The Response of the Criminal Justice System to Bias Crime, An Explanatory Review."

21. Such organizations include the National Institute Against Prejudice and Violence, the Center for Democratic Renewal (formerly known as the National Anti-Klan Network), the Anti-Defamation League of B'nai B'rith, the Anti-Violence Project of the Gay and Lesbian Task Force, and the Southern Poverty Law Center.

22. Congress, House, Committee on the Judiciary, *Report Amending Chapter 13 of Title 18, United States Code, to impose criminal penalties for damage to religious property . . .* , 100th Cong., 1st sess., 2 October 1987, p. 3.

23. Ibid., 4; and "But Who's Counting? Violent Racial Incidents Add Up," *Village Voice*, 14 July 1987, p. 34.

24. Concern about the rise in violence against religious property led the National Council of Churches to warn that it has reached "epidemic proportions." See National Council of Churches, "They Don't All Wear Sheets: A Chronology of Racist and Far-Right Violence: 1980–86" (1988).

25. Ibid.

26. Congress, Senate, Committee on the Judiciary, Subcommittee on the Constitution, *Hate Crimes Statistics Act of 1988*, 100th Cong., 2nd sess., 21 June 1988, p. 125.

27. State laws prohibiting hate crime already existed in Maryland, Pennsylvania, Illinois, Connecticut, Oklahoma, and North Carolina. These states plus the Los Angeles County Human Relations Commission and the police departments of Chicago, New York and Boston have been compiling data on hate crime since the early 1980s.

28. See Congress, House, Committee on the Judiciary, Subcommittee on Criminal Justice, *Crimes against religious practices and property*, 99th Cong., 1st sess., 16 May and 19 June 1985, p. 11.

29. A few state governments and community organizations monitor the incidence of hate crimes. See notes 24 and 27.

30. See Senate Bills 702 (to provide for the collection of data about crimes motivated by racial, religious, or ethnic hatred) and 797 (to require the Attorney General to collect data and report annually about hate crimes) and 2000 (to provide for the acquisition and publication of data about crimes that manifest prejudice based on race, religion, affectional or sexual orientation, or ethnicity). One Hundredth Congress, Second Session (1988).

31. Dymally's remarks, Congress, House, "Religious Hate Violence . . . ," p. E4990.

32. Ibid.

33. Ibid.

34. "Hate Crime Statistics Act," p. 33.

35. In announcing new police investigation guidelines in Massachusetts, Priscilla Douglas, the assistant public safety secretary, said that when investigating alleged hate crimes, police departments are instructed to look for such "bias indicators" as the differing race of the victim and the offender, and whether the crime occurred in an area where hate crimes have been known to occur, e.g., "in an area frequented by homosexuals." If there is sufficient evidence that the attack was motivated by bias, then the act will be classified as a hate crime as well as an assault. An allusion to the potential for abuse by local police, in using the new laws as a means to monitor closely certain communities to the point of harrassment, is contained in Douglas' oblique warning that "communities must not be "stigmatized" early on for reporting relatively high numbers of hate crimes. That may merely indicate compliance with the law. . . ("Rules on 'Hate Crime' Set for Police by State," *Boston Globe*, 12 September 1991, p. 51).

36. The Uniform Crime Report program was revised so that the FBI can collect data through a computerized system identifying approximately twenty-five categories of crime. Implementation of the redesigned system began in the summer of 1988. Proponents of the Hate Crime Statistics Act successfully argued that the FBI could easily add an additional category— hate crime—to its data collection instrument.

37. For instance, see Congress, House, "Dissenting Views of Mr. Gekas, Mr. McCollum, Mr. Coble, Mr. Dannemeyer, and Mr. Smith to H.R. 3193," *Hate Crime Statistics Act*, 100th Cong., 2nd sess., *Congressional Record*, p. 12, where the Representatives state that the legislation "seeks to acquire too much information about too many crimes at too great an expense for everyone." See also Congress, Senate, "Additional Views of Mr. [Strom] Thurmond," *Hate Crime Statistics Act*,101st Cong., 1st sess., *Congressional Record*, pp. 9–10, where Senator Thurmond argues that the standard for data collection needs further clarification, that a definition of what constitutes "intimidation" must be provided to avoid undue vagueness in the law, and that the cost of the legislation is an appropriate concern.

38. The Community Relations Service was established under Title X of the Civil Rights Act of 1964, 42 U.S.C. section 2000(g) to provide assistance to communities and individuals in resolving disputes, disagreements, or difficulties relating to discriminatory practices based on race, color, or national origin.

39. See *Federal Register* 56 (June 13, 1991) for the Department of Justice, Community Relations Service, Notice of availability of funds re: Prejudice and Bigotry Related Crimes, 27269–72; quote on 27270.

40. Ibid., 27269.

41. Ibid.

42. Ibid., 27270.

43. Ibid.

44. Examples of such organizations include any of the groups previously identified as monitoring hate violence, such as the Klanwatch Project of the Southern Poverty Law Center which monitors white supremacist activities across the country. See note 24.

45. Lawyers, police, and civil rights groups, as examples of "communities of interpretation in the criminal justice field," are communities which do not ordinarily work in concert. Conflict often arises among them, and their relations can be adversarial.

46. See *Federal Register*, p. 27271, where the award announcement stipulates that the agency will not continue the program beyond the initial project and budget periods, which will not exceed twelve months.

47. See Mitchell, pp. 77–96.

48. Ibid., p. 95.

49. Ibid., p. 90.

50. Ibid., p. 95.

51. *Federal Register*, p. 27269.

52. Mitchell, p. 91.

53. Ibid., p. 94.

54. Ibid., p. 95.

55. Ibid., p. 90.

56. *Boston Globe*, 12 September 1991, p. 51.

57. Mitchell, p. 94.

58. Ibid.

59. "Bush Signs Act Requiring Records on Hate Crimes," *Washington Post*, 11 January 1990. The complexity of pluralism and of state-society relations is evident in the concerted action of the disparate groups that pressured Congress to adopt the hate crimes legislation. The American Civil Liberties Union called the Hate Crime Statistics Act the "fruit of an unprecedented collaboration" among law enforcement personnel, civil liberties groups, and religious and gay and lesbian organizations. Tim McFeeley, executive director of the Human Rights Campaign Fund, a national gay and lesbian political organization, lauded the bill and President Bush's support of it. Gay and lesbian activists who endorsed the bill were official guests at the White House signing ceremony, marking the first time that representatives of such groups had been invited to the White House.

60. Dr. Maher Hathout is one of the founders of the Muslim Public Affairs Committee (MPAC). In 1982 he was part of a select group of leaders of Southern California religious communities to be granted an audience with the Roman Catholic Pope during his 1982 visit to Los Angeles. During the Persian Gulf war he was actively involved, with the Reverend George Regis of All Saint's Episcopal Church in Pasadena among others, in an inter-faith movement to call for an end to the hostilities.

61. Chazanov.

62. See *The Minaret (An Islamic Magazine)*, Winter 1991, p. 23.

63. As an aside, it is worth pointing out here that the most vocal critics in Congress objected to a particular class of persons potentially protected by the legislation; they voiced their objections to the addition of the term "sexual orientation" to the legislation. They argued that an earlier version of the bills, passed by the House during the 99th Congress, which made no reference to sexual orientation, was the version they supported. For instance, Reps. Dannemeyer, McCollum, Gekas, Coble and Smith argued that the

expanded definition of protected classes, which by the 100th Congress included homosexuals, was excessive and unfair *vis à vis* other affinity groups such as religious groups which were, in their estimation, properly covered by the legislation. They also stated that "there is no mention of homosexual rights in the Constitution." See Congress, House, "Dissenting Views of Mr. Gekas, Mr. McCollum, Mr. Coble, Mr. Dannemeyer, and Mr. Smith to H.R. 3193," *Hate Crime Statistics Act,* 100th Cong., 2nd sess., *Congressional Record,* p. 12.

64. See "FBI Quest Leaves Many Arab-Americans Fearful," *Los Angeles Times.*

65. Ibid.

CHAPTER 6: THERE GOES THE NEIGHBORHOOD:
MOSQUES IN AMERICAN SUBURBS

1. Editorials in major metropolitan newspapers warn well-to-do suburbanites that they must recognize "that one-half of the nation cannot afford to build barriers of any sort against the other half," whether in the form of racial discrimination, prohibitive housing costs, or any other arrangements that benefit the wealthy and middle-class residents of the suburbs at the expense of the poor. See Michael N. Danielson, "The Politics of Exclusionary Zoning in Suburbia," *Political Science Quarterly* 91 (Spring 1976): pp. 1–18; quotation, p. 2.

2. Cited in Geoffrey Shields and L. Sanford Spector, "Opening Up the Suburbs: Notes on a Movement for Social Change," *Yale Review of Law and Social Action,* 2 (Summer 1972): p. 305. See also Danielson, p. 1.

3. See Douglas S. Massey and Nancy A. Denton, "Trends in the Residential Segregation of Blacks, Hispanics, and Asians: 1970–1980," *American Sociological Review* 52 (Dec. 1987): pp. 802–825; and John M. Stahura, "Blacks Still Segregated in Suburbs," *USA Today,* 30 November 1984.

4. Carol A. O'Connor, "Sorting Out the Suburbs: Patterns of Land Use, Class and Culture," in *American Quarterly* 36 (1984): pp. 382–394; quotation, p. 394. See also Kenneth Jackson, "A Nation of Suburbs," *Chicago History* 13 (Summer 1984): pp. 6–25; and "Race, Ethnicity and Real Estate Appraisal: The Home Owners Loan Corporation and the Federal Housing Administration," *Journal of Urban History* 6 (1980): pp. 419–452; Carol A. O'Connor, *A Sort of Utopia: Scarsdale, 1898–1981* (Albany: State University of New York Press, 1983); Zane L. Miller, *Suburb: Neighborhood and Community in Forest Park, Ohio, 1935–1976* (Knoxville: University of Tennessee Press, 1981); Elizabeth K. Burns, "The Enduring Affluent Suburb," *Landscape* 24 (1980): pp. 33–41; Constance Perin, *Everything in its Place: Social Order and Land Use in America* (Princeton: Princeton University Press,

1977); Michael N. Danielson, *The Politics of Exclusion* (New York: Columbia University Press, 1976); and Anthony Downs, *Opening Up the Suburbs: An Urban Strategy for America* (New Haven: Yale University Press, 1973). For an annotated bibliography of suburban studies, see Joseph Zikmund II and Deborah Ellis Dennis, *Suburbia: A Guide to Information Sources* (Detroit: Gale Research, 1979).

Examples of literature on Canadian suburbs include Peter C. Pineo, "Socioeconomic Status and the Concentric Zonal Structure of Canadian Cities," *Canadian Review of Sociology and Anthropology* 25, (1988): pp. 421–38; M. Goldberg and P. Horwood, *Zoning: Its Costs and Relevance for the 1980s* (Vancouver, B.C.: Fraser Institute, 1980); S. D. Clark, *The New Urban Poor* (Toronto, and New York: McGraw-Hill Ryerson, 1978); and Samuel Delbert Clark, *The Suburban Society* (Toronto: University of Toronto Press, 1966).

Comparative of the U.S. and Canada is *Land Rites and Wrongs: the Management, Regulation and Use of Land in Canada and the United States,* ed. Elliot J. Feldman and Michael A. Goldberg (Cambridge, Massachusetts: Lincoln Institute of Land Policy, 1987).

5. See Perin.

6. David E. Dowall, *The Suburban Squeeze, Land Conversion and Regulation in the San Francisco Bay Area* (Berkeley and Los Angeles: University of California Press, 1984), p. 31; cf. Richard F. Babcock, *The Zoning Game.* (Madison: University of Wisconsin Press, 1966).

7. Perin, p. ix.

8. O'Connor, 1984, p. 382.

9. According to Arthur Hertzberg, former president of the American Jewish Congress, "Between 1945 and 1965, about a third of all American Jews left the big cities and established themselves in the suburbs.. . . In the 1950s and 1960s, at least a billion dollars were raised and spent building a thousand new synagogue buildings. It was the largest building boom in the history of American Jews" (*The Jews in America: Four Centuries of an Uneasy Encounter* [New York: Simon and Schuster, 1990], pp. 321–333; quote at p. 321).

See also Marshall Sklare and Joseph Greenblum, *Jewish Identity on the Suburban Frontier, A Study of Group Survival in the Open Society,* 2nd. ed. (Chicago: University of Chicago Press, 1979 [1st. ed. 1967]).

10. Ibid., p. 203.

11. However new immigrant patterns signal a shift in the distribution of recent arrivals to North America. Census figures show that instead of settling in urban enclaves—"the traditional barrios, ghettos, and China-towns"—many immigrants now choose to bypass the big port-of-entry cities altogether and, upon arrival, settle in small towns and suburbs. This new

trend has resulted in suburban growth due to direct immigration as well as to immigrant urban dwellers who have also sought refuge in smaller communities. See "More Newcomers Bypass Big Cities," *Christian Science Monitor*, 5 March 1991, p. 6.

12. Dowall, 3. The police power gives the state the right to regulate for the common good, protecting the general health and safety of the community under its jurisdiction. In terms of zoning practices, residential, industrial, and commercial properties are generally separated and confined to their respective areas for the sake of the common good (e.g., noise abatement). Modern zoning practices specify not only permissible uses and minimum lot sizes, but also dimensions—the length and width of the lot, setback limits, and building height. See Ibid., p. 77.

13. Ibid., p. 11. Neither I nor Dowall wish to argue that the development of regulations sensitive to the ecology of a neighborhood is "entirely pernicious" (4). However, these controls affect residential development more than industrial and commercial, and are often relaxed in the face of pressing economic conditions such as high housing prices. Thus, to suggest that land use controls exist solely for the benefit of the natural environment is overly simplistic.

14. Ibid., p. 31.

15. See for example, *State ex. rel. Lake Drive Baptist Church v Bayside*, 12 Wis. 2d 585, 108 N.W. 2d 288 (1961).

16. 348 US 98 (1954).

17. 458 S.W. 2d 305 (Mo. 1970).

18. *People v Stover*, 12 NY 2d 462, 240 NYS 2d 734, 191 NE 2d 272, appeal dismissed 375 US 42 (1963). Subsequent cases have cited *Stover* as the "leading case" on the "aesthetics only" rule. See *Cromwell v Ferrier*, 19 NY 2d 263, 279 NYS 2d 22, 225 NE 2d 749 (1967).

19. The individual's property rights in the American context are seen as constitutionally protected. Thus, there is a constitutional guarantee that no individual shall be deprived of property without due process of law, a tradition which serves in part as a basis for citizens' participation in community planning and development. The claim that certain types of development might adversely effect the *value* of private property gives citizens groups some authority in deciding property questions such as zoning and land use. For a brief discussion of American property rights and how they differ from the Canadian conception of property rights, see John Brigham, "The 'Giving Issue': A View of Land, Property Rights and Industrial Development in Maine and Nova Scotia" in Feldman and Goldberg, pp. 247–268, especially p. 253.

20. *Edmonton Journal,* 18 December 1980, p. A9; cited in Baha Abu-Laban, "The Canadian Muslim Community," in *The Muslim Community in North America,* ed. Earle H. Waugh, Baha Abu-Laban, and Regula B. Qureshi (Edmonton: University of Alberta Press), pp. 91–92, n. 24.

21. Ibid.

22. Ibid.

23. Ibid.

24. Information about the mosque and Islamic center of Rochester is based on an interview with Professor M., History Professor, interview by author, 16 March 1991.

25. *Masjid* is one of the Arabic words, used in the United States and Canada, which means mosque.

26. Professor M., interview on 16 March 1991.

27. Ibid.

28. Each municipality has its own procedures. In general the proposed construction must fit within the general plan of the city and not violate any bylaws.

29. Dowall, p. 32.

30. Professor M., interview on 16 March 1991.

31. Ibid.

32. Dowall, p. 47.

33. Ibid., p. 79.

34. Information about the Grand Masjid and Islamic Center project of the Islamic Society of East Bay-San Francisco, located in Fremont, is taken from an interview with Rifaat, a founding member of the project, interview by author, 30 March 1991 and issues of *Al-Mashriq,* the monthly publication of the Islamic Society of East Bay-San Francisco.

35. Rifaat, interview on 30 March 1991.

36. Ibid.

37. Ibid.

38. Ibid.

39. *al-Mashriq,* July 1990, p. 7.

40. *al-Mashriq,* August 1989, p. 6.

41. Rifaat, interview on 30 March 1991.

42. Dr. Speight, interview by author, 19 March 1991.

43. In our conversation, Dr. Speight made it a point to say that another witness for the Muslims was a local Jewish woman and that the Muslims' attorney was Jewish.

44. Dr. Speight, interview on 19 March 1991.

45. Ibid.

46. Information about the Dearborn community is taken from an interview with the Reverend William Gepford, Presbytery of Detroit Interfaith Ministry and Rector, Littlefield Presbyterian Church, Dearborn, Michigan, interview by author on 4 April 1991. I was referred to the Reverend Gepford by Dr. Marston Speight as a leading and well-informed advocate for interfaith relations within the Arab-American community in the greater Dearborn area.

47. "Muslims Call to Prayer Arouses the Neighbors," *Christian Science Monitor*, 18 September 1979, p. 2.

48. Gepford, interview on 4 April 1991.

49. Ibid.

CHAPTER 7: REACHING A CROSSROAD

1. Jim Thomas, p. 13.

2. "From the Special Issue Editors," *Law and Society Review* 22 (1988): 631.

3. Minow, p. 310.

4. Ibid., p. 90.

5. Ibid.

6. Ibid., p. 293.

7. Ibid.,

8. Ibid., pp. 294–295.

9. For a discussion of accommodation and isolation as models of minority identity, see Yvonne Y. Haddad, "The Challenge of Muslim Minorityness: The American Experience," *The Integration of Islam in Western Europe*, ed. W. A. R. Shadid and P. S. van Koningsveld (Kok Pharos Publishing House), pp. 134–151.

10. Ibid., p. 136.

11. "Muslims' Call to Prayer Arouses the Neighbors," *Christian Science Monitor*, 18 September 1979, p. 2.

12. Jacobs, p. 63.

BIBLIOGRAPHY

Abilla, Walter D. *The Black Muslims in America, An Introduction to the Theory of Commitment.* Kampala, Nairobi, and Dar es Salaam: East African Literature Bureau, 1977.

Abou, Selim. "Ethnical History and Migration." *Cultures* 7 (1980): 75–100.

Abu-Laban, Baha. "The Arab-Canadian Community." In *The Arab-Americans: Studies in Assimilation,* edited by Elaine C. Hagopian and Ann Paden, 18–36. Wilmette, Illinois: Medina University Press, 1969.

———. "The Canadian Muslim Community: The Need for a New Survival Strategy." In *The Muslim Community in North America,* edited by Earle H. Waugh, Baha Abu-Laban, and Regula B. Qureshi, 75–92. Edmonton: University of Alberta Press, 1983.

"Additional Views of Mr. Thurmond," Hate Crime Statistics Act, Senate Report, *Congressional Record,* 101st Congress, 1st Session.

Ahmed, Gutbi Mehdi. "Muslim Organizations in the United States." In *The Muslims of America,* edited by Yvonne Yazbeck Haddad, 11–24. New York and Oxford: Oxford University Press, 1991.

Aleinikoff, T. Alexander. "Citizens, Aliens, Membership and the Constitution." *Constitutional Commentary* 7 (1990): 9–34.

"Americans Facing Toward Mecca, The Fast-Growing Muslim Community is Invisible No Longer." *Time,* 23 May 1988.

Askari, Hossein G., and John Thomas Cummings. "The Middle East and the United States: A Problem of 'Brain Drain'." *International Journal of Middle East Studies* 8 (1977): 65–90.

Austin, Allan D. *African Muslims in Antebellum America: A Source-book.* New York: Garland Publishing, 1984.

Barclay, Harold B. "The Perpetuation of Muslim Tradition in the Canadian North." *The Muslim World* 59 (1969): 64–73.

Beckley, Gloria T., and Paul Burstein. "Religious Pluralism, Equal Opportunity, and the State." *Western Political Quarterly* 44 (March 1991): 185–208.

Bercovitch, Sacvan. "The Rites of Assent: Rhetoric, Ritual and the Ideology of American Consensus." In *The American Self: Myth, Ideology and Popular Culture,* edited by Sam B. Girgus, 5–42. Albuquerque: University of New Mexico Press, 1981.

Brigham, John. *The Cult of the Court.* Philadelphia: Temple University Press, 1987.

———. "The 'Giving Issue': A View of Land, Property Rights and Industrial Development in Maine and Nova Scotia." In *Land Rites and Wrongs: the Management, Regulation and Use of Land in Canada and the United States,* edited by Elliot J. Feldman and Michael A. Goldberg, 247–268. Cambridge, Massachusetts: Lincoln Institute of Land Policy, 1987.

———. "Judicial Impact Upon Social Practices: A Perspective on Ideology." *Legal Studies Forum* 9 (1985): 47–58.

Buckley, Jr., William F. "Keep out Muslim Fundamentalists," in *Providence Journal-Bulletin,* 12 July 1993.

Burns, Elizabeth K. "The Enduring Affluent Suburb." *Landscape* 24 (1980): 33–41.

Burns, W. Haywood. "The Black Muslim in America: A Reinterpretation." *Race* 5 (1963): 26–37.

"Bush Signs Act Requiring Records on Hate Crimes." *Washington Post,* 11 January 1990.

"Bush's Holy War: The Crusader's Cloak Can Grow Heavy on the Shoulders." *New York Times,* 3 February 1991.

"But Who's Counting? Violent Racial Incidents Add Up." *Village Voice,* 14 July 1987.

Caldwell, Wallace F. "A Survey of Attitudes Toward Black Muslims in Prison." *Journal of Human Relations* 16 (1968): 220–238.

"A Call to Prayer." *Los Angeles Times*, 24 January 1991.

Clark, S. D. *The New Urban Poor*. Toronto and New York: McGraw-Hill Ryerson, 1978.

Clark, Samuel Delbert. *The Suburban Society*. Toronto: University of Toronto Press, 1966.

Cohen, Arthur A. *The Myth of the Judeo-Christian Tradition*. New York: Harper and Row, 1970.

Comment, *The Religious Rights of the Incarcerated*. University of Pennsylvania Law Review 125 (1977).

Danielson, Michael N. *The Politics of Exclusion*. New York: Columbia University Press, 1977.

―――. "The Politics of Exclusionary Zoning in Suburbia." *Political Science Quarterly* 91 (1976): 1–18.

Denton, Nancy A. "Trends in the Residential Segregation of Blacks, Hispanics, and Asians: 1970–1980." *American Sociological Review* 52 (1987): 802–825.

DiIulio, John J., Jr. *Courts, Corrections, and the Constitution, The Impact of Judicial Intervention on Prisons and Jails*. New York and Oxford: Oxford University Press, 1990.

"Dissenting Views of Mr. Gekas, Mr. McCollum, Mr. Coble, Mr. Dannemeyer, and Mr. Smith to H.R. 3193," Hate Crime Statistics Act, *Congressional Record*. 100th Congress, 2d Session.

Dowall, David E. *The Suburban Squeeze, Land Conversion and Regulation in the San Francisco Bay Area*. Berkeley and Los Angeles: University of California Press, 1984.

Downs, Anthony. *Opening Up the Suburbs: An Urban Strategy for America*. New Haven: Yale University Press, 1973.

Elkholy, Abdo A. *The Arab Moslems in the United States: Religion and Assimilation*. New Haven: College and University Press, 1966.

Erickson, Paul. *Reagan Speaks, The Making of an American Myth*. New York: New York University Press, 1985.

Esposito, John L. "Isma'il R. al-Faruqi: Muslim Scholar and Activist." In *The Muslims of America*, edited by Yvonne Y. Haddad, 65–79. New York and Oxford: Oxford University Press, 1991.

Essien-Udom, E. U. *Black Nationalism: A Search for Identity in America*. New York: Dell Publishing, 1962.

Fardan, Dorothy Blake. *Understanding Self and Society, An Islamic Perspective*. New York: Philosophical Library, 1981.

Faruqi, Isma'il Raji al-, edited by *Trialogue of the Abrahamic Faiths*, Second Edition (Issues of Islamic Thought no. 1). Herndon, Va: International Institute of Islamic Thought, 1986.

"FBI Quest Leaves Many Arab-Americans Fearful." *Los Angeles Times*, 24 January 1991.

"Federal Prisons Giving Considerations to Muslims." *New York Times*, 18 November 1979, 57.

Federal Register 56, no. 114 (June 13, 1991). Notice of availability of funds re: Prejudice and Bigotry Related Crimes, Department of Justice, Community Relations Service, pp. 27269–72.

Feeley, Malcolm, and Roger A. Hanson. "The Impact of Judicial Intervention on Prisons and Jails: A Framework for Analysis and a Review of the Literature." In *Courts, Corrections, and the Constitution*, edited by John J. DiIulio, Jr., 12–35. New York and Oxford: Oxford University Press, 1990.

Feldman, Elliot J., and Michael A. Goldberg, edited by *Land Rites and Wrongs: the Management, Regulation and Use of Land in Canada and the United States*. Cambridge, Ma: Lincoln Institute of Land Policy, 1987.

Freeman, George C., III. *The Misguided Search for Constitutional Definition of "Religion."* Georgetown Law Journal 71 (1983): 1519–1565.

"From the Special Issue Editors." *Law and Society Review* 22 (1988): 629–636.

Frye, Northrup. "Letters in Canada: 1952. Part I: Publications in English." *The University of Toronto Quarterly* (April 1953): 269–280.

Geertz, Clifford. *The Interpretation of Cultures*. New York: Basic Books, Inc., 1973.

Ghuyur, Arif. "Ethnic Distribution of American Muslims and Selected Socio-Economic Characteristics." *Journal Institute of Muslim Minority Affairs* 5 (1983/84): 47–59.

———. "Muslims in the United States: Settlers and Visitors." *Annals of the American Academy of Political and Social Science*, Special Issue (America As a Multicultural Society), edited by Milton M. Gordon (March 1981): 150–163.

Gilman, Stuart C. "Degeneracy and Race in the Nineteenth Century: The Impact of Clinical Medicine." *Journal of Ethnic Studies* 10 (1983): 27–50.

Goldberg, M., and P. Horwood. *Zoning: Its Costs and Relevance for the 1980s*. Vancouver: Fraser Institute, 1980.

Goldman, Sheldon, and Thomas P. Jahnige. *The Federal Courts as a Political System*. 3rd edited by New York: Harper and Row, 1985.

Gordon, David C. *Images of the West, Third World Perspectives*. Savage, Maryland: Rowman & Littlefield Publishers, 1989.

Grant, Madison, and Charles Stewart Davison, eds. *The Alien in Our Midst*. New York: Galton Publishing, 1930.

Greenhouse, Carol. "Courting Difference: Issues of Interpretation and Comparison in the Study of Legal Ideologies." *Law and Society Review* 22 (1988): 687–707.

Haddad, Yvonne Y. "Arab Muslims and Islamic Institutions in America: Adaptation and Reform." In *Arabs in the New World, Studies of Arab-American Communities*, edited by Sameer Y. Abraham and Nabeel Abraham, 64–81. Detroit: Wayne State University, 1983.

———. "A Century of Islam in America" (*The Muslim World Today* Occasional Paper No. 4). Washington, D.C.: The Washington Institute for Islamic Affairs, 1986.

———."The Challenge of Muslim Minorityness: The American Experience." In *The Integration of Islam and Hinduism in Western Europe*, edited by W. A. R. Shadid and P.S. van Koningsveld, 134–151. Kok Pharos Publishing House.

———. *Contemporary Islam and the Challenge of History*. Albany: State University of New York Press, 1982.

———. "The Impact of the Islamic Revolution in Iran on the Syrian Muslims of Montreal." In *The Muslim Community of North*

America, edited by Earle H. Waugh, Baha Abu-Laban, and Regula B. Qureshi, 165–181. Edmonton: University of Alberta Press, 1983.

———. "Muslims in America: A Select Bibliography." *The Muslim World* 76 (April 1986): 93–122.

———. "Muslims in Canada: A Preliminary Study." In *Religion and Ethnicity,* edited by Howard Coward and Leslie Kawamura, 71–100. Waterloo, Ontario: Wilfrid Laurier University Press, 1978.

———. "Muslims in the United States." In *Islam: The Religious and Political Life of a World Community,* edited by Marjorie Kelly, 258–74. New York: Praeger Press, 1984.

———. "Sayyid Qutb, Ideologue of Islamic Revival." In *Voices of Resurgent Islam,* edited by John L. Esposito, 67–98. New York: Oxford University Press, 1983.

Haddad, Yvonne Yazbeck, and Adair T. Lummis. *Islamic Values in the United States: A Comparative Study.* New York: Oxford University Press, 1987.

Haddad, Yvonne Yazbeck, and Jane Idleman Smith. *Mission to America: Five Sectarian Communities in North America.* Gainesville, Florida: University Press of Florida, 1993.

Haley, Alex, and Malcolm Little. *Autobiography of Malcolm X.* New York: Ballantine Books, 1964.

Handlin, Oscar. *Race and Nationality in American Life.* Garden City, N.Y.: Doubleday Anchor Books, 1957.

Herberg, Will. *Protestant, Catholic, Jew. An Essay in American Religious Sociology.* Garden City, New York: Doubleday Anchor, 1960.

Hertzberg, Arthur. *The Jews in America: Four Centuries of an Uneasy Encounter.* New York: Simon and Schuster, 1990.

Hess, Gary R. "The 'Hindu' in America: Immigration and Naturalization Policies and India, 1917–1946." *Pacific Historical Review* 38 (1969): 55–79.

Hierstead, Ganong Carey, and Richard Warren Pearce. *Law and Society.* Homewood, Illinois: Richard D. Irwin, Inc., 1965.

Higham, John. *Send These to Me, Immigrants in Urban America*

(Revised Edition). Baltimore and London: Johns Hopkins University Press, 1984 (1st. edited by 1975).

Hitti, Philip K. *The Syrians in America.* New York: George H. Doran Co., 1924.

Hooglund, Eric J., edited by *Crossing the Waters, Arabic- Speaking Immigrants to the United States Before 1940.* Washington, D.C.: Smithsonian Institution Press, 1987.

Horsman, Reginald. *Race and Manifest Destiny, the Origins of American Racial Anglo-Saxonism.* Cambridge, Massachusetts: Harvard University Press, 1981.

Hudson, Michael C., and Ronald G. Wolfe, edited by *The American Media and the Arabs.* Washington, D.C.: Center for Contemporary Arab Studies, 1980.

Huntington, Samuel P. *American Politics: The Promise of Disharmony.* New York: Belknap Press, 1981.

———. "The Clash of Civilizations?" in *Foreign Affairs*, Vol. 72. no. 3 (Summer 1993): 22–49.

Hussain, Asaf. "Islamic Awakening in the Twentieth Century: an Analysis and Selective Review of the Literature." *Third World Quarterly* 10 (1988): 1005–1023.

"Inquiries on Arab-Americans by FBI Raise Concern." *New York Times,* 12 January 1991.

Irwin, John. *Prisons in Turmoil.* Boston: Little, Brown and Co., 1980.

Islam in America Series in *New York Times* 2–7 May 1993.

"Islam in Canada." *The Canadian Encyclopedia*, 1097–8. Edmonton: University of Alberta Press, 1988.

Jackson, Kenneth. "A Nation of Suburbs." *Chicago History* (1984): 6–25.

———. "Race, Ethnicity and Real Estate Appraisal: The Home Owners Loan Corporation and the Federal Housing Administration." *Journal of Urban History* 6 (1980): 419–452.

Jacobs, James B. *New Perspectives on Prisons and Imprisonment.* Ithaca and London: Cornell University Press, 1983.

Jensen, Joan M. *Passage from India, Asian Indian Immigrants in North America*. New Haven: Yale University Press, 1988.

Johnston, Hugh. "The Development of the Punjabi Community in Vancouver since 1961." In *Canadian Ethnic Studies* 20 (1988): 1–19.

Jones, Maldwyn Allen. *American Immigration*. Chicago: University of Chicago Press, 1960.

Jones, Oliver, Jr. "The Black Muslim Movement and the American Constitutional System." *Journal of Black Studies* 13 (June 1983): 417–437.

Karpat, Kemal H. "The Ottoman Emigration to America, 1860–1914." *International Journal of Middle East Studies* 17 (1985): 175–209.

Kayal, Philip M., and Joseph M. Kayal. *The Syrian- Lebanese in America, A Study of Religion and Assimilation*. Boston: Twayne Publishers, 1975.

Khalaf, Samir. "The Background and Causes of Lebanese/Syrian Immigration to the United States Before World War I." In *Crossing the Waters, Arabic-Speaking Immigrants to the United States Before 1940*, edited by Eric J. Hooglund, 17–36. Washington, D.C.: Smithsonian Institution Press, 1987.

Khan, Salim. "A Brief History of Pakistanis in the Western United States." M.A. thesis, California State University at Sacramento, 1981.

———. "Pakistanis in the Western United States." *Journal Institute of Muslim Minority Affairs* 5 (1983/84): 43–46.

Kly, Y. N. "The African-American Muslim Minority: 1776–1900." *Journal Institute of Muslim Minority Affairs* 10 (1989): 152–160.

Konvitz, Milton R. *The Alien and the Asiatic in American Law*. Ithaca, N.Y.: Cornell University Press, 1946.

Leonard, Karen. "The Pakhar Singh Murders: A Punjabi Response to California's Alien Land Law." *Amerasia* 11 (1984): 75–87.

Lesser, Jeff H. "Always 'Outsiders': Asians, Naturalization and the Supreme Court." *Amerasia* 12 (1985/86): 83–100.

Levinson, Sanford. *Constitutional Faith*. Princeton: Princeton University Press, 1988.

Levy, Leonard W. *Blasphemy: Verbal Offense Against the Sacred, From Moses to Salman Rushdie*. New York: Alfred A. Knopf, 1993.

Lewis, Bernard. *Islam and the West*. New York: Oxford University Press, 1993.

————. "The Roots of Muslim Rage," *The Atlantic Monthly*, September 1990.

Lincoln, Charles Eric. *The Black Muslims in America*. Rev. edited by Boston: Beacon Press, 1973.

Lipset, Martin Seymour. "Historical Traditions and National Characteristics: A Comparative Analysis of Canada and the United States." *Canadian Journal of Sociology* 11 (1986): 113–155.

McCloud, Beverly Thomas. "African-American Muslim Women." In *The Muslims of America*, edited by Yvonne Y. Haddad, 177–187. New York and Oxford: Oxford University Press, 1991.

Marsh, Clifton E. *From Black Muslims to Muslims: The Transition from Separatism to Islam, 1930–1980*. Metuchen, New Jersey: The Scarecrow Press, 1984.

Marty, Martin E. "A Judeo Christian Looks at the Judeo Christian Tradition." *The Christian Century*, 8 October 1986, 858–859.

Mashriq, al- (Publication of the Islamic Society of East Bay-San Francisco). August 1989–June 1991.

Mehdi, Beverlee Turner. *The Arabs in America 1492–1977*. New York: Oceana Publications, Inc., 1978.

Michalak, Laurence. "The Arab in American Cinema: A Century of Otherness." *Cineaste* 17 (1989): 3–9.

————. *Cruel and Unusual: Negative Images of Arabs in American Popular Culture*. 2d. edited by (Issue Paper no. 15, ADC Issues). Washington, D.C.: American-Arab Anti-Discrimination Committee, n.d.

"Middle Eastern Enclave Fears Reprisals in U.S." *Washington Post*, 11 January 1991.

Miller, Zane L. *Suburb: Neighborhood and Community in Forest Park, Ohio, 1935–1976.* Knoxville: University of Tennessee Press, 1981.

The Minaret (An Islamic Magazine), (Magazine of the Islamic Society of Southern California), Winter 1991.

Minow, Matha. *Making All the difference: Inclusion, Exclusion, and American Law.* Ithaca: Cornell University Press, 1990.

Mitchell, Timothy. "Everyday Metaphors of Power." *Theory and Society* 19 (1990): 545–577.

———. "The Limits of the State: Beyond Statist Approaches and Their Critics." *American Political Science Review* 85 (1991): 77–96.

Mitchell, Timothy, and Roger Owen. "Defining the State in the Middle East: A Workshop Report." *Middle East Studies Association Bulletin* 24 (1990): 179–184.

Moore, Kathleen. "Muslims in Prison: Claims to Constitutional Protection of Religious Liberty." In *The Muslims of America,* edited by Yvonne Yazbeck Haddad, 136–156. New York and Oxford: Oxford University Press, 1991.

Moore, R. Lawrence. *Religious Outsiders and the Making of Americans.* New York: Oxford University Press, 1987.

"More Newcomers Bypass Big Cities." *Christian Science Monitor,* 5 March 1991.

"Moslem Faithful in USA Tackle Misconceptions." *USA Today,* 1 September 1989.

"Mosque has a U.S. Flavor." *Los Angeles Times,* 25 January 1991.

Muhammad, Akbar. "Muslims in the United States: An Overview of Organizations, Doctrines, and Problems." In *The Islamic Impact,* edited by Yvonne Yazbeck Haddad, Byron Haines, and Ellison Findly, 195–217. Syracuse: Syracuse University Press, 1984.

———. "Some Factors Which Promote and Restrict Islamization in America." *American Journal of Islamic Studies* 1 (1984): 41–50.

Muhammad, Elijah. *How to Eat to Live.* Chicago: Muhammed Mosque of Islam No. 2, 1967.

————. *Message to the Blackman.* Chicago: Muhammed Mosque of Islam No. 2, 1965.

————. *The Supreme Wisdom: The Solution of the So-Called Negroes' Problem.* Chicago: University of Islam, 1957.

Mukerji, Dhan Gopal. *Caste and Outcast.* New York: E. P. Dutton and Company, 1923.

"Muslims a Growing U.S. Force." *Los Angeles Times,* 24 January 1991.

Naff, Alixa. *Becoming American, The Early Arab Immigrant Experience.* Carbondale and Edwardsville, Illinois: Southern Illinois University Press, 1985.

National Council of Churches. "They Don't All Wear Sheets: A Chronology of Racist and Far-Right Violence: 1980–86" (1988).

Niebuhr, R. Gustav. "American Moslems." *The Wall Street Journal,* 5 October 1990, 5.

Note, *Beyond the Ken of the Courts: A Critique of Judicial Refusal to Review the Complaints of Convicts.* Yale Law Journal 72 (1963): 500–544.

Note, *Soul Rebels: The Rastafarians and the Free Exercise Clause.* Georgetown Law Journal 72 (1984).

O'Connor, Carol A. *A Sort of Utopia: Scarsdale, 1898–1981.* Albany: State University of New York Press, 1983.

————. "Sorting Out the Suburbs: Patterns of Land Use, Class and Culture." *American Quarterly* 36 (1984): 382–94.

Orfalea, Gregory. *Before the Flames, A Quest for the History of Arab-Americans.* Austin, Texas: University of Texas Press, 1988.

Perin, Constance. *Everything in its Place: Social Order and Land Use in America.* Princeton: Princeton University Press, 1977.

Pineo, Peter C. "Socioeconomic Status and the Concentric Zonal Structure of Canadian Cities." *Canadian Review of Sociology and Anthropology* 25 (1988): 421–38.

Pipes, Daniel. "The Muslims are Coming! The Muslims are Coming!" *National Review,* 19 November 1990.

Poston, Larry Allan. "The Future of Da'wah in North America." *The American Journal of Islamic Social Sciences* 8 (1991): 501–511.

———. *Islamic 'da'wah' in North America and the Dynamics of Conversion to Islam in Western Societies (Vols. I and II)*. Ph.D. diss., Northwestern University, 1988.

"Religious Hate Violence Targets Islamic Mosques," *Congressional Record* 133, no. 206 (December 22 1987), p. E4990.

Roberts, Barbara. "Doctors and Deports: the Role of the Medical Profession in Canadian Deportation, 1900–20." *Canadian Ethnic Studies* 18 (1986): 17–36.

Roof, Wade Clark, and William McKinney. *American Mainline Religion, Its Changing Shape and Future*. New Brunswick, New Jersey: Rutgers University Press, 1987.

Rothman, David J. *Conscience and Convenience: The Asylum and its Alternatives in Progressive America*. Boston: Little, Brown, & Co., 1980.

———. "Decarcerating Prisoners and Patients." *Civil Liberties Review* 1 (1973): 9–30.

Said, Edward W. *Covering Islam: How the Media and the Experts Determine How We See the Rest of the World*. New York: Pantheon Books, 1981.

———. *Orientalism*. New York: Vintage Books, 1978.

Scheingold, Stuart A. *The Politics of Rights*. New Haven: Yale University Press, 1974.

Schuck, Peter H., and Rogers M. Smith. *Citizenship Without Consent, Illegal Aliens in the American Polity*. New Haven and London: Yale University Press, 1985.

Sheler, Jeffrey L. "Islam in America." *U.S. News and World Report*, 8 October 1990, 69.

Shields, Geoffrey, and L. Sanford Spector. "Opening Up the Suburbs: Notes on a Movement for Social Change." *Yale Review of Law and Social Action* 2 (1972).

Silk, Mark. "Notes on the Judeo-Christian Tradition in America." *American Quarterly* 36 (1984): 65–85.

Smith, Rogers M. "The 'American Creed' and American Identity: The Limits of Liberal Citizenship in the United States." *Western Political Quarterly* 41 (1988): 225–251.

Stahura, John M. "Blacks Still Segregated in Suburbs." *USA Today*, 30 November 1984.

Stone, Carol L. "Estimate of Muslims Living in America." In *The Muslims of America*, edited by Yvonne Y. Haddad, 26–36. New York: Oxford University Press, 1991.

Suleiman, Michael W. "Arab-Americans: Community Profile." *Journal Institute of Muslim Minority Affairs* 5 (1983/84): 29–35.

———. "Early Arab Americans: the Search for Identity." In *Crossing the Waters, Arabic Speaking Immigrants to the United States Before 1940*, edited by Eric J. Hooglund, 37–54. Washington, D.C.: Smithsonian Institution Press, 1987.

Sweeney, Harry A., Jr. *A. Joseph Howar, the Life of Muhammed Issa Abu Al-Hawa*. Washington, D.C.: the Howar Family, 1987.

Takaki, Ronald. *Iron Cages, Race and Culture in Nineteenth Century America*. New York: Alfred Knopf, 1979.

———. "Reflections on Racial Patterns in America." In *From Different Shores, Perspectives on Race and Ethnicity in America*, edited by Ronald Takaki, 26–38. New York: Oxford University Press, 1987.

Terry, Janice J. *Mistaken Identity: Arab Stereotypes in Popular Writing*. Washington, D.C.: American-Arab Affairs Council, 1985.

Thernstrom, Stephen, edited by *Harvard Encyclopedia of American Ethnic Groups*. Cambridge, Massachusetts: Harvard University Press, 1980. S.v., "Mormons," by Dean L. May: 720–731; and s.v. "Naturalization and Citizenship," by Reed Ueda: 734–748.

Thomas, Jim. *Prisoner Litigation, The Paradox of the Jailhouse Lawyer*. Totowa, New Jersey: Rowman & Littlefield, 1988.

Tumeh, George. *Al-Mughtaribūn al-Arab fi Amrika al- Shamaliyyah (The Arab Immigrants in North America)* (In Arabic). Damascus: *Wizarat al-Thaqafah wa al-Irshad al-Qawmi*, 1965.

Turner, William Bennet. "Establishing the Rule of Law in Prisons: A Manual for Prisoners' Rights Litigation." *Black Law Journal* 1 (1971): 106.

U. S. Congress. House. Commission on Immigration, *Abstract of Reports, Vol. II.*, 61st Cong., 3rd sess., 1910–1911.

————. Commission on Immigration, *Statements and Recommendations by Societies*, 61st. Cong., 3rd sess., 1910–1911.

————. Committee on Immigration and Naturalization, *Hearings on Admission of Near East Refugees*, 67th Cong., 4th sess., Sec. 15, 16, and 19, 1922.

————. Committee on Immigration and Naturalization, *Hearing on Immigration*, 61st Cong., 2d sess., 1910.

————. Committee on Immigration and Naturalization, *Hearings on Hindu Immigration* (Restriction of Immigration of Hindu Laborers), 63rd Cong., 2d sess., 1914–1915.

————. Committee on the Judiciary, *Hearing on Polygamy*, 58th Cong., 1st sess., 1902.

————. Committee on the Judiciary, "Crimes Against Religious Practices and Property," *Hearings before the Subcommittee on Criminal Justice*, 99th Cong., 1st sess., 1985.

U. S. Congress. Senate. Commission on Immigration, *Immigrant in Industries: Japanese and Other Immigrant Races in Pacific Coast and Rocky Mountain States, 3 vols.*, 61st Cong., 2d sess., 1909–1910.

————. Committee on the Judiciary, "Hate Crime Statistics Act of 1988," *Hearing Before the Subcommittee on the Constitution*, 100th Cong., 2d sess., 1988.

"US Moslems say Crisis Distorts Peaceful Faith." *Boston Globe*, 22 September 1990.

Ward, W. Peter. *White Canada Forever, Popular Attitudes and Public Policy Toward Orientals in British Columbia*. Montreal: McGill-Queen's University Press, 1978.

Waugh, Earle H., Baha Abu-Laban, and Regula B. Qureshi, edited by *The Muslim Community in North America*. Edmonton: University of Alberta Press, 1983.

Waxman, Chaim I. *America's Jews in Transition*. Philadelphia: Temple University Press, 1983.

Weiner, Myron. *Sons of the Soil, Migration and Ethnic Conflict in India*. Princeton: Princeton University Press, 1978.

———. "Immigration: Perspectives from Receiving Countries." *Third World Quarterly* 12 (1990): 140–165.

Weinfield, M., W. Shaffir, and I. Cotler. *The Canadian Jewish Mosaic.* Toronto and New York: J. Wiley, 1981.

Weisbrod, Carol. *The Boundaries of Utopia.* New York: Pantheon Books, 1980.

Williams, Raymond Brady. *Religions of Immigrants from India and Pakistan.* Cambridge and New York: Cambridge University Press, 1988.

Wills, Garry. *Under God, Religion and American Politics.* New York: Simon and Schuster, 1990.

Wittke, Carl. *We Who Built America: The Saga of the Immigrant.* 2d. edited by Cleveland: Ohio University Press, 1964.

Wolf, C. Umhau. "Muslims in the American Mid-West." *Muslim World* 50 (1960): 39–48.

Younis, Adele L. "The First Muslims in America: Impressions and Reminiscences." *Journal Institute of Muslim Minority Affairs* 5 (1983/84): 17–28.

1979 International Press Seminar. *The Arab Image in Western Mass Media.* London: Morris International Ltd., 1980.

CASES CITED

Abdullah v Kinnison, 769 F.2d 345 (1985).

Abernathy v Cunningham, 393 F.2d 775 (1968).

Africa v Commonwealth of Pennsylvania, 662 F.2d 1025 (3d Cir. 1981), *cert. denied*, 456 U.S. (1982).

Banks v Havener, 234 F. Supp. 27 (1964).

Banning v Looney, 213 F.2d 771 (10th Cir. 1954), *cert. denied*, 348 U.S. 266 (1954).

Barnes v Virgin Islands, 415 F. Supp. 1218 (D.V.I. 1976).

Barnett v Rodgers, 410 F.2d 985 (D.C. Cir. 1969).

Battle v Anderson, 376 F. Supp. 402 (1974).

Berman v Parker, 348 US 98 (1954).

Bethea v Dagget, 329 F. Supp. 796 (N.D.Ga. 1970).

Brown v Peyton, 437 F.2d 1228 (1971).

Bryant v Wilkins, 265 N.Y.S. 2d 995 (1970).

Burgin v Henderson, 536 F.2d 501 (2d Cir. 1976).

Cantwell v Connecticut, 310 U.S. 296 (1940).

Chae Chan Ping v United States, 130 U.S. 581 (1889) (Chinese Exclusion Case).

Church of Latter Day Saints v United States, 136 U.S. 1 (1890).

Cochran v Sielaff, 405 F. Supp. 1126 (S.D. Ill. 1976).

Cooper v Pate, 378 U.S. 546 (1964).

Cox v New Hampshire, 312 U.S. 569 (1944).

Cromwell v Ferrier, 19 NY 2d 263, 279 NYS 2d 22, 225 NE 749 (1967).

Davis v Beason, 133 U.S. 333 (1890).

Dow v United States, 226 Fed. 145 (Circuit Court of Appeals, Fourth Circuit. September 14, 1915).

Elam v Henderson, 472 F.2d 582 (5th Cir.), *cert. denied,* 414 U.S. 868 (1973).

Ex Parte Shahid, 205 Fed. 812 (1913) (District Court, E. D. South Carolina, June 24 1913).

Finney v Hutto, 57 L.Ed. 2d 522 (1976).

Fong Yue Ting v United States, 149 U.S. 698 (1893).

Founding Church of Scientology of Washington v United States, 409 F.2d 1146 (D.C. Cir. 1969).

Fulwood v Clemmer, 206 F. Supp. 370 (1962).

In re Dow, 213 Fed. 355 (District Court, E.D. South Carolina. April 15, 1914).

In Re Ferguson, 361 P.2d 417 (1961).

In re Feroz Din, 27 F. 2d. 568 (1928) (District Court, N. D. California, S. D., at San Francisco).

In re Halladjian, 174 Fed. 834 (Circuit Court, D. Massachusetts, Dec. 24 1909).

In re Najour, 174 Fed. at 736 (Circuit Court, N. D. Georgia. December 1 1909).

In the Matter of Brown v McGinnis, N.Y.S. 2d 497 (1962).

International Society for Krishna Consciousness, Inc. v Barber, 650 F.2d 430 (2d Cir. 1981).

Jihaad v Carlson, 410 F. Supp. 1132 (1976).

Knuckles v Prasse, 302 F. Supp. 1036 (E.D. Pa. 1969), *cert. denied*, 403 U.S. 936 (1971).

Long v Parker, 455 F.2d 466 (3d Cir. 1972).

Madyun v Franzen, 704 F.2d 954 (1983).

Melnack v Yogi, 592 F.2d 197 (3d Cir. 1979).

Minor v Happersett, 88 U.S. (21 Wall.) 162 (1874).

Monroe v Bombard, 422 F. Supp. 211 (S.D.N.Y. 1977).

Moorish Science Temple of America, Inc. v Smith, 693 F.2d 987 (1982).

Northern v Nelson, 315 F. Supp. 687 (1970).

O'Lone v Shabazz, 107 S.Ct. 2400 (1987).

People ex rel. Rockey v Krueger, 306 N.Y.S. 2d 359 (1969).

People v Ruggles, 8 Johns. (N.Y.) 290 (1811).

People v Stover, 12 NY 2d 462, 240 NYS 2d 734, 191 NE 2d 272, appeal dismissed 375 US 42 (1963).

People v Woody, 394 P.2d. 813 (Sup. Ct. of Ca. 1964).

Pierce v LaVallee, 203 F.2d 233 (1961).

Reynolds v United States, 98 U.S. 145 (1878).

Robinson v Foti, 527 F. Supp. 1111 (E.D. La. 1981).

Ross v Blackledge, 477 F.2d 616 (4th Cir. 1973).

Rowland v Sigler, 327 F. Supp. 821 (D. Neb.), *aff'd. sub nom. Rowland v Jones* 452 F.2d 1005 (8th Cir. 1971).

Ruffin v Commonwealth, 62 Va. 790 (1871).

SaMarion v McGinnis, 284 N.Y.S. 2d 508 (1967).

Scott v Sandford, 60 U.S. 393 (1857).

Sewell v Pegelow, 291 F.2d 196 (1961).

Shabazz v Barnauskas, 598 F.2d 345 (1979).

Sherbert v Verner, 374 U.S. 398 (1963).

Sostre v McGinnis, 334 F.2d 905 (2d Cir. 1964), *cert. denied*, 378 U.S. 382 (1964).

State ex rel. Lake Drive Baptist Church V. Bayside, 12 Wis. 2d 585, 108 N.W. 2d 288 (1961).

State ex rel. Stoyanoff v Berkeley, 458 S.W. 2d 305 (Mo. 1970).

State ex rel. Tate v Cubbage, 210 A.2d 555 (Del. Super. Ct. 1965).

Thomas v Review Board of Indiana Employment Security Division, 450 U.S. 707 (1981).

Thompson v Kentucky, 712 F.2d 1078 (1983).

United States v Ali, 7 Fed. 2d. 728 (1925) (District Court, E. D. Michigan, S. D.).

United States v Baghat Singh Thind, 261 U.S. 204 (1922).

United States v Ballard, 322 U.S. 78 (1944).

United States v Balsara, 180 Fed. 694 (Circuit Court of Appeals, Second Circuit, July 1, 1910).

United States v Kahane, 396 F. Supp. 687, *aff'd. sub nom. Kahane v.Carlson*, 527 F.2d 492 (2d Cir. 1975).

United States v Lee, 102 S.Ct. 1051 (1982).

United States v Seeger, 380 U.S. 163 (1965).

Waddell v Aldredge, 480 F.2d 1078 (1973).

Walker v Blackwell, 411 F.2d 23 (5th Cir. 1969).

Witmer v United States, 75 S.Ct. 392 (1955).

Wright v Wilkins, 26 Misc. 2d 1090, N.Y.S. 2d 309 (Sup. Ct. 1961).

Wolff v McDonnell, 418 U.S. 539 (1974).

INTERVIEWS

Gepford, The Reverend William, Minister, Presbytery of Detroit Interfaith Ministry, and Rector, Littlefield Presbyterian Church, Dearborn, Michigan, April 4, 1991.

M., Professor [pseud.]. Telephone interview by author, Rochester, New York, March 16, 1991.

Rifaat [pseud.]. Telephone interview by author, Fremont, California, March 30, 1991.

Speight, Dr. Marston, Director for Christian-Muslim Relations, National Council of Churches. Telephone interview by author, Hartford, Connecticut, March 19, 1991.

INDEX